LIONS OF THE NORTH

Lions of the North

SOUNDS OF THE NEW NORDIC RADICAL NATIONALISM

Benjamin R. Teitelbaum

OXFORD

UNIVERSITY PRESS

OXFORD
UNIVERSITY PRESS

Oxford University Press is a department of the University of Oxford. It furthers
the University's objective of excellence in research, scholarship, and education
by publishing worldwide. Oxford is a registered trade mark of Oxford University
Press in the UK and certain other countries.

Published in the United States of America by Oxford University Press
198 Madison Avenue, New York, NY 10016, United States of America.

Library of Congress Cataloging-in-Publication Data
Names: Teitelbaum, Benjamin R., author.
Title: Lions of the north : sounds of the new Nordic radical nationalism / Benjamin R. Teitelbaum.
Description: New York, NY : Oxford University Press, [2016] | Includes bibliographical references and index.
Identifiers: LCCN 2016029444| ISBN 9780190212599 (hardcover : alk. paper) |
ISBN 9780190212605 (pbk. : alk. paper) | ISBN 9780190212629 (oxford scholarly online)
Subjects: LCSH: Popular music—Sweden—Political aspects—20th century. | Popular
music—Sweden—Social aspects—20th century. | Popular music—Sweden—20th century—History and
criticism. | Radicalism in music. | Nationalism in music.
Classification: LCC ML3917.S94 T45 2017 | DDC 306.4/84240985—dc23 LC record available
at https://lccn.loc.gov/2016029444

This volume is published with the generous support of the AMS 75 PAYS Endowment of
the American Musicological Society, funded in part by the National Endowment for
the Humanities and the Andrew W. Mellon Foundation.

For Kajsa

Contents

Acknowledgments

THIS BOOK DEMANDED considerable time and energy, and had it not been for the support of others I would never have seen it through to completion. I am indebted to many friends and colleagues who commented on or otherwise helped shape my writing, including Juliana Madrone, Sienna Wood, Francesca Ingelse, Aleysia Whitmore, David Fossum, Nancy Jakubowski, David Kaminsky, Kay Kaufman Shelemay, Loren Kajikawa, Sheila Morris, Patrick Sutton, Dana Sutton, Mikael Grafström, Olof Göthlin, Saskia Reimann, Jacob Senholt, Roger Griffin, Jay Keister, Thomas Riis, Carlo Caballero, Beverly Weber, Laura Osterman, Sasha Senderovic, Tamir Bar-On, Sherrill Harbison, and Catrin Lundström. I must pay special thanks to those mentor figures who have guided me in this project and in my research more generally, especially Marc Perlman, David Josephson, and Thomas Zeiler.

During the research and writing phases of this project I have been kept honest by the scrutiny of those moving in or closely observing the circles I study. I received invaluable criticism, suggestions, and assistance from Mattias Karlsson, Erik Almqvist, Chang Frick, Jonathan Leman, Niklas Orrenius, Tobias Hübinette, Lina, Daniel, Anders, Vávra Suk, Daniel Friberg, John Morgan, Jonas De Geer, and Magnus Söderman.

This book would not have been possible without the careful reading of my editor, Suzanne Ryan, and editorial assistants at Oxford University Press, as well as my anonymous reviewers. Likewise, travel grants from Brown University, the University of Colorado, Boulder, and Mångkulturellt centrum allowed me to conduct fieldwork in Scandinavia, and a subvention award from the American Musicological Society helped ease the costs of publication. I am grateful to my former chairs

Davide Stimilli and Mark Leiderman as well as my current chair Carlo Cabellero at the University of Colorado, Boulder for their steadfast encouragement. And thanks also to the many outstanding undergraduate students in my courses Radical Nationalism in Northern Europe (SCAN 3301) and Global Neofascism (IAFS 3000), whose thoughtful questions and sharp analyses revealed insights I never could have arrived at on my own.

Most affectionate thanks to my mother, father, step-parents, sister, nephew, grandmother, and in-laws. To my infant daughter Signe, who in little more than a year has already given me courage and joy to last a thousand lifetimes. And finally to my wife Kajsa, whose unfailing care, brilliance, and strength sustained me and this project through highs and lows. It is to her that this book is lovingly dedicated.

Prologue

I TRAVELED BY train in eastern Sweden on July 28, 2012. For over two years I had been following circles of anti-immigrant activists in the region, and gatherings I visited on this day revealed why they were transforming themselves and how they were using music, of all things, to do it. I'll describe my day in reverse order, starting where it ended—late at night in a muddy countryside field fifty miles south of Stockholm that was the site of Kuggnäs Festival, the largest annual skinhead gathering in the Nordic countries.

I arrived at Kuggnäs to find a crowd of about 2,500—more than double that of the previous years as I recall—and these people had come for a special event. At midnight, punk-metal band Ultima Thule would give their final performance. Ultima Thule shook Sweden's cultural landscape during the 1990s by rallying opponents of immigration and multiculturalism in ways no politician could. But in 2012, nearly twenty years beyond their heyday, the members of Ultima Thule decided to disband. The rise of illegal downloading had made music less profitable for groups like themselves, and the skinhead subculture they played to had begun to age and fade. Further, as singer Jan Thörnblom stated in newspaper interviews, band members felt they were no longer needed following the breakthrough election of the nationalist, anti-immigrant Sweden Democrats party to parliament in 2010.

Band members always denied that they were racists. At Kuggnäs, singer Thörnblom declared on stage that they were only "patriots" seeking the protection and celebration of Swedish identity rather than hatred of minorities. Those statements resonated with some: leaders of the Sweden Democrats—even as they struggle to counter accusations of racism directed at themselves—have never felt the need to hide the fact that Ultima Thule was instrumental in inspiring their political activism. But the band's relationship with white activism and neo-Nazism has always been dubious, and outsiders have often suspected that what is said on stage is not always felt beyond.

Ultima Thule's denunciation of racism during their final concert did not receive unanimous applause. I saw that coming. T-shirts in the crowd told the story: "White Pride World Wide," "Weisse Macht" (White Power), "Blod och ära" (Blood and Honor), and everywhere the name of the flagship British white-power band "Skrewdriver." Tattoos featured swastikas and images of Adolf Hitler mixed with messages in Old Norse runic script. And walking through the parking lot and camp-grounds adjacent to the concert area, I heard the music of classic Swedish white-power bands like Storm, Odium, and Pluton Svea blasting from car radios.

Though they sing in Swedish, Ultima Thule enjoys considerable renown among skinheads globally. Visitors at Kuggnäs that year had come from throughout the Nordic countries, as well as Germany, England, Australia, the United States, Italy, Poland, and Hungary. At the youth hostel where I slept, "skins" from Spain sur-rounded me on nearly all sides. And looking out at the audience that evening, I wondered if there wasn't more hair on my head than on the heads of all other men combined. And yes, they were mostly men; I guessed there were five to six for every woman.

Though previous festivals erupted in brawls, this year was relatively calm, with only a handful of reported assaults. There were still confrontations here and there—I nearly found myself in one after having accidentally knocked four cups of beer out of a Finnish skinhead's arms and onto a middle-aged German couple. Violence aside, the atmosphere was far from reverent. At the lower edges of the field, attract-ing the audience's attention as much as what was happening on stage, men took turns urinating through the fence, occasionally dropping their pants to the ground so as to moon all onlookers.

Everything about Kuggnäs seemed so different from the gathering I attended ear-lier that same day in Stockholm. It began when I arrived a little after noon outside of a subway station in the central city district, at a meeting place designated for par-ticipants in a seminar called "Identitarian Ideas." We were to congregate and await a representative who would lead us on foot to the site of the event. This was a standard exercise intended to prevent attacks from left-wing groups.

Participants in the seminar condemned non-European immigration and, with varying degrees of reservation, identified as nationalists. Still, they were hardly a homogeneous bunch. Some were openly anti-Semitic, some feared the arrival of Islam, some worked to protect white racial purity, and some advocated the assimila-tion of immigrants for the sake of preserving Nordic national cultures. They aligned with different, sometimes obscure subcategories of radical nationalism, be it Nazism, race materialism, pan-Aryanism, white nationalism, ethnopluralism, traditionalism, right-wing anarchism, counterjihad, or ultraconservatism. The individuals hosting the event called themselves "identitarians"—adherents of a French-inspired school of thought seeking the establishment of subnational, ethnically homogenous communities across the continent.

Clad as I was in a polo shirt, tidy jeans, and loafers, my attire seemed formal. But those waiting at the preseminar gathering place had thoroughly outdressed me. Pressed khakis, wingtips, suits, and cherry-red sweaters on top of button-up shirts: the dress code here was nothing like that in the muddy field to the south. After a long wait in the sun, our guide finally got the call and began walking us to the seminar location. It was only after the roughly ninety-person procession entered the hall that we were able to have a good look at each other.

Everyone was there: notorious former leaders of National Socialist street gangs and militant groups, founders of ethnic separatist propaganda organizations, editors of far-right media outlets, and celebrity authors from antiliberal blog portals. Active members of semimainstream, anti-immigration parties in the region knew about the meeting and wanted to attend, but most refrained for fear of association with anti-Semites and race ideologues. Save those absences, nearly every major Nordic nationalist organization, party, club, and think tank was represented in that room.

The seminar theme was "Identity and Geopolitics: Towards a Multi-Polar World." The half-dozen speakers highlighted what they predicted was a fast-approaching breakdown of modern American hegemony in global affairs; the rise of political and military power in the East; and the possible ramifications this change could have for racial, ethnic, and cultural pluralism throughout the world. Prominent Russian intellectual and purported mastermind of Vladimir Putin's expansionist foreign policy, Alexander Dugin, gave the keynote address.

Participants mingled and bought refreshments between lectures. As I worked my way through the hall, others noticed that I was wearing a Kuggnäs Festival wristband. I had kept it on from earlier, and would need it to get back into the festival later that night. They had few kind words for Kuggnäs, even though most had been passionate Ultima Thule fans during the 1990s. A member of a youth activist group saw my wristband and said proudly, "Ah, Kuggnäs—that's not my scene." A famous blogger in attendance, whose writings often lampoon skinheads as culturally bankrupt, later expressed that same sentiment to me in harsher tones.

I asked seminar organizer Daniel Friberg to describe the people at Identitarian Ideas, and he characterized them as "intellectuals and academics." While that was true of a portion of attendees, the atmosphere was not one of a standard academic gathering. Many at the seminar had once moved in nationalist skinhead circles, and that legacy continued to mark them in subtle ways. The overwhelmingly male assembly, dapper as it was, featured what seemed to me a disproportionate number of close-cropped haircuts and tattoos, and many listened to lectures while downing lavish servings of beer and wine. No, Daniel Friberg's response to me would have been more valid as a mission statement rather than a description: he and others like him hoped to refine radical nationalism in the Nordic countries, and they created Identitarian Ideas for that purpose. Seeking utmost distance from events like Kuggnäs, they attempted to replace muddy fields, boots, and decadence with seminar rooms, wingtips, and decency. Above all, whereas Kuggnäs was a concert, Identitarian Ideas featured lectures rather than music. This, Friberg said, was far more appropriate for serious political activism.

But the outward appearance of nationalists rallying around a single vision for the future concealed deeper complexities, as well as an enduring commitment to the very artform excluded from the seminar. The newspaper editor who greeted me at the door had been waging a multiyear campaign to champion Scandinavian folk music through his publications. Former members of the Sweden Democrats in attendance had also devoted part of their political careers to promoting folk music, and the seminar's official photographer had just started taking fiddle lessons—all with the goal of refocusing nationalism on the uniquely Swedish. The famous woman author who cast a suspecting glance at me between lectures was also a vocalist in multiple acoustic singer-songwriter acts that aimed to project a more mainstream sound and image of anti-immigrant campaigning. The wine-drinking former skinheads in attendance had made some of their most notable contributions as activists by writing about white power music and its alleged perversion of the nationalist message. The peppy youths who sold me a sandwich at the refreshments counter were part of a controversial initiative to produce nationalist reggae and rebrand their cause as a fight against oppression. The blogger who commented on my Kuggnäs wristband was better known to insiders as rapper Zyklon Boom, whose rhymes savaged liberalism and multiculturalism while showcasing bookish smarts and wit. Even organizer Daniel Friberg was a music producer involved in some of the most innovative and celebrated nationalist albums in the Nordic countries.

Music, in other words, saturated the activism of Nordic nationalists in muddy fields and seminar rooms alike. And the hidden music in Stockholm had a story to tell, namely, that those attending the seminar differed in their visions of themselves and their cause. Through music they identified variously as wholesome, down-to-earth, victimized and oppressed, or learned and intelectual. What they held in common was their shared antithesis: none at the seminar were interested in associating with the music others expected them to like, the music featured in the muddy field to the south—skinhead music.

As I sat on the train heading from Stockholm to the night performances at Kuggnäs, it seemed as though I traveled between eras. Most of the individuals in Stockholm had their nationalist awakenings in settings like that at Kuggnäs, inspired by the very artists who would perform on that stage. They were moving on, however. Through creative expression they were inventing new selves and finding new nations to defend. They are the reformers, the anti-skinheads, the New Nationalists. Their organizations and initiatives exploded during the past decade to fundamentally and forever change Nordic society. Skinheadism, on the other hand, had crumbled. Yes, the numbers at the festival were far greater than those in Stockholm. But the skinheads did not gather in that field to sing of brighter futures. They were there to say goodbye.

Sitting on the train, it seemed I was ideally positioned to present what follows: a story about music and the transformation of Nordic radical nationalism in the early twenty-first century. The transition I study is unreconciled and incomplete, and it remains a movement of processes rather than conclusions. My focus lies therefore not in the muddy fields of nationalism's past, nor in the halls it is preparing for its future, but rather on the spaces and tracks in between, where anxiety reigns and new music resounds.

LIONS OF THE NORTH

1

INTRODUCTION

OUTSIDERS CALL THEM "right-wing extremists," "organized racists," or "neofascists," but they call themselves "nationalists." They are a fractured and chaotic population of activists who see themselves as struggling for the survival of European societies. Some advocate white racial or ethnic purity, while others claim to be defending cultural or religious norms. Despite intense ideological differences among nationalists, all fight against the growth of immigration and multiculturalism. And since World War II, theirs has been the most reviled political cause in the west.

Though certain nationalists consider themselves heirs of the Third Reich, their activism often has far more recent roots. Skinhead subculture seized and rebranded opposition to immigration during the late twentieth century. Its fashion, literature, and—above all—punk and metal music mobilized masses of white working-class youths across Europe, making what was officially a political rebellion also an engine of expressive culture. Record labels became key sources for fundraising, songs voiced core beliefs, music magazines served as core media organs, concerts hosted the largest nationalist gatherings, and musicians rather than politicians emerged as the cause's foremost celebrities (Brown 2004; Pieslak 2015).

Nordics—and Swedes in particular—always held an exceptional status in this global scene. Revolutionary white nationalists and neo-Nazis throughout the world have long showcased imagery of the North in their artwork, myths, and songs, praising Swedes as the quintessential members of the community they championed—as the "whitest of all whites" (Hübinette 2012:45). However, Sweden rejected even the most tempered and politically effective expressions of Europe's late-twentieth-century nationalist explosion. Throughout the 1980s, 1990s, and early 2000s, anti-immigrant political parties entered parliaments in France, Austria, Germany, Belgium, Holland, Hungary, and Italy, as well as in Denmark and Norway. Yet no such party could establish itself in Sweden (Green-Pedersen and Odmalm 2008);[1] this was vital to the country's cherished reputation as a global beacon of tolerance (Andersson and Hilson 2009; Hübinette and Lundström 2011). Having kept anti-immigrant forces out of its government, Sweden would by 2013 become the recipient of more refugees per capita than any other country in Europe.[2]

Although nationalists failed to enter Sweden's parliament, they flourished in the country's underground. Sweden became a center for skinhead subculture and militant neo-Nazism during the 1980s and 1990s, and the bedrock of this movement was the growth of a peerless nationalist skinhead music industry (Lööw 1998a; Lagerlöf 2012). By 2005, the country had nearly three times the number of nationalist bands that could be found in all the other Nordic countries combined and a higher rate of bands per capita than any other country worldwide.[3] The fortunes of Sweden's skinheads and anti-immigration politicians, however, would soon reverse.

During the first decade of the twenty-first century, the country's once-mighty skinhead culture came undone as its militant leaders were imprisoned, its gatherings were prohibited, and its many record labels were liquidated. On the heels of this downfall, in 2010, a political party called the Sweden Democrats earned 5.7 percent of the national vote, thereby gaining representation in parliament. The Sweden Democrats weren't just an anti-immigrant party. Unlike most of their counterparts in Western Europe, they were also self-identified nationalists, born in part from the same skinhead movement that fueled militant Nordic neo-Nazism. Their meager but symbolic share of the electorate would more than double in the 2014 elections, and by early 2016 opinion polls showed them contending to become the largest party in the country. They had not only tarnished Sweden's reputation as a global liberal flagship—the party threatened to dismantle that reputation entirely.

The collapse of skinheadism and the rapid rise of the Sweden Democrats have a common impetus. As long as skinhead subculture and anti-immigrant activism have been synonymous in the North, there have been disgruntled insiders claiming that their movement's brutish image was counterproductive. Visions for an alternative to skinheadism were as numerous as the insider critics themselves. The push to cultivate an ideologically moderate, democratic nationalist force—which eventually found expression in the Sweden Democrats—was but one of multiple sites in a mass exodus from nationalism's hooliganistic stereotype. These reformist efforts ushered in a new era of anti-immigrant, antiliberal activism in Sweden and, by extension, the wider Nordic region. Further, just as skinheadism was forged through style, so too did reformers negotiate and craft their new identities via creative expression.

In this book, I offer a glimpse into Nordic radical nationalism during this process of change, and I do so focusing on an artform with peculiar importance to the anti-immigrant, antiliberal cause. The transformation of nationalism in the North has been perpetuated by a dramatic shift in activists' musical practices. Organizations seeking to rebrand their cause as a fight against alleged white oppression now spread this message through hip-hop and reggae. Others refashion themselves as wholesome champions of an idyllic Nordic past, rallying behind traditional folk music. Still others seeking to portray themselves as victims turn to sorrowful pop ballads to express their fear and desperation. More importantly, these unorthodox projects sparked extensive controversy and discussion among nationalists and prompted insiders to reflect upon their essence and declare their dreams for the future. Music and the discourses surrounding it thus offer insight into this shrouded population as it transitions from a marginal subculture into a powerful political and cultural force.

This book diverges from standard scholarship on European nationalists in both its interest in music and its research methods. It is based on several years of ethnographic fieldwork I conducted among nationalists in Sweden and the surrounding Nordic countries. From 2010 until 2012, and later during the summers of 2013, 2014, and 2015, I traveled throughout the region interviewing and observing ideologues, politicians, activists, and musicians. Various watershed events in Nordic radical nationalism punctuated this timespan. I was in the field during the Sweden Democrats' entry into parliament as well as when Anders Behring Breivik carried out a pair of racially motivated (Teitelbaum 2016) terrorist attacks in Oslo and Utøya, Norway that left seventy-seven people—most of them children—dead. My fieldwork provided experiences that were compelling, electrifying, and horrifying, along with a host of unresolved ethical dilemmas. But they also left me astounded at music's awesome potential to forge new identities for people and social movements alike (Frith 1996; Born and Hesmondhalgh 2000).

In what follows I introduce the actors at the center of this work, the techniques I used to study them, and the antecedents and agendas shaping their current moment of transformation.

> I don't know if you were quoted correctly in today's *Aftonbladet*, but if you were, I must
> question your use of the term "nationalist pop" to describe Saga. From what I can see, she is an
> outspoken Nazi who sings white power music. I don't know what in the world that has to do with
> nationalism. Nazism is an anti-nationalist ideology. (electronic message, August 7, 2011)[4]

The Sweden Democrats' chief ideologue, Mattias Karlsson, sent me this message following an interview I gave to the newspaper *Aftonbladet*. The interview dealt with Saga, a Swedish singer whose core audience consists of self-identified National Socialists, whose lyrics express sympathy for historic Nazism, and whose stage performances often include right-arm *Sieg Heil!* salutes. The relatively moderate Karlsson rejects all association with Saga, arguing that the singer's manifest racialism and overtures to the Third Reich—which he considers an imperialist movement that violated the national sovereignty of others—mark an irreconcilable opposition between his and her worldviews. But, like Saga, Karlsson insists on calling himself a "nationalist." If actors so different can adopt this label, then what does it mean?

The population I study in this book is difficult to define. A subset of all anti-immigrant forces in the Nordic region, its boundaries do not follow those of any organization or voting bloc. Nationalists diverge over issues as fundamental as the nature of identity, the origins and consequences of immigration to the North, and the lineage of their cause. At times, disagreements lead them to deny affiliation with each other, and occasionally lead to acts of violence. Given such discord, one can reasonably question whether these actors ought to be treated as an integrated whole—whether the affinities among nationalists go any deeper than their shared name.

Broadly speaking, nationalism in the Nordic countries is aligned among three ideological and methodological camps: race revolutionaries, cultural nationalists, and identitarians.[5] The three camps, represented in Figure 1.1, are seldom equal to each other in terms of size or influence, and their relationships have long been in flux. The first camp, race revolutionaries, encompasses individuals who often call themselves "white nationalists" or "National Socialists." Typically celebrating the cause and mythology of historical Nazism, these actors rally behind a racial community—conceived along national ethnic lines or as transnational Nordic, Aryan, or white populations—and tend to identify Jews as the ultimate enemies of their people. Operating in a postwar west in which their ideals are banished from mainstream politics, many race revolutionaries abandon hope of creating a populist mass movement through democratic processes, and instead opt to form violent paramilitary groups or youth street gangs. Having been at the center of the nationalist skinhead

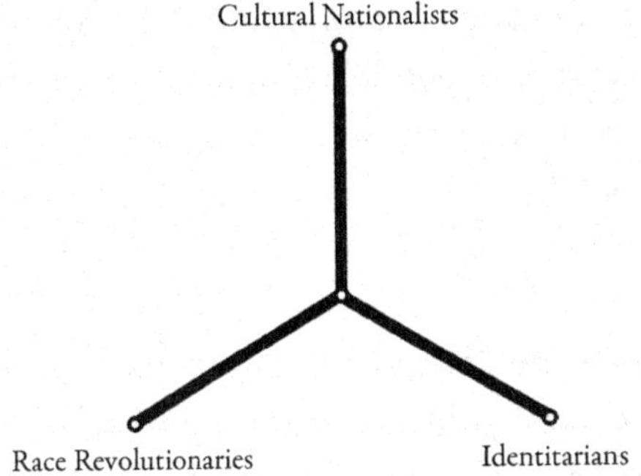

FIGURE 1.1 Three-part map of the contemporary Nordic radical nationalist scene.

movement during the 1980s and 1990s, they are now highly marginalized and few in number. The foremost Nordic race revolutionary organization today is the Sweden-based Nordic Resistance Movement.[6]

Whereas race revolutionaries declare national identity to be a matter of blood, the second camp of nationalists—cultural nationalists—claim that one's status as a Swede, Dane, or Norwegian derives from cultural practices that can be adopted by any individual regardless of their ethnicity. Often philosemitic and pro-Israel, they train their criticisms on Muslim immigration in addition to social liberalism, alleging that Islam poses the greatest threat to the cultural integrity of the national people. With this comparatively mainstream agenda, cultural nationalists are poised to achieve wider appeal than race revolutionaries, and most of them operate in democratic political parties. Cultural nationalists are the most numerous of all nationalist camps in the Nordic countries today, and they find their chief representation in the leadership of the Sweden Democrats.

Activists associating with a school called "identitarianism" make up the third, most complicated camp. These actors often assert that race and ethnicity are indispensable elements of identity—a position that places them opposite cultural nationalists in a broad ethnonationalist field, together with race revolutionaries. However, and in contrast with white nationalists and National Socialists, identitarians do not strive toward racial or ethnic purity as an end in itself. Their aim to preserve biological fellowship is one piece of a larger campaign to promote social diversity in nearly all ways imaginable. Rather than opposing any particular ethnic or religious Other, they claim to oppose movements that homogenize human society, such as liberalism, Marxism, capitalism, or evangelical monotheism. Identitarians often dismiss the possibility of affecting change through revolution or parliamentary politics. Instead, they commit themselves to propagandizing and intellectual activism—to shaping ideas—often through media, expressive culture, or nonviolent public spectacles. Only handfuls of Nordic nationalists call themselves "identitarians": numerically, it is the smallest of the three nationalist camps. However, their influence is considerable. Identitarians are chiefly responsible for producing the cultural and expressive forms that dominate post-skinhead Nordic nationalism. The identitarian cause is represented in the region by online journalism, publishing, and social networking initiatives sprung from an organization called the Nordic League.

There are many exceptions to this classificatory scheme, with alternative configurations of ideology and methodology appearing frequently. Some white nationalists and National Socialists form political parties and participate in elections, such as Vigrid in Norway, the Party of the Danes, and the Party of the Swedes (formerly the National Socialist Front). Activists like Norwegian terrorist Anders Behring Breivik, in contrast, publicly espoused a cultural nationalist, anti-Muslim agenda while embracing militancy as a method of activism. Additionally, organizations and initiatives migrate between these camps. The Sweden Democrats, for example, first emerged with an ideological profile nearer to race revolutionaries and a methodology like identitarians, but they have since become the standard-bearers of democratic cultural nationalism. Race revolutionaries, cultural nationalists, and identitarians thus do not account for all nationalist activism in the North. Instead, they serve as end points on a three-way continuum.

Scholarly and journalistic observers have been quick to dismiss nationalists' internal dividing lines. The field of critical race studies has long alleged that discourses like cultural nationalism are merely the new public façade of race nationalism—that when nationalists talk about irreconcilable "cultural differences" among peoples, they are simply describing race in less incriminating language.[7] Similarly, Scandinavian media personalities like Henrik Arnstad (2013) allege that fascist conceptual frameworks appear in the agendas of both so-called moderate activists like Mattias Karlsson and historical and contemporary National Socialists;[8] thus they view apparent variations among nationalists as deriving from shifting political strategies or activists' efforts to deceive outside observers. Such accounts are powerful tools in the hands of antiracist commentators as they strive to undermine ascendant nationalist political parties and their claims to moderation.

Though this paradigm enjoys widespread celebration in media circles, it fails to grasp the often genuinely felt and socially consequential ideological differences among activists, as well as the extra-ideological forces that bring them together. In a move likely to frustrate political activist readers of all types, I argue in this book that while nationalists share a broad ideological profile they are ultimately united by their affiliation with select media, lifestyles, and expressive culture. It is when we regard Nordic nationalism as both an ideological and a sociocultural phenomenon that the connections between actors like Mattias Karlsson and singer Saga become clearer.

I will briefly introduce these defining ideological and sociocultural aspects of nationalism, along with the terms I use to describe them. What unites these actors politically is their aim to effect dramatic societal changes to promote the purity of a national people. This profile, general and encompassing as it is, can be better described with the insider term, "radical nationalist," than with the umbrella term most commonly used by commentators, "right-wing extremist."[9] Whereas nationalist groups in other parts of the western world may welcome association with political rightism, Nordic nationalists do not always feel closer to rightists than to leftists in their own country. Association with the right may seem intuitive to them in some senses. Nationalist rhetoric often longs for the past, to times when the Nordic countries were allegedly more culturally or ethnically homogenous. The will to return society to one of its earlier forms could be seen as a hallmark of rightism via conservatism. Additionally, the major establishment Swedish right-wing party today, the Moderates, contained a significant number of Nazi sympathizers in its youth organization during World War II (Lööw 2004). However, free-market liberalism, rather than social conservatism or opposition to immigration, has defined rightism in contemporary mainstream Nordic politics. Conversely, nearly all nationalist political parties and organizations in the North reject economic liberalism and advocate a robust welfare state—a stance in line with Nordic social democracy, and one that further hinders them from identifying with rightists abroad.

Like the label "right-wing," "extremism" also seems a word ill-suited to describe the population of nationalists as a whole. In his masterful conceptual history of extremism, German political scientist Uwe Backes maps centuries of attempts to define extremism, and highlights an understanding of the concept emerging from the Aristotelian tradition. According to that tradition, extremism aspires to monism over pluralism, egotistical interest over a common goal, despotism instead of a legal state, and outside determination over self-determination. And, Backes adds, "in the social psychological realm, [extremism] can be interpreted as a consequence of ambiguity intolerance, refusal to accept the heterogeneity and ambiguity of the world" (2010:184). Were we to use the term "extremism" in this sense to describe Nordic nationalists, we would be calling them essentially antidemocratic and uncompromising. Although some nationalist organizations are openly antidemocratic, others assert that they support democracy, and virtually all see themselves as fierce advocates of free speech. Further, and perhaps more problematically, by calling nationalists "extremists," we might be declaring ourselves privy to an ultimate reality—some particular state of heterogeneity and ambiguity inherent in the human condition—of which they are ignorant.

"Radical nationalism" is by no means a perfect descriptor. Contemporary nationalisms in the postcolonial world and parts of Eastern and Southern Europe target entirely different national Others than the forces I describe in this book—foreign governments rather than domestic minorities, respectively—and their agendas do not always differ radically from their local political mainstreams. National borders can also be of secondary importance to neo-Nazi and white nationalist movements, whose members at times prioritize the boundaries of a transnational white or Nordic race over those of specific nation-states. Ideologues associated with the identitarian school, in contrast, emphasize both pan-European and regional ethnic identities over those of the nation—an entity they regard as a modernist construct blind to organic ethnic communities. Despite these shortcomings, "radical nationalism" remains an attractive heading in the Nordic countries because it avoids problematic distinctions between right and left;[10] encompasses both democratic and antidemocratic methods of political engagement; signals these actors' affinity with classic nationalist thought; and captures their commitment to an imagined national people in the face of overwhelming social, political, and cultural odds.

However, though all nationalists oppose immigration, not all who oppose immigration are nationalists. If we are to understand what makes someone a nationalist in the Nordic countries today, we must look beyond ideology. Whether they belong to a moderate political party or a National Socialist militant group, most nationalists are young or middle-aged men. In addition, most share a history of violent confrontation with anarchist and anti-fascist activists; most consume each other's media and believe that mainstream journalistic and academic establishments deliberately misrepresent and undermine their cause; and most maintain a body of insider language (terms like "ZOG [Zionist Occupation Government]," "oikofobi," and "metapolitik" are opaque to average Swedes, Danes, or Norwegians but understood by virtually all nationalists). Most nationalists also have past relationships to skinheadism, either as participants themselves or through close friends and fellow activists; and finally, most are familiar with a body of nationalist music, featuring in particular songs by the Viking rock band Ultima Thule and the ethnonationalist singer-songwriter project Svensk Ungdom.

Nationalism in the Nordic countries today is not only an ideology; it also encompasses a social and cultural identity. Elsewhere in Europe race revolutionaries, cultural nationalists, and identitarians do not belong to the same sociocultural or political sphere. However, these forces are driven together in the North because of their interpersonal histories, their alleged or actual association with 1990s skinheadism, their shared demographic features, and their shared experience of being confronted en masse by a mainstream devoted to keeping them all—moderates as well as utmost fringe actors—at bay. The unity of the three nationalist camps is especially pronounced in Sweden. There, social conservatism and opposition to immigration have long been absent from standard political discourse, and the rise of the

Sweden Democrats has been fiercely contested by major parties across the political spectrum. Banished from the political and media establishment, diverse nationalists in Sweden often consume each other's texts and endure a similarly hostile reception in public, and this helps imbue their expressions with a deviant and defiant character befitting a protest subculture. Indeed, whereas leaders in Nordic anti-immigrant parties like the Danish People's Party, Norway's Progress Party, and the Finns Party are seldom nationalist insiders, many in the Sweden Democrats' party leadership are.

I describe this composite nationalist ideological and sociocultural community and the infrastructure sustaining it as "the nationalist scene." I use the term "scene," not in Irwin's sense as a collectivity built around "a central leisure activity, a set of special symbols and meanings, relative availability, and action" (1977:30), but more specifically as real or virtual spaces for exhcnage among individuals who share concern for a cluster of issues and familiarity with unconventional modes of expression.[11] The communicative channels and sociocultural practices that construct such scenes at any given time must encompass diverse ideological impulses. They must mark participants as insiders while also providing factions room to differentiate themselves. But the discursive and symbolic forms that demarcate a scene are seldom static. Instead, they adjust in response to the broader political climate, internal power struggles, or changes in technology. The phenomena I explore in this book are the result of one such shift in the nationalist scene—a shift away from skinhead subculture and toward new ways of looking, acting, and sounding like a nationalist.

Thus, while scholars of radical nationalism typically investigate the varying manifestations of a core ideology over time and among groups,[12] the nature of the Nordic nationalist scene—and perhaps of those beyond—compels us to examine the ongoing transformations of expressive behaviors and social identities. The study of contemporary Nordic radical nationalism is therefore not the exclusive domain of political science or intellectual history. Rather, it requires insights into the production of culture, the dynamics of interpersonal relationships, and the metamorphosis of style: it requires humanistic ethnography.

Studying Radical Nationalism

This book is the product of a multiyear ethnography I conducted among a wide network of nationalists in the Nordic countries.[13] My activities during fieldwork centered on face-to-face conversations and interviews, repeated observations of concerts and other events, and informal contact—the "deep hanging out" (Geertz 1998) that cultivates trust and unleashes ethnography's explanatory force. As common as these approaches are within the fields of anthropology and ethnomusicology, they are scarce in studies of radical nationalism. A handful of exceptions notwithstanding,[14] scholars of nationalist groups seldom pursue sustained, direct, and transparent contact with insiders during the research and writing process. My departure from that trend stems from my goals as a scholar, my understandings of nationalism, my personal background, and my complicated relationship with those I study.

Since my teenage years I have yearned to be Swedish; perhaps because of the deep love I felt for my Swedish grandmother, perhaps because the Jewish side of my background—more apparent in my name and appearance—felt burdensome as a youth in suburban Denver, Colorado. I devoted the bulk of my young adult life to cultivating a Swedish identity through language study, genealogical research, and especially Swedish folk music.

While still in secondary school during the early 2000s, I began traveling to Sweden every summer to study music and discover sites and people linked to my grandmother's family. It was during those visits when I first encountered nationalists. I spotted skinheads in small towns, saw them profiled on television news, and heard them discussed around the kitchen tables of my newfound Swedish relatives. I was confused by my initial reactions to these actors. Their politics, looks, and lifestyles were far from my own. Yet theirs were also the only patriotic voices I heard in the supremely postmodern, postnational nation, and I felt drawn to them for that reason. I was at the time attempting to experience and celebrate my own Swedishness, and I identified nationalists as those most aligned with the logic of my thinking and its implied assertion that belonging in Sweden depended on ethnicity. The nationalists asserted ownership of, and sought to police, that which I so coveted. However, I also assumed that they among all people were most likely to reject my claim to Swedish identity on account of who I was: a liberal, half-Jewish, American academic. My emotions were as memorable as they were conflicted, and I came to view nationalists with an arresting mix of disgust, fear, sympathy, and fascination.

Perhaps owing to my early experiences, questions about nationalists' rightness or wrongness were of secondary interest to me. What captivated me instead were the mysteries of their inner workings and the powers of their expression. I wanted to understand—rather than criticize—their symbols, visions, and lives. It seems fitting that when I returned to study nationalists in 2010 as a scholar, I grappled not with my own but with their identity crises and strained attempts to reinvent themselves through music.

I thus approach the study of this population with an uncommon agenda. Most researchers of radical nationalism in the Nordic countries operate with the primary goal of undermining the movements they study. Their projects often strive to expose the unsightliness of nationalist thought or to outline techniques for blunting its political advance.[15] Active opposition limits research potential, however, for few scholars can convince insiders to participate in such politically engaged studies. This was vividly illustrated when independent scholar Anna-Lena Lodenius attempted to arrange interviews with members of the militant Nordic Resistance Movement as part of a government-funded study on nationalists' recruitment efforts. The e-mail response to her query, which the Resistance Movement posted online, did not surprise:

> Hello Anna-Lena! The question is whether we would like to participate in a government study where we would explain details about how we recruit. Details that would then be used to try to stop our recruiting. It's quite strange that you even took the time to ask. How stupid do you think we are, really?[16]

Because combining transparent insider contact with antinationalist activism promises awkward results, most scholars either conceal their intentions or forgo direct interaction with insiders. Daniel Poohl, for example, infiltrated a Swedish ethnic separatist party in 2001 by posing as a sympathizer, and he even traveled with a party delegation to Prague before exiting the organization and turning over large amounts of damning video footage to the media. Alternately, Mattias Wåg based his research (2010) on a large collection of hacked e-mails among nationalist leaders.

In few other fields of inquiry would the academic community tolerate such relationships between scholars and insiders, and rarely have researchers been willing to say so much about living people with whom they have such little and strained interaction. Yet the broad acceptance of these methods is as much intellectual as it is political. Once nationalists are regarded as but ideologies incarnate, the need to study them as multifaceted individuals weakens, as does the appeal of research methods that might bring scholars into deeper contact with insiders and their idiosyncrasies.

Activist agendas, an analytical focus on ideology, and a lack of productive contact with insiders are mutually reinforcing tendencies in the study of radical nationalism. They never seemed options to me as I began my own research. I was convinced that the unidimensional nature of much activist scholarship left an unacceptable amount of the nationalist experience unexamined. Further, I thought that gaining greater understanding of the complex ways nationalists think and live required more than an impersonal survey of their musical and extramusical "texts," and more than could be found by intruding on their private correspondences or infiltrating their communities in disguise.[17]

I aspired to base both my research and my writing on extensive contact and exchange with insiders—an approach drawing from what is often called "collaborative ethnography" (Lassiter 2005). My success in recruiting and partnering with nationalists relied on my topic: I once overheard one insider say to another, while discussing my request for an interview, "He's safe to talk to. He's not interested in anything serious. Just music." But I most attribute my ability to forge a broad network of informants to my disavowal of an activist agenda. When approaching nationalists, I always explained that I had no connections to any official antiracist organization or initiative and clarified that I aimed to produce scholarship focused on understanding their cause rather than undermining it. My rapport with informants deepened as I worked to involve them in the writing process. I gave all interviewees ample time to review instances where I quoted them, and I consulted with many about this book as a whole.[18] Likewise, I worked to write about nationalists in prose free from the condemnations and admonitions standard in academic and journalistic commentary. I did all this not because I see radical nationalism as a political cause like any other, nor because I champion the silly fetish of an unattainable neutrality as a commentator. Rather, I hoped that by abandoning terms like "racist" and "fascist" I might deny readers their expectations and challenge them to approach the topic with curiosity.[19]

While my approach to research spares me from some concerns and liabilities, it introduces others. Scholars of contemporary social behavior advocate collaborative ethnography and similar techniques for reasons both ethical and epistemological. Working in partnership with the people we study counteracts the type of exploitative research that marred early-twentieth-century anthropology (Wolf and Jorgensen 1970; Asad 1973) and helps us access the expertise of insider scrutiny of our claims and ideas. Notions of how relationships between scholars and informants ought to manifest have shifted throughout the past decades. Since the 1970s, official ethical codes produced by anthropological and ethnomusicological academic societies have called on scholars to reject research practices that harm or deceive informants in the field.[20] Writings on ethnographic ethics outside official settings tend to look beyond practices of nonintervention, advocating collaboration as well as reciprocity, advocacy,[21] and even care and empathy in field relationships—a so-called friendship model of fieldwork (Pelto and Pelto 1973; Cooley 2003; Beaudry 2008; Shelemay 2008; Titon 2008).

Warranted as these approaches may be, they were not designed for projects like my own. Calls for collaboration and advocacy appear ethical because they assume scholars will study groups whose cause is virtuous. Theorists of ethnography might be excused for such presumption. Historically, anthropologists in particular have gravitated toward the disenfranchised, the oppressed, or the marginalized (Kulick 2006), and acting in solidarity with such communities is often uncontroversial. But collaboration and advocacy lose their aura of righteousness as soon as scholars venture beyond the study of subjugated peoples. In my case, some might say that adopting standard ethnographic practice would be anything but ethical. Nationalists of all kinds pursue agendas that would harm or marginalize others, and their shared goal of homogenizing heterogeneous populations augurs spectacular acts of injustice. Further, a culture of violence shrouds the Nordic nationalist scene. Militant organizations like the Nordic Resistance Movement are linked to strings of assaults on ethnic and religious minorities, homosexuals, and antifascist activists. Political parties and intellectual organizations rarely inflict violence on others or themselves, although they occasionally harass political and ideological opponents in ways that traumatize, such as publishing opponents' addresses and personal information online, writing defamatory articles, and vandalizing property.

Though collaborative ethnography may lose its claim to moral superiority in the study of such groups, its use is essential nonetheless. Mutual respect, honesty of purpose, and partnership in interpretation are indispensable to the type of close contact demanded by today's research standards. When we refuse that level of contact with people, we refuse to know them. And it would be naïve, further, to think that we could spend hundreds of hours among a group of people and remain only disinterested observers. Despite passionate claims to the contrary (Lassider 2005; Holmes and Marcus 2008), many ethnographers see collaboration and advocacy as byproducts of successful long-term fieldwork (e.g., Kemper and Royce 2002; Stuart 2002:178)—as outcomes of close interaction with insiders that scholars are now acknowledging as a resource rather than engineering anew. Indeed, throughout the course of my fieldwork, I became friends with some of my informants. I grew to know and enjoy their families. I came to hear of their personal struggles and pains, and they heard of mine. I spent days touring Viking-era archaeological sites with them, afternoons teaching their children how to throw an American football, and nights drinking copious amounts of alcohol. Was I functioning as a researcher in all of these instances? I am not sure. But it was during those occasions when I gained key insights into the questions that guide this study—into who these people are, why they are nationalists, and what and how music means to them.

The question of whether friendship turned into sympathy and advocacy is not as simple as it seems. Just as I seek to study nationalists as dynamic sociocultural and political actors, so too are my feelings toward them multifaceted and conflicting. Throughout the course of my fieldwork, I gained a greater appreciation for the grievances they hold regarding their treatment. The majority of those we will meet in this book report having been assaulted by communist, anarchist, and antifascist activists. They have been pelted with cobblestones, tear-gassed in front of their families, and beaten with iron pipes. One had a swastika knifed into his forehead, and another suffered a gang attack that police would later classify as an attempted murder.[22] While objecting to these blatant acts of violence, I have also grown critical of journalistic commentary on nationalists, particularly in Sweden. All too often it seems the Swedish mainstream uses nationalists to avoid grappling with its own shortcomings, whether they be practical problems in immigration and integration policies or, alternately, its own tendancies toward racism.[23]

Scattered points of agreement like these allowed the sympathy I felt toward individual nationalists to creep beyond the interpersonal, and left me—and I suspect some of my informants—wondering if affinities between us might run deeper yet. Certainly, the complicated attraction to Swedish nationalism I felt as a youth continued to lurk in my mind, and at times it felt as though I was occupying something like what Susan Harding calls "narrative space" between between belief and unbelief in her study of Born-Again Christians (2001:xii). But a conversation, a joke, a chorus, a word, a gesture, a drag, or a glance always served to remind me that I am and will remain an outsider to those I study—socially, culturally, and politically.

The text emerging from my experiences is neither dispassionate nor ethically reconciled. Nationalists are people to me rather than ideologies, and I cannot write about them in the demonizing language demanded by activist audiences or with the unbiased remove I might once have coveted. You will no doubt sense my affection for some of these individuals. My tendency to dwell on their personal eccentricities, histories, and tastes—combined with the lack of critical language in my narration—can be faulted for helping to normalize controversial and widely discredited positions. Further, I anticipate that my friendships with insiders, my relative disinterest in assessing the truth of their claims, and my past fascination with the scene may be bedfellows all too suspicious for some readers. I trust, though, that this book will not act as an espousal or defense of radical nationalism. Allowed to speak freely and without interference, insiders describe their cause in ways that reveal its core assumptions and ambitions.

Historical Background

The overwhelming majority of contemporary nationalists in the Nordic countries are Swedes, and for that reason Sweden dominates my attention in this book. Historical circumstances helped position the country in this flagship role. Sweden escaped military confrontation during World War II, thanks in part to its geographic position and also to its willingness to collaborate with Germany during the conflict's early stages. Each of Sweden's Nordic neighbors, in contrast, experienced invasion. Nazi troops occupied Denmark and Norway in 1940 and would remain in these countries until the end of the war. To the east, the Soviets attempted to annex Finland, prompting the Finns to align with the Germans in defense of their border. Facing a strengthening Red Army, Finland would sign an armistice with the Soviet Union in 1944 that compelled the country to cede land in the east and expel German brigades within its territory.[24]

The aftereffects of World War II varied among the Nordic countries. Denmark, Norway, and Finland emerged from the conflict with their sovereignty intact, which energized national pride. Further, after years of occupation, anti-German sentiment in Denmark and Norway was intense, as was contempt for local Nazi collaborators. The various war-era fascist and National Socialist organizations in these countries were quickly dissolved after 1945, and some of their leaders were executed in what would be the last instances of capital punishment in the North. In Finland, fascist organizations were suppressed in accordance with the country's armistice with the Soviet Union.

The commonplace nature of public patriotism among Danes, Norwegians, and Finns, combined with their entrenched hostilities toward Nazism, would leave subsequent generations less receptive to future attempts to forge a radical nationalism through Third Reich nostalgia. The situation in Sweden was different. With an infrastructure largely undamaged by military conflict, Sweden emerged from the war era by embarking on a campaign of hypermodernization. These efforts enabled considerable economic development and a cultural transformation centered on expanding rationalistic, liberal values in opposition to romanticized nationalism and religion (Löfgren 1993). And whereas discourses in surrounding Nordic countries pitted local patriotism against German National Socialism, the component pieces of such sentiment were absent in the Swedish context.

A scattering of small, anti-Semitic, race-nationalist organizations surfaced in Sweden in the decades following World War II. Most of these groups faded quickly after their inception. Those organizations that survived into the 1970s—most notably the war-era fascist group the New Swedish Movement and the postwar Nordic Reich Party—existed as social clubs as much as activist groups.[25] However, demographic change and the rise of an international white youth subculture would later ignite a surge of radical nationalism within Sweden and in the Nordic region by extension, lifting the cause out of dormancy and into the public eye.

Scandinavia embraced a wave of refugee immigration in the early 1970s. Refugees had been arriving in the region during previous decades, many from Soviet Eastern Europe. During the 1970s, however, this immigration increased dramatically and expanded to include individuals from more distant sites like Yugoslavia, Iran, Iraq, Lebanon, and Chile. And though the Nordic region as a whole was attractive to refugees, Norway and Sweden became the most common destinations because of their relatively generous asylum policies and economic strength (Runblom 1995:293–306).

Sweden's vision for integrating immigrants shifted throughout these decades. Although policies resembling both assimilationism and multiculturalism reigned throughout the country's past, the state grew to favor a multiculturalist model when refugees began constituting a larger portion of its immigrant population. In 1974 the sitting administration in parliament adopted changes to its integration policy aimed at recognizing and accommodating minorities' cultural difference. The reforms declared that cultural identity in Sweden would be built on "freedom of choice [*valfrihet*]" in forging cultural loyalties, "equality [*jämlikhet*]," and "cooperation [*samverkan*]."[26]

As years went on, the Swedish state gradually strengthened this position in its constitution, moving from language that permitted minorities to maintain their own cultural allegiances to language that encouraged and even sanctioned such identification. In 2002, the government altered the constitution to declare, "Ethnic, linguistic, and religious minorities' ability to preserve and develop their own culture and social life should be promoted." Eight years later, in fall 2010, the concluding statement, "should be promoted," was changed to "shall be promoted" (Chapter 1, 3§).[27] Support for constitutional multiculturalism in Sweden has been remarkably steady throughout periods of left-wing and right-wing rule. Indeed, Ålund's and Schierup's claim during the 1990s that "stable consensus (in terms of right-left politics) on the importance of multicultural rights . . . is probably unique to Sweden" (1991:4) remained valid into the 2010s.[28]

The expansion of immigration and multiculturalism stirred resentment among the native-born population. By the mid-1980s, radical nationalist groups in the country were experiencing unprecedented gains. The Nordic Reich Party enjoyed moderate growth during the late 1980s and early 1990s. However, more dramatic expansion occurred when a kaleidoscope of small, semimilitant organizations rose up throughout Scandinavia, and Sweden in particular. These "groupuscules"[29] typically espoused Nazism, draping themselves and their cultural and intellectual output in references to the Third Reich. Nationalist organizations and political parties tended to struggle against each other as much as they challenged their sworn political opponents, and instances of sabotage and violence among nationalists were common. But many understood themselves as being united in a larger whole, which they often referred to as "the national movement [*den nationella rörelsen*]."

Though its most vocal and visible actors were self-identified National Socialists, the early national movement encompassed ideological diversity. Its cause and public image would be transformed by an activist group with a generic nationalist profile called "Keep Sweden Swedish" (*Bevara Sverige Svenskt*). Emerging in 1979, Keep Sweden Swedish's official output prophesized cultural and economic devastation due to immigration, as well as the loss of racial purity and the inability for nonwhites to function in Swedish society. However, it almost never celebrated Hitler or presented

Jews as a significant threat to the North. This ideological orientation spurred a heated rivalry between Keep Sweden Swedish on the one hand and the conglomerate National Socialist groupuscules and parties on the other. The Nordic Reich Party even alleged that the activist group was filled with disguised Zionists bent on undermining National Socialism and the resurgence of the Nordic race (Ekman and Poohl 2010:25).

The surface antagonisms between these groups belied the fact that many members of Keep Sweden Swedish—including leading figures like Leif Zeilon and Niels Mandell—were formerly associated with the Nordic Reich Party. Nonetheless, this new organization attracted more moderate activists, and as years went by it drifted further from its National Socialist counterparts. With an agenda less offensive to mainstream sociopolitical taboos, the organization set its sights on something that had eluded all nationalist groups since World War II: elected office. Throughout the 1980s, leaders grew enthusiastic about expanding their role from that of a propaganda organization to a political party. They made this change in 1986, joining forces with the anti-immigrant, tax-populist Progress Party. At first, the new organization called itself the Sweden Party. However, two years later, and in the wake of some minor administrative turnover, they changed their name to the Sweden Democrats—the same name the party would use when they entered Sweden's national parliament twenty-two years later.

Skinhead Song

> Were our spiritual leader Adolf Hitler alive today, I am sure he would not be running around with a whip and riding pants. Every era has its own strategies, and today music is our weapon and our white skin is our uniform! (Matti Sundquist, *Nordland*, no. 3 (1995:33))

The explosion of nationalist organizations in 1980s and 1990s Sweden, as well as in Norway and Denmark, relied on factors beyond rising resentment toward non-western refugee immigration. Like many of their counterparts throughout Europe and North America, Nordic activists propelled the dramatic expansion of radical nationalism by importing British skinheadism. Skinhead style first emerged as an offshoot of the London hard-mod scene during the late 1960s. Early British skinheads abandoned the typical mod-style dress suit for jeans and combat boots and began cropping their hair—a style borrowed from West Indian immigrants living in London (Mercer 1987:18, 1994; Hebdige 1988). Though at first the scene contained diverse demographics and political causes, skinheadism grew to become a voice for urban, working-class, race-nationalist whites.

Historians trace the yoking of neo-Nazi activism and skinhead subculture to the late 1970s and early 1980s, a time when nationalist organizations in Britain like the National Front and the British Movement began recruiting skinheads to their cause (Marshall 1991:99). Music was the main vessel for this union. Nationalist Oi! punk and metal musicians—most notably the English band Skrewdriver—would craft an image that mixed odes to Hitler and Rudolph Hess, critiques of contemporary immigration and multiculturalism, and the skinhead style. The genre came to be known as white power, and its spread throughout Europe nourished by perceptions that skinheadism and neo-Nazism were one and the same (Brown 2004).

Music also fueled the rise of skinheadism and nationalist activism in Sweden. Dozens of Swedish white power record labels emerged in the country throughout the 1980s and 1990s, including Ragnarock and Svea Musik, and later Nordvind and Midgård. White power music was allowing radical nationalists in the country to recruit new members and raise funds more safely than ever before—particularly since earlier means of fundraising included tactics like bank robbery (Corte and Edwards 2008:16). Most importantly, the new culture of music consumption also calmed infighting by providing a center around which the fractious scene could rally.[30]

Not all nationalist skinheads were the same, however. The ideological split in the early nationalist movement—that between race revolutionaries and increasingly moderate groups like Keep Sweden Swedish—had its parallel in the youth skinhead scene. Sweden Democrat ideologue Mattias Karlsson recalled this separation as it manifested in his hometown during the 1990s:

> It divided fairly quickly into what were called NS [National Socialist] skins—those who became Nazis quite simply and who were violent—and those who were called Thule skins—who listened to Ultima Thule and just said that they were patriots and that they didn't have any problem with immigrants, said that as long as they adjust to our culture they are welcome, but we must have the right to be proud of the fact that we are Swedes, etc. [NS skins] were very organized. Also, the [Thule skins] weren't real skins, most of them had hair. What united everybody was that we all had bomber jackets, maybe with a Swedish flag on the jacket. (Interview, Mattias Karlsson, March 31, 2011)

Karlsson alludes to the fact that Thule skins were a variation of the NS standard, and that the divisions in this broad community were colored by music. Indeed, though 1990s nationalist skinhead music was often referred to collectively as "white power" by outsiders, it divided into two broad genres in the Nordic countries: white power and Viking rock.[31] Both genres had similar instrumental styles, employing a basic punk format with trap set, bass, one or two guitars, and vocals. However, the musics diverged in their textual themes as well as their political and social affiliations. Just as neo-Nazi organizations nurtured white power, political parties like Keep Sweden Swedish invested in music to support more moderate skinheads, funding the first album of leading Viking rock band Ultima Thule in 1985.

For an example of the common lyrical content of Nordic white power music, we can turn to famed 1990s Swedish band Odium ("Hate" in Latin) and their song "Our Honor Is Loyalty."[32]

> Our Swedish kingdom stands ablaze,
> Zionism is swallowing our country.
> And as darkness slowly falls,
> Svensson[33] stands there, just looking on.
> Dark forces encircle us,
> many give up without a fight.
> Yet our eternal loyalty lifts our spirits,
> an eternal loyalty to our fatherland.
>
> (chorus:) In our loyalty there is hope,
> there is a banner flying at the top,
> there is a pride in our country and our race.
>
> Black-clad troops march on all cities,
> NS [National Socialist] groups are sitting in parliament.
> The constitution is changed so that Sweden will be free,
> from the demons of Zion we shall be rid.
> Leaders hold speeches on the streets;
> never again will there be an election.
> Now we have power—we took it by force,
> now we will reign for eternity![34]

White power songs like "Our Honor Is Loyalty" are unequivocal in their contempt for Jews, their affirmation of race nationalism, and their vision for a violent revolution that gives National Socialists absolute power in their society.

Viking rock lyrics typically lack all of these themes. Consider, for example, "My Country" by Ultima Thule:

> Carried over the fields, through the forest,
> sign of our kingdom's soil.
> Banner beautiful, yellow and blue.
> Forever proud, in the wind you fly.

Rushing river, great tundra.
Places, carved in stone.
Hand on the heart, my friend.
For Sweden's best, we live on.

(chorus:) My country, my country,
my dear fatherland.
My country, my country,
my dear fatherland.

We play and we sing for our country,
proud and without shame.
Sweden, our place in the world.
Sweden, our place in the North.

The text does not mention any ethnic or religious minority, it does not speak of race or ethnicity, nor are there any obvious celebrations of violence. Instead, the song tells of Sweden's virtues. The band itself claimed that these are patriotic, rather than racist, lyrics. Textual themes of Ultima Thule and groups like Odium diverge so much that scholarly attempts to classify Viking rock bands as "white power" (e.g., Corte and Edwards 2008:14) must be rejected.

Though their words may seem banal and harmless, groups like Ultima Thule still antagonized mainstream sensibilities. In their punk accompaniment and in lines like "proud and without shame," the group acknowledged that their messages were controversial in a postwar Sweden where public expressions of national pride often accompanied xenophobia. The band was always dogged by allegations of racism, and such charges were often based on the group's collaboration during festivals, compilation albums, and retailing ventures with white power acts like Brutal Attack, Svastika, Vit Aggression, and Skrewdriver, as well as their open identification as skinheads. But given the wholesome nature of their lyrics, Ultima Thule seemed intent on undermining their critics. Lyrics like those to "My Country" imply that Ultima Thule and their followers face condemnation for something as innocent as loving their homeland.

Whether it was white power punk or Viking rock, radical nationalist music reached its widest audience in the 1990s. A 1997 study of listening habits among sixth- through twelfth-grade students throughout Sweden revealed that 12.2 percent of youth overall listened to "white power music" (a category that was likely understood as including Viking rock) sometimes or often. That number was 15.3 percent when limited to boys overall, and 18.9 percent when limited to boys in grades 10–12 (Lange, Lööw, Bruchfeld, and Hedlund 1997). The fusion between skinhead subculture, its musics, and nationalist activism was doomed to break, however, and it is there I find my point of departure in this book.

New Nationalism

> Think of that music. A shame. A shame! It's deeply destructive, modern music. I don't get it. You have to ask yourself, is this the music, is this the culture, that is going to save Europe? (Interview, Mr. X, May 25, 2011)

A confluence of factors contributed to the dramatic decline of skinheadism during the late 1990s and early 2000s. In Sweden as throughout Western Europe, this turn of events was perpetuated by the rise of online file-sharing and a corresponding drop in record sales; harsher enforcement of hate speech laws; the aging of the subculture's core population; and activists' realization that, for all skinheadism's mobilizing power, it had yielded few concrete political achievements (see Dyck 2012; Lagerlöf 2012). The withering of record labels, magazines, festival circuits, and street gangs created a power vacuum where latent divisions among activists sharpened, and insiders with longstanding grievances toward nationalism's thuggish reputation found new opportunity to effect change.

The following chapters in this book examine Nordic nationalists' efforts to craft an alternative image for their cause in the post-skinhead era. For activists like the young Swede quoted above, music served as a token for what was wrong with nationalism's past, and many would also consider music key to forging a new future. Reformist campaigns and the music that propelled them scattered in multiple directions, and the three-part structure of today's nationalist scene—with race revolutionaries, cultural nationalists, and identitarians—reflects that fragmentation. Despite their differences, however, reformers shared a distain for skinheadism and a desire to recast their relationship with mainstream society. Those common drives provided a degree of uniformity in reformist campaigns, and they allow us to talk about changes to Nordic radical nationalism in general terms.

I call this movement and the activism it bore "New Nationalism." I adopt the term in an attempt to channel insider terminology and to emphasize the wide-ranging influence reform has had throughout the contemporary Nordic radical nationalist scene. Additionally, I intend to highlight links between New Nationalism and the concept of New Europe as described by Philip V. Bohlman.[35] Bohlman (2011) claims that contemporary Europe is typified by the rise of multiculturalism and its simultaneous rejection and affirmation of borders in social, cultural, and political life. Likewise, though New Nationalists often present themselves as opponents of multiculturalism, we find the movement's signature in the way it mimics activism designed for minority groups.

For an introduction to the ways post-skinhead nationalism borrows from multiculturalism, we can first turn to Charles Taylor and his landmark work *Multiculturalism and the Politics of Recognition* (1992). There Taylor argues that liberal democracies have come to regard inadequate recognition of cultural difference as an act of oppression. This oppression may occur through misrecognition, as when society perpetuates false stereotypes about a group. Alternately, elites may oppress by way of nonrecognition and the refusal to acknowledge a group's status as culturally distinct. Taylor's thoughts on nonrecognition evoke what other scholars have described as multiculturalist societies' call for minorities to accentuate and display cultural uniqueness. Lundberg, Malm, and Ronström (2000) argue that the ability to project and receive confirmation of difference in such contexts is vital to a group's existence in a social and economic sense. Multiculturalism cultivates a state of affairs where uniqueness is vital to visibility, visibility is vital to recognition, and recognition is vital to enfranchisement: it forges a market of difference (Gladney 2004).

Members of white majority groups are likely to experience themselves as invisible nonactors in such contexts. Scholarship from critical race studies frequently reports on whites in western countries who experience themselves as "unraced" or "non-ethnic."[36] Works like Ashley Doane's article (1997) and those that built from it[37] further argue that white majorities' experienced unmarkedness is a symptom of their ongoing structural privilege in society—a token of their exemption from competitions for resources. Nonetheless, multiculturalism offers the claim of oppression to whites who want it: they can label their unmarkedness as an instance of nonrecognition and a violation of the universal right to difference.

Understanding the position of the invisible white subject in multiculturalist society helps us make sense of emerging agendas and creative expression in Nordic radical nationalism. Reformers have a burgeoning interest in adopting popular techniques for defining and defending group identity, and this parallels their rejection of skinheadism. If nationalist skinheads strove to isolate themselves in a marginalized underground—in a universe of "hidden spaces" (Simi and Futrell 2010) forged through symbol and deed—New Nationalists instead envisioned increased participation in the mainstream and collaboration with outside partners.

Reformers are also abandoning the rhetoric and ideologies of supremacy. Instead, and in step with multiculturalist logic, they tend to defend ethnic or cultural separatism as a means of preserving nonhierarchical human diversity. Much of their activism now centers on explaining how their contribution to diversity—their difference—is being blunted in ways most unjust. New Nationalists in the Nordic countries often argue that elites fail to recognize whites, Nordics, or national majorities as distinct or valued peoples. In Sweden, activists from the moderate Sweden Democrats to militant neo-Nazi circles fixated on statements by leaders of the country's two major political parties that seem to reinforce this claim. In 2002, when the magazine *Euroturk*—a publication produced by and primarily for Turkish immigrants living in Sweden—asked former Social Democrat party leader Mona Sahlin to define Swedish culture, she responded:

> I am often asked that question, but I can't think of what Swedish culture is. I think that, in part, is what makes many Swedes jealous of immigrant groups: You have a culture, an identity, a history, something that binds you together. And what do we have? We have Midsummer and nerdy things like that. (*Euroturk*, 2002: no. 2)

Four years later, during a visit to the ethnically diverse town of Ronna to the south of Stockholm in 2006, then center-right Swedish Prime Minister Fredrik Reinfeldt told an assembly of immigrants that

> the core of Swedishness is nothing but barbarism. All progress has come from the outside. (*Dagens Nyheter*, November 15, 2006)

Nationalists from the 1990s and up to the present often cite quotes like these to argue that, though Sweden's reigning political elite may disagree about taxes or healthcare, they are united in their contempt for and denial of the Swedish.

Perceived non-recognition of difference, the ideological mechanisms that label it oppression, and the assumption that society might regard backlash as an act of justice underlie most agendas in the New Nationalism. These guideposts position activists to create identities blatant in their divergence from a chauvinistic, reclusive, and politically ineffectual skinheadism. However, nationalists' interaction with multiculturalism also introduces a core tension to the scene, one that fuels both discord among insiders and a flowering of expressive culture and music.

The New Nationalist Double Imperative

New Nationalist thought often features a pair of differing, at times competing agendas. One the one hand, those seeking distance from 1990s skinheadism emphasized the need for a nondeviant nationalism. Organized opposition to immigration and globalization in their minds should employ unremarkable language, political methods, and cultural attributes so as not to repulse mainstream audiences. On the other hand—and in the spirit of multiculturalism—reformists also argued for a renewed commitment to national or subnational distinctiveness rather than transnational subcultures (like skinheadism) or foreign impulses. Ideal nationalists should not sport close-cropped hairstyles and combat boots, nor should they embrace American pop culture or adorn their bodies or propaganda with references to Germany: instead, they should be exceptionally native. The New Nationalism thus contains contrasting attitudes toward difference, striving at once toward integration and dis-integration with society at large.

I call this conceptual paradox the "New Nationalist double imperative." Nationalists pursue the first imperative, that based on integration with society at large, when they portray themselves as champions of the oppressed and guarantors of diversity. Equalizing their cause with that of minority group activists, these nationalists attempt to align themselves with prevailing multiculturalist values—those of defending the disenfranchised and promoting pluralism. They render their activism unremarkable when they forgo militarism and sect-like social practices for parliamentary politics and think-tank initiatives. Likewise, they attempt to bring their cultural practices in line with the mainstream when they abandon skinheadism for various other, less inflammatory cultural trends. All of these developments serve to hinder outsiders from labeling nationalist rhetoric, methodology, and behavior as extreme or deviant.

Nationalists pursue the second imperative when they wear traditional folk costumes at public events, or when they memorize and perform all four verses of Sweden's national anthem (most Swedes do not know that verses three and four exist). They establish annual gatherings where they learn and practice folk dancing, study Old Norse poetry and mythological tales, and make Viking-era crafts. Some also assert their commitment to their national identity by linking themselves to domestic sources of ideological inspiration, turning away from Adolf Hitler and toward historic Nordic ultraconservatives like Swede Rudolf Kjellén or Norwegian Vidkun Quisling.

Both sides of the double imperative expose nationalists to internal critique. Activists may brand attempts to integrate with popular culture as acts of capitulation. Given that such efforts often entail a softening of language, dress, and expressive modes, some insiders claim that the New Nationalism lacks a vital oppositional ethos. Some may also charge that in the process of fitting their message to mainstream sensibilities, nationalists have stripped themselves and their activism of a core white, Nordic, or national essence. An activist named "Robert" for example, criticizes the nationalist organization Nordic Youth's efforts to spread their message through popular expressive forms:

You have unfortunately fallen to the enemy's propaganda, so much so that you have begun to be assimilated into the society of multiculturalism.[38]

Just as agendas of assimilation meet internal resistance, so too do campaigns aimed at enhancing national distinctiveness. Insiders attempting to free themselves of foreign influence occasionally encounter criticism and ridicule from other activists who highlight the proliferation of ideas, products, and expressive forms from abroad in historical and contemporary Nordic societies. For example, fervent race nationalist and anti-Semite Richard Langéen offered the following response to other activists who complained about foreign influence in nationalist propaganda:

> Most of what is around you is probably "non-Swedish"; your computer, your tv, your clothes, the food you eat, etc. So take off all of your clothing, starve, don't move anymore in case you rub against something that isn't pure-bred Swedish.[39]

The cognitive dissonance inherent in popularizing a cause that has long conceived of itself as oppositional, and the futility of an agenda aspiring to absolute purity, leaves the New Nationalism fiercely contested from within.

Internal contradictions like the double imperative are hardly unique to contemporary Nordic radical nationalism. Rather, they appear in nearly all kinds of establishment and subcultural nationalist imaginaries, the most studied of which is what Tom Nairn famously calls nationalism's Janus face. Nairn claims that nationalisms typically aspire to a forward-looking modernism and a backward-looking traditionalism simultaneously (Nairn 1977, 1998). Nationalists may similarly espouse cosmopolitanism and nativism, materialism and spirituality, and rationalism and emotionalism (Chatterjee 1986, 1993; McClintock 1997). The modernist school of nationalism scholarship suggests that these ideological dualisms help preserve asymmetrical power relations in national societies as they move toward ostensible unification. Ideologues may delegate different aspects of a nationalization project to different demographics—calling on some members of society to be modernistic, cosmopolitan, and rational while demanding that others be traditional, provincial, and mystified. These contrasting directives often build upon existing class (Gellner 1983), gender (Collier 1997; Yuval-Davis 1996, 1997; Weismantel 2001; Goluboff 2008), or racial (Crook 1993) divisions. But whereas the dualisms underlying establishment movements prescribe behavior and identities to large communities, Nordic radical nationalists attempt to impose their Janus-faced, double imperative on themselves—a population smaller and far more homogenous than that of any nation-state, and thereby less able to neutralize self-contradicting programs by delegating different roles to different social actors.

Though some insiders rally behind just one of the opposed imperatives, most seek conceptual and operational strategies that might reconcile agendas of assimilation and particularity. These strategies typically center on assigning different domains of their activism, lifestyle, and identity to different New Nationalist drives. At times, assignments hinge on insiders' conceptions of national identity. Activists who believe that being Swedish is essentially a racial distinction, for example, typically become more receptive to sociocultural practices they consider un-Swedish. In such instances, race becomes the site of particularity, freeing other aspects of their identity and behavior for assimilation. Insiders may observe similar divisions within the realm of sociocultural practices. They may pursue an agenda of rigid purity in the food they consume but embrace cosmopolitan attitudes toward spirituality and religion. They may clothe themselves in traditional folk costumes and compete in motocross sporting events. And they may write with antiquated spelling and grammatical forms but use Facebook and Twitter to spread their message. Here too, decisions as to whether nationalists ought to invest a behavior, institution, or expressive form with either integrating or particularizing power rely on their understandings of the essence of national identity. If activists regard an item or practice as containing a distinctly Swedish, Norwegian, or Danish variant, they can showcase it as an emblem of their difference. If instead they consider it neutral, it could present an avenue for expanding into the mainstream.

Music and the New Nationalism

As we will see, music has served as a key arena in which reformist nationalists develop and perform their new post-skinhead identities. The character of their creations and the spirit in which they are received often interact with the foundations of New Nationalism I outlined above—its double imperative in particular. The movement's internal tension compels insiders to reconsider the defining characteristics of the population they fight for and whether the media of their activism possess inherent ideological, ethnic, or cultural associations. Some treat music as a manifestation of national distinctiveness—typically one condescended to by Sweden's elite. For example, former Sweden Democrat and leading folk musician Marie Stensby blamed the absence of immigrants at Swedish folk music events on Swedish self-contempt. She said of the absences:

> It has to do in part with how Swedish politics and Swedish politicians—they have always belittled and talked about how [Swedish culture] isn't worth anything, "so why should we go to something like that?" (Interview, Marie Stensby, November 19, 2010)

For Stensby, elites' rejection of Swedishness more generally leads to a rejection of folk music. Accordingly, she and likeminded nationalists rally behind folk music as a means of defending an allegedly besieged Swedish identity. Insiders may alternately exclude music from the set of phenomena that define a people, and this allows them to think of music a tool for integrating the nationalist cause with mainstream society. Often, these sentiments entail a deconstruction of the notion of purity in music, the likes of which nationalists would seldom tolerate in questions of race, ethnicity, or culture more generally.

The theoretical framework I have provided in this chapter does not account for all musical activity in reformist radical nationalism. While insiders use music to pursue political and social agendas, they also use it to escape the imperatives of their convictions altogether. Some insiders claim that music's status as a form of free expression hinders attempts to shape not only its production but also its consumption in the scene. Nordic Youth activist Andreas Nyberg channels this sentiment when he argues,

> You can't say to people, "don't listen to this type of music," because music is so incredibly personal. (Interview, Andreas Nyberg, July 4, 2011)

Musical taste and musical practice, according to Nyberg, are involuntary aspects of human identity and behavior. For that reason, attempts to shape another's musical practices will lead to inauthentic results. Nationalists may offer defenses like this to justify their consumption of musics that seem antithetical to the New Nationalism— whether it be leftist music, mainstream pop, or, most of all, 1990s white power—or to claim that music ought not be involved in activism at all.

The increasing variety of uses for music in the scene coincides with a dramatic proliferation of styles. Whereas punk and metal dominated radical nationalism during the 1990s, activists today produce and consume light pop, folk music, singer-songwriter balladry, techno, and even rap and reggae. Though nationalists use music to rally behind national distinctiveness, to integrate with popular culture, or to find temporary relief from their declared political programs, they seldom agree as to which musics best serve these functions. It is for this reason that most of my analyses in this book focus on the discourses surrounding musical practice, rather than the musical sound itself.

Chapter 2 investigates in greater depth the intellectual underpinnings of New Nationalist ideology in its nonmusical manifestations, highlighting Swedish activists' importation and modification of American white nationalist and European antiliberal thought. Following this, I move to three case studies of musical practice—one for each of the three wings of Nordic radical nationalism today. Chapter 3 explores the black/white musical dynamic in the nationalist scene by studying the emergence of anti-immigrant rap and reggae among identitarian-oriented nationalists in Sweden.

The chapter traces these musical projects and shows how the discussions surrounding them helped to perpetuate reform. Chapter 4 examines a burgeoning interest in traditional folk music among nationalists—cultural nationalists in particular—and frames this as part of an effort to reject skinheadism and assert a commitment to national distinctiveness. Chapter 5 analyzes efforts to soften race-revolutionary nationalist music through the introduction of women singers. Focusing on singer Saga, the chapter describes how musical performances of an ultratraditional femininity cultivate beliefs that nationalists and white Nordics at large are oppressed. Finally, chapter 6 traces the overall decline of nationalist music-making, highlighting how agendas of rationalization and internal criticisms of subculture have driven activists toward new expressive modes and forms of social behavior.

"VI ÄR OCKSÅ ETT FOLK!"

A New Nationalism Rises

I CAUGHT ONLY a glimpse of the banner as three members of the Sweden Democrats' youth wing carried it down Central Avenue in Gothenburg on April 10, 2011. Rows of their fellow demonstrators marched behind, clad in the organization's hallmark of bright yellow polo shirts. Some carried flags, some held small signs, and some filmed the event on their cell phones. Onlookers next to me whispered to each other as the procession went by: "That one looks like he's straight out of the *Hitlerjugend*." "I think I've seen that bimbo type on TV before." "What's up with the dark-skinned guy?" Few reactions were this benign, however. For as the hundred or so youths advanced down the avenue, nearly six hundred counterdemonstrators from various socialist, communist, and immigrant organizations attempted to stop them, flinging a barrage of tomatoes, eggs, fireworks, and glass bottles that a massive police force—tasked with shielding marchers and observers alike—struggled to contain.

Happy to have been struck only with eggs in the crossfire, I followed the marchers and counterdemonstrators as they moved to Kungsportsplatsen Square. There the Sweden Democrats assembled behind police barricades and listened to speeches by party leaders and guests from partner organizations in Germany and Italy. Though these politicians spoke through an amplified sound system, I couldn't hear a word they said. I was standing among the counterdemonstrators, and their chorus of whistles, rattlers, blow horns, and screams easily drowned out the speeches. In fact, from the time the youth marchers arrived until they left in police-escorted buses, the only statement they managed to communicate to me was their banner slogan: *Vi är också ett folk!* (We are also a people!).

Nordic radical nationalism is changing. Following the turn of the twenty-first century, internal reformers attempted to purge the scene of its aggressive, undisciplined, and chauvinistic skinhead subculture. These newer voices strived to refashion themselves in opposition to the hooligan cliché, claiming an alternative identity as peaceful, professional, erudite, and victimized. Their efforts were seldom identical or coordinated, but they combined to propel the scene into a new era—a "New Nationalism," as I call it in this book—distinguished by unorthodox strategizing, by novel partnerships, and above all by a yearning to transcend nationalism's recent past. To prepare for a close investigation of the musical phenomena that have been both the vessels and the objects of change, I devote this chapter to a focused investigation of New Nationalism in its nonmusical forms.

New Nationalism's signature appears throughout the scene today, from the propaganda of fringe militant groups to the rhetoric of moderate parliamentarians, and it resounded during the Sweden Democrats' demonstration I attended in Gothenburg. On that day the young marchers cast themselves as anti-skinheads through looks, behavior, and messaging. While the sight of nationalists marching with flags evoked images of neo-Nazism for some spectators, the youths' presentation was otherwise wholesome and plain. They walked calmly and quietly down the avenue, barely flinching—and never retaliating—as shards of glass danced about their white tennis shoes, as tomatoes stained their polo shirts, and as raw egg dripped from their hair. Nationalists' once-standard ensemble of boots, bomber jackets, fists, and howls was nowhere to be seen.

The most distinguishing manifestation of New Nationalism, however, was the slogan written on the Sweden Democrats' banner: "We are also a people!" With rhetoric unlikely to have rallied nationalists of decades past, the phrase pleads with a society that recognizes the unique value of some peoples but allegedly denies such consideration to the majority. It makes a seemingly modest request by calling for Swedes to receive only the same recognition that society provides minority groups—a move echoing what Dyer (1997) describes as white "me-too-ism" and Wiegman (1999) calls "white minoritization." The phrase, in other words, seeks to complete the spread of a universal principle acknowledging and respecting difference. And by characterizing majority Swedes as threatened and oppressed, nationalists portray themselves as champions of justice and pluralism rather than hate.

With their statement, the marchers in Gothenburg thus embraced and repurposed multiculturalist ideals—the inherent virtue of diversity and the accompanying notion that all groups have a right to recognized difference. In ways like this, New Nationalist activism attempts to work via popular values, expressive forms, and institutions. But its assimilationist bent is typically paired with efforts to exoticize national distinctiveness. Most attempts to integrate with a broad mainstream—most statements of "We are also"—appear alongside calls to withdraw into particularism and promote the uniqueness of "a" distinct "people." I describe the pairing of these two agendas as the New Nationalist double imperative (see also chapter 1).

The Sweden Democrats captured New Nationalism's conceptual world and inner tension with their slogan, but they are not the primary source of this kind of thinking. To understand why nationalists' rejection of skinheadism manifests as it does, and how they remain linked in an era of apparent fragmentation, we must first turn our attention away from the political parties and militant street gangs that captivate popular imagination, and toward a lesser-known community of Nordic and continental European actors who operate beyond the public gaze and whose output unites disparate activists today: identitarians.[1]

In chapter 1, I describe identitarians as one of three outlining camps in contemporary Nordic radical nationalism together with race revolutionaries and cultural nationalists. We see their unmistakable influence throughout the scene today, including in the Sweden Democrats' slogan, "We are also a people!" That phrase's simultaneous appeal to the universal and the particular—its drive to mainstream the movement's activism while exoticizing its chosen national people—builds from two key identitarian ideas. Channeling concepts of a French antiliberal school known as the *Nouvelle Droite*,[2] Nordic identitarians promote an activist strategy of cultural infiltration they call "metapolitics"; they also advocate an ostensibly nonhierarchical global separatism to create a "pluriversum," where differences among peoples are preserved and celebrated. The concepts of metapolitics and the pluriversum are the most formal articulations of the New Nationalist double imperative to social integration and disintegration that today shapes the activism of militant National Socialists and moderate Sweden Democrats alike.

In what follows I present a genealogy of these ideas in the North, tracing Nordic identitarianism's breakaway from the white power music movement, its conceptual roots in American and French antiliberal thought, and its rise to shape nationalist activism in a post-skinhead era. Though I write of a New Nationalism, few of the ideas I discuss here are genuinely new. Radical nationalists' emerging drives toward professionalism, their claims to victimization, their renunciation of chauvinism, even their fetishizing of "diversity" have extensive precedents in the Nordic region and beyond.[3] The novelty of New Nationalism resides instead in the way insiders mobilized these ideas against skinhead subculture and aligned them with the logic of multiculturalism. The events I describe in this chapter therefore remind us of Ernst Gellner's edict that "whatever has been said, has also been said by someone else on an earlier occasion" (1985:9); thus, intellectual histories ought not dwell on when ideas originated but rather on how and to whom they became compelling. Accordingly, to examine New Nationalism, I will first explore the settings and experiences that stoked its call to reform.

Of Boots and Razors

Mattias Karlsson had his nationalist awakening as a teenager during the mid-1990s. He was born to working-class parents whose political sympathies alternated only between the left-wing Social Democrats and the far-left (former communist) Left Party. The family lived in a rural village outside of the southern Swedish city of Växjö. It was a community Karlsson describes as rich in social cohesion, where neighbors shared culture, values, and identity, and where life felt secure. But when Karlsson moved to the city at age sixteen to attend secondary school, he found himself in a context that was neither homogeneous nor safe. There, immigrant boys from the Middle East, the Balkans, and Africa coalesced into violent gangs. These youths were often part of the "kickers" hip-hop subculture that spread throughout Sweden at the time,[4] and their main targets—Karlsson claims—were ethnic Swedes. He recalls being attacked at discotheques and on the street, and he had friends who were severely injured in knife fights. Never did he see police punish this aggression, and his parents back home never took seriously his claims that in the city one could be attacked "just for being a Swede" (Interview, February 11, 2011).

At the same time, 150 miles to the west in the Swedish city of Gothenburg, another young man felt similarly victimized. Daniel Friberg grew up considering himself an antiracist. His parents were highly educated, and like most of those living in his quiet, wealthy Gothenburg suburb, his family identified with the political left. Friberg's politics began to change when he entered a regional secondary school with a high percentage of immigrant students. He claims to have witnessed expansive and unrestrained ethnic violence targeting Swedes at his new school, all while family, teachers, and the media praised multiculturalism as beneficial and unproblematic.

Opportunities for backlash were available to youths like Karlsson and Friberg. They came of age as 1990s neo-Nazi skinheadism in Sweden was at its peak (Lööw 1998). Dubbing itself "the national movement" (*den nationella rörelsen*), this cause was powered by frustrated young men like themselves who resented the lack of Swedish solidarity and the authorities' alleged refusal to address their concerns. With shaved heads, combat boots, and bomber jackets, and adorned with Swedish flags, Celtic crosses, and Nordic rune symbols, packs of skinheads roamed city streets confronting hip-hop gangs and nonwhite youths. Though the skinhead wave enveloped the entire nation, Karlsson and Friberg grew up in two of its centers. The country-side village of Karlsson's childhood was home to the infamous neo-Nazi leader Mats Nilsson, whose followers were dotted throughout the surrounding municipalities as well as in the nearby city of Växjö. Alternately, Gothenburg played host to Midgård Records—the North's most prolific source for white power music—as well as a field of smaller action groups and gangs.

By the midpoint of their teenage years, both these young men had come in contact with their local nationalist skinhead scenes. Karlsson began donning a bomber jacket with a Swedish flag, and mutual acquaintances introduced him to neo-Nazi leader Nilsson, who provided him a copy of Hitler's *Mein Kampf* and offered to school him—just as he had scores of other young boys in the region—in National Socialism and racial consciousness. Likewise, at age sixteen, Friberg shaved his head, began wearing Midgård Records t-shirts, and started attending white power concerts in the Gothenburg area.

Though the nationalist skinhead scene seemed an ideal antidote to their troubles with immigrants, neither of these young men felt at home in it. Karlsson had earlier considered himself a "punk rocker," and his transition into skinhead style was easy. But ideological conflicts with the scene prevented him from integrating into it fully. Despite Nilsson's pressure, he held no sympathies for Nazism. In Karlsson's mind, the problem with immigrants was not their race, but rather their alienation from Swedish culture—an alienation that was ghettoizing society, and one that could be remedied through cultural assimilation. Though he had no name for his ideology at the time, he was what would later be called a "cultural nationalist"—a nationalist who asserts that any person, regardless of their ethnic background, can become Swedish by assimilating a select body of beliefs, values, practices, and traditions. Because Karlsson so stubbornly advocated this perspective, Nilsson abandoned his efforts to indoctrinate him and began calling Karlsson a "meatball patriot" (Interview, Mattias Karlsson, February 11, 2011).

Friberg, on the other hand, was more receptive to the prevailing ideology in nationalist skinhead circles. He agreed with neo-Nazi voices that true Swedishness came only through blood: he was an ethnonationalist. Still, he did not identify as a National Socialist, and considered nostalgia for the Third Reich irrelevant to contemporary struggles over immigration in Scandinavia. After having once shaved his head, he gradually turned on the skinhead scene, which he regarded as undereducated and delinquent. Exiled from mainstream Swedish society because of his political ideals, class and lifestyle differences also made him an outsider in 1990s radical nationalism. "The national movement had the right basic ideas, they saw actual problems," he thought, "but it was filled with the dregs of society and was completely incapable of achieving anything real" (Interview, Daniel Friberg, June 30, 2014).

Mattias Karlsson and Daniel Friberg were hardly alone in their simultaneous attraction to and disgust with 1990s nationalist activism. Scatterings of disgruntled insiders throughout the previous years had bemoaned their cause's association with white power skinheadism. In newspaper articles and during speeches, those voices argued that the fight against immigration, multiculturalism, and liberalism needed to have more upstanding ambassadors if it was to achieve anything beyond petty violence and musical rabble-rousing.[5] Their cries vanished like arrows shot into a dark sky. Skinhead subculture energized radical nationalism, providing a measure of funds, participants, and vigor that had seemed unthinkable in the postwar era. Its champions filled the ranks of major nationalist political, journalistic, and cultural initiatives, while its critics were slow to organize.

At the dawn of the twenty-first century, however, skinheadism's grip on anti-immigrant activism began to weaken. The white power music scene at its core faced attacks on multiple fronts. During the late 1990s, the Swedish government pressured its police force to react more quickly and decisively against the white power music industry and its frequent violation of hate speech laws.[6] Mass arrests at concerts established a new order where the staging of large-scale performances became nearly impossible. Further, Internet music sites like Napster, and later YouTube, offered free access to white power, undermining sales for virtually all nationalist music labels. From the late 1990s and into the 2000s, scores of Nordic nationalist record companies went bankrupt or dormant, including Alternative Action in Finland; NS Records in Denmark; Boot Boys Records in Norway; and Nordland, Ragnarock, and Svea Musik in Sweden.[7] As its cultural practices dwindled, neo-Nazi skinheadism's crippling association with criminality deepened. The summer of 1999 alone saw revolutionary nationalists commit a string of high-profile car bombings, robberies, and murders, leading commentators to speak of a "wave" of nationalist violence (Deland et al. 2010:5), and allowing police to jail many of the scene's highest-profile members and dissolve their organizations.[8]

By the early 2000s, opportunity was rife for disaffected nationalists seeking alternatives to skinheadism, and Mattias Karlsson and Daniel Friberg were poised to capitalize. Their grievances with nationalism's status quo varied, with Karlsson finding its dominant ideological profile unacceptable and Friberg objecting to its forms of expression. Likewise, these young men held visions for the future that were irreconcilable, both with neo-Nazi skinheadism and with each other. Their paths would eventually cross in open conflict. But each would serve as a driving force to push the anti-immigrant cause into a new era and transform what was broadly a one-part scene into three camps.

Karlsson's story from this point forward is well chronicled (e.g., Mattsson 2009; Ekman and Poohl 2010; Orrenius 2010; Jalving 2011; Teitelbaum 2013). After having found a temporary refuge for his more moderate activism in the Ultima

Thule–inspired "Thule skins" wing of the nationalist skinhead scene (see chapter 1), he turned to his local chapter of the Sweden Democrats. The party was then working to shape itself like the right-wing populist parties harrying in parliaments throughout continental Europe, and the first stage in this effort involved addressing its own links with youth-based hooliganism and ethnonationalism. During the mid-1990s, the Sweden Democrats led a charge to wash all forms of skinheadism from their ranks. In 1995, the party issued new rules for official events, prohibiting the use of alcohol, cigarettes, symbols connected with World War II, and the shouting of slogans other than those endorsed by the party. At the party congress a year later, Stockholm Sweden Democrats' Tomas Johansson defended this new agenda:

> The average Swede does not want to be linked with beer-drenched kids sporting shaved heads, steel-toed boots, and screaming "Seig Heil!" and "out with them all," which is the media's image of the Sweden Democrats. The Sweden Democrats' chances are not helped by the fact that the party's leaders have a hard time distancing themselves from nostalgia for the 1930s. (Quoted in Larsson and Ekman 2001:167)

While rejecting skinheadism, the party also began formalizing its cultural nationalism. By 2002, Mattias Karlsson had risen in the party ranks and would become the chief architect of that initiative, shaping the party platforms from that point forward and specifying that they advocated an "open Swedishness" (*öppen svenskhet*) that any individual could assimilate into. He would later find himself in the party's leading circle when they made their electoral gains in 2010.

While Karlsson found existing—if underdeveloped—venues through which to escape the race-revolutionary standard, Friberg was not so fortunate. His commitment to ethnonationalism left him fewer alternatives to National Socialist skinheadism and its attendant class-based associations. His path forward would be more strenuous and contested, and it remains a mystery to many commentators. Rather than joining a party, he created a network of media initiatives aimed at importing ideas and strategies from abroad. The outcome of his efforts was considerable: he at once cultivated a new wing of the nationalist scene and built a foundation upon which reformist nationalists of various kinds would craft their visions for the future.

The Nordic Press

Daniel Friberg's work as a reformer began in earnest during the early twenty-first century when he joined forces with three other activists who, for reasons both personal and ideological, also found themselves marginalized within Swedish ethnonation-alism. Together with Lennart Berg, Anders Lagerström, and Peter Melander he sought to forge new forms and forums of activism, and in 2001, this group of four established the publishing and retail outlet, the Nordic Press (*Nordiska förlaget*).[9] They declared that the Press would be devoted to "educating" and "inspiring" Nordic nationalists, and they designated specific media for advancing these goals. They clarified their method on their website:

> The education side consists mostly of the production and distribution of books. . . . The inspiration side consists in part of books, in part of the production and distribution of CDs.[10]

In other words, the Press considered literature a means for pursuing both of their goals, while music could inspire but not educate. Relative to other nationalist cultural organizations at the time, leaders thus outlined a limited role for music.

At first, the Nordic Press struggled to break from staid forms of radical nationalism. At the turn of the twenty-first century, white power skinhead circles remained the scene's social and organizational centers, as well as its most prolific producers of culture. Just as latent cultural nationalists once maintained types of skinheadism more compatible with their political ideologies (i.e., Thule skinheadism), so too was the Press initially adapted to current cultural trends in the scene—trends built around music making and nostalgia for the Third Reich.

Music constituted the largest portion of the Press's retail offerings, and this despite its demoted position behind literature in the organization's official agenda. Virtually all retailers in the Nordic scene sold music, and the Press could not afford to deny itself that market. Further, leaders disagreed about the need to reduce Nazi iconography and music in nationalist activism. Nordic Press cofounder Peter Melander was a veteran performer and producer of Swedish white power music, and because of his influence, the overwhelming majority of the Press's music offerings were staple Swedish and international white power punk bands like Brigad Wotan, Division S, and Brutal Attack.[11] In addition to selling CDs from other labels, the Nordic Press produced a small number of its own music recordings, ten albums from five groups. These projects—the most popular of which were Fyrdung and the three-CD project Svensk ungdom—diverged from standard radical-nationalist acts in musical style more than in ideological content. The Press's own output lacked skinhead punk, featuring instead dark metal, neofolk, and acoustic singer-songwriter genres. But while employing then-uncommon styles, these releases nonetheless celebrated National Socialism in their lyrics, occasionally by setting music to the poems of historic Swedish Nazi sympathizers.

The Nordic Press thus catered to entrenched forms of activism via its music sales, and to a slightly lesser extent via its own music production. But its literary output also held closely to then-prevailing models in radical ethnonationalism. Early on, writings by historical National Socialists like Adolf Hitler were rare in its offerings. However, a general fixation on alleged Jewish treachery was ubiquitous. The Press published translations of American books like David Duke's *Jewish Supremacism* and Kevin MacDonald's *The Culture of Critique*,[12] and sold a Swedish translation of Norman Finkelstein's *The Holocaust Industry*.

In sum, while functioning to expand literature consumption in the scene, the Nordic Press initially offered few ideological or methodological alternatives to the ethnonationalist status quo. However, Press leaders and other reformers gradually came in contact with emerging schools from abroad, and these foreign ideas became powerful tools in attempts to reshape the Nordic scene.

American and European Alternatives

The initial wave of outside reformist ideology came to the North from two American activists, David Duke and Richard McCulloch. Throughout the 1980s and 1990s, Duke—a former Ku Klux Klan leader and notorious household name in American society—attempted to reform race-nationalist circles in the United States. He encouraged activists to abandon violence and deviant dress. But his efforts focused on refashioning the way insiders spoke about their cause. He called on activists to avoid expressing hatred for nonwhites and instead to defend white Americans' need for the same political advocacy as other ethnic groups. Further, based on the claim that whites did not receive such advocacy, Duke described his activism as a civil rights movement, a campaign to balance power relations among races. He would pursue this approach in part though the establishment of initiatives like the National Association for the Advancement of White People (NAAWP)—a name that mimics that of the National Association for the Advancement of Colored People (NAACP) in an attempt to equalize white and African American struggles (see Berbrier 1998:439).

As Duke spread his message of white victimization and the right to race-based political mobilization, fellow American Richard McCulloch made a similar, more theorized attempt to reconcile white activism with mainstream values. McCulloch's paramount publication is his book *The Racial Compact*, released in 1994. There he claims that, in step with United Nations resolutions on biological and cultural diversity, the global community ought to encourage racial diversity through separatism. In contrast with rhetoric that opposes pluralism, McCulloch accepts the inherent value of difference. His reasoning in *The Racial Compact* is encapsulated in what he calls the "Racial Golden Rule":

> The Racial Golden Rule asserts the right of every race to racial freedom through racial separation and independence. To secure racial freedom and separation it respects the requirement of every race for its own exclusive racial territory or homeland, its own independent and sovereign government. It declares for every race the freedom to follow its own path, to control its own life and existence, to determine its own course of development and to pursue its own happiness and evolutionary destiny. It is a declaration of racial independence, freedom and diversity, holding it to be self-evident that all races were created different, and have a right to be different, to be themselves, with equal rights to life, liberty, and the pursuit of their own happiness.[13]

For McCulloch, separatism is needed not because of one race's superiority, but because it would ensure all races' universal right to continued difference, or "life." Borrowing language from the U.S. Declaration of Independence, he presents his ideology as a logical outgrowth of broadly accepted sentiments in American society, including the inherent virtue of diversity.

During the 1990s, Swedish, Norwegian, and Danish nationalist newspapers disseminated Duke's calls for a more upstanding, less militant, and less hateful activism, and delegations from Sweden frequently attended his events in the United States (Wåg 2010; Interview, Vávra Suk July 14, 2011). Duke was and remains celebrated in nearly all ethnonationalist circles in the Nordic countries, and the Nordic Press invited him to speak at their Nordic Festival in 2005. However, as the twentieth century drew to a close, reformist activists outside of the Nordic Press began celebrating Richard McCulloch. In 1999, Swedish activists Robert Almgren and Omar Filmersson—the latter a former translator for the white power music magazine *Nordland*—founded the Organization for the Peoples' Future (*Föreningen för folkens framtid*), with the goal of translating and disseminating Richard McCulloch's writings (Sexton 2008:74–75). In the preface to their translations, they framed McCulloch's ideas as the reasonable alternative between two extremist poles—between chauvinistic and supremacist "immoral racism" and a "race nihilism."[14]

The Nordic Press began selling these Swedish translations of *The Racial Compact* in its first years. The Press's inclusion of McCulloch's work—a piece of literature that advocated a universal right to difference rather than supremacy and that lacked explicit demonization of Jews and nonwhites—was largely the agenda of leaders Daniel Friberg and Lennart Berg who worked against their colleague, white power music enthusiast Peter Melander. It constituted a minor counterweight to the retailer's extensive offerings in musical and literary emblems of neo-Nazi skinheadism.

What began as a small body of unconventional nationalist texts grew exponentially when Press leaders and other reformist nationalists came in contact with a foreign school emanating from the continent: the European New Right, also known as the *Nouvelle Droite*. The school emerged during the late 1960s and early 1970s in intellectual circles surrounding French philosopher Alain de Benoist, and it was inspired by the thinking of pre–World War II German conservatives like Arthur Moeller and Oswald Spengler, as well as traditionalists and esotericists like Julius Evola and René Guénon.

The *Nouvelle Droite* offered Nordic nationalists many of the same features as McCulloch's works. Like McCulloch, these European thinkers formulated a separatist cry through the language of diversity. However, they also aspired to academic legitimacy. Their thinking embeds criticisms of immigration, multiculturalism, and interracialism within relatively sophisticated, wide-ranging analyses of modernity—commentary committed as much to scrutinizing economic systems, spirituality, democracy, and gender relations as ethnic politics. Further, they spread their critiques via seminars and conferences, as well as self-produced and occasionally mainstream academic journals.[15] Daniel Friberg and those who shared his drive to forge a more literate nationalism thus saw in the *Nouvelle Droite* not only an attractive ideological platform but also an appealing cultural model, whose emblematic intellectualism rendered it antithetical to skinhead subculture. Before describing the ways Nordic activists imported and adapted this school, I will first outline its defining features and core critiques.[16]

The *Nouvelle Droite*

Thinkers of the *Nouvelle Droite* advocate political, social, and spiritual systems that they believe will nurture a "pluriversum"—that is, a global society that embraces "the plurality and variety of races, ethnic groups, languages, customs, even religions [that] has characterized the development of humanity since the very beginning" (De Benoist and Champetier 1999:130–31). Such diversity not only has value in itself, it is also allows individuals to gain a vital sense of belonging and embeddedness—to link themselves to a particular place, history, and society and thereby to possess an identity. Members of this school claim that liberalism and its agenda of equality threatens their vision of a diverse world. Their use of the term "equality" refers not to the concept of equal access to political influence but rather to the notion that all are identical to one another. As such, equality is poised to homogenize, to mask and erase what the school regards as humanity's "irreducible plurality." The forces of equality are necessarily imperialist, absolutist, and totalitarian. And, the *Nouvelle Droite* claims, they reign in Europe today.

As Michael Torigian aptly summarizes (1999), the *Nouvelle Droite* sees Europe as being in a state of alienation from itself, having in effect been ruled by foreign powers—the United States and Russia—since the onset of the world wars. These occupying political forces, and with them capitalism and communism, represent only the latest instance of foreign ideological and spiritual intrusion. American capitalism and Bolshevik communism replaced the regime of Christianity in Europe, itself a transplant to the continent from the Levant that erased the multitude of indigenous European pagan spiritualities. The foreignness of these three forces is not their only flaw, however. Rather, they fed a social movement devoted to advancing equality at the expense of difference: modernity.

With its individualization, desacralization, massification, rationalization, and universalization, modernity erases older forms of community life, standardizes behavior and beliefs, and asserts itself as absolute. Modern society, according to the *Nouvelle Droite*, destroys the infrastructure for maintaining authentic diversity, and thereby one's ability to obtain identity and function socially. The instruments of modernity's destruction appear varied, and may thereby be seen as offering some compensatory dynamism and heterogeneity. However, its central oppositions, such as the political right–left dichotomy, have always been illusory. De Benoist and Champetier write:

> [D]espite their mutual hostility, liberalism and Marxism basically belong to the same universe and are both the heirs of Enlightenment thought: they share the same individualism, even the same universal egalitarianism, the same rationalism, the same primacy of economics, the same stress on the emancipatory value of labor, the same faith in progress, the same idea of an end of history. (1999:121)

Modernity's internal oppositions ultimately reduce to replications and restatements of itself. Further, members of the *Nouvelle Droite* assert that the conceptual matter shared by ostensibly opposed forces like Marxism and capitalism derives from Judeo-Christian thought, particularly Protestantism. This religious tradition not only asserts its primacy above all other descriptions and prescriptions of human life, it further equalizes all humans in the pursuit of its goal at the end of history: communion with God. Marxism, capitalism, and modernity as a whole did not abolish this conceptual framework. Rather, they repackaged it, maintaining its claims to absolute truth, and erecting an earthly utopia, personal wealth, or the abstract notion of social progress as ersatz substitutes for union with the divine.

Thus, according to this perspective, Marxism, capitalism, Christianity, and secular humanism all compel their subjects to embrace egalitarianism and shed their ties to the past. Mass immigration—with its implicit assumption that individuals can be recontextualized without it having an appreciable impact on their lives or the lives of those around them—is a byproduct of this multifaceted modernist regime. However, voices of the *Nouvelle Droite* do not believe that such developments erased our natural allegiances and inherent differences. Rather, as Canadian professor and school sympathizer Andrew Fraser argues, modern liberalism has simply devised methods for diverting and delaying their expression. He writes, "To keep a lid on the simmering stew of racial, ethnic, and religious resentments, managerial multiculturalism depends entirely on steady economic growth" (2011:330). This shackling of our true nature does not come without a cost. As De Benoist and Champetier argue:

> [M]odern societies tend to bring together individuals who experience each other as strangers. . . . In becoming more solitary, man also has become more vulnerable and more destitute. He has become disconnected from meaning, because he can no longer identify himself with a model, and because there is no longer any way for him to understand his place in the social whole. (1999:125)

Those living in modern society cannot ignore the very real differences between themselves and their neighbors—differences that modernity's agents would deny exist—and they respond to this cognitive dissonance through traumatic social withdrawal. To compensate for the loss of community, modernity showcases progress in economic, spiritual, or political spheres. But beneath its veneer of structure, organization, and direction, modernity advances what Tomislav Sunic calls "formless politics, formless life" and "formless values" (2011 [2009]:58), formless because it does not belong to any context or to any people.

To remedy this situation, the *Nouvelle Droite* seeks to forge out of modernity "social systems that used to ascribe individuals their place in a clearly understood social order" (De Benoist 2004:133). Contemporary societies that deny and rebel against human diversity are not failing to advance to new heights of emancipation, as philosophers like Charles Taylor argue (1992). Instead, the school claims they are dismissing pluralistic worldviews that are ancient and natural, models that need to be reinvigorated rather than created anew.[17] Inspired by the esoteric traditionalism of Julius Evola and René Guénon, many of these thinkers see in pre-Christian or pre-Reformation Europe a hierarchical social model where the naturally occurring diversity in human life was respected, and thereby where the process of realizing one's identity was not shrouded in anxiety. This stance leads a portion of those affiliated with the *Nouvelle Droite* to follow Indo-European paganism (Miller 1974) or conservative forms of Catholicism on account of these traditions' inherent spiritual variation or social stratification. Likewise, these actors strive to invigorate local and pan-European identities—regarding them as more reflective of Europe's organic diversity than nation-states, which the school regards as modernist, homogenizing constructs.[18]

Voices of the *Nouvelle Droite* often present the pluriversum concept as the one virtuous universal, describing it as relevant to all peoples at all times. In such cases, activists' calls for a Europe of local identities are part of a larger, global agenda.[19] With words evocative of Richard McCulloch and his Racial Golden Rule, De Benoist and Champetier write, "the right to difference is a principle which has significance only in terms of its generality. One is only justified in defending one's difference from others if one is also able to defend the difference of others" (1999:133–34). Accordingly, these actors described themselves "differential anti-racists" who respect "the irreducible plurality of the human species," just as they call themselves "differential feminists" championing "the equal value of [men's and women's] distinct and unique natures" (ibid.:134, 136). They do this while opposing ideologies of racial supremacy. Nazism, for the *Nouvelle Droite*, was an imperialist, modernist movement that asserted its cause as absolute and disregarded others' right to self-determination and difference.

Methodologies of the *Nouvelle Droite*

The *Nouvelle Droite* thus champions social particularism, calling on individuals to withdraw from large-scale homogenizing entities into small collectivities that are spiritually, politically, and ethnically distinct. However, they seek to achieve this transformation through contradictory means: by pulling themselves and like-minded activists out from the margins of public life and injecting their message into the mainstream. They call this methodological approach "metapolitics," and it emerged when members of the *Nouvelle Droite* studied their ideological opposites. Seeking to understand how modern social and economic liberalism had entrenched itself in contemporary Western Europe, *Nouvelle Droite* thinkers found an explanation in the writings of neo-Marxist Antonio Gramsci. Gramsci, in a reversal of classical Marxist theory, argued that any meaningful political or economic change always proceeds from a shift in the cultural sphere, and thus that efforts to change the political status quo must begin their struggle in culture. Echoing this thinking, members of the *Nouvelle Droite* asserted that the triumph of liberalism in the west— its ascent to the level of taken-for-granted common sense and its unfettered persistence throughout left- or right-wing rule—derived from its prior dominance in the cultural realm. As Alain de Benoist writes, "[T]he French Revolution would not have been possible without the Enlightenment. Before any Lenin, there must always be a preceding Marx" (2011[2009]:19).

Accordingly, the *Nouvelle Droite* attempted to replicate its foes' tactics, devoting itself to "[t]he social diffusion of ideas and cultural values for the sake of provoking profound, long-term, political transformation" (Faye 2011:193), or "metapolitics." With this agenda, activists dismissed the need to run for public office or incite revolution. Instead, their primary activity was intellectualism and the waging of culture wars—campaigns to change hearts and minds rather than to gain political power. The *Nouvelle Droite* lacks a unified understanding of culture and how it differs from politics, but the school's writing and activism implies that arenas of intellectual and cultural production, like film, literature, art, theater, scholarship, and music, are valid targets for metapolitical campaigning.[20]

Metapolitics typically takes one of two forms: either activists seek to inject their message seamlessly into existing educational institutions and expressive and communicative outlets, or they aim to create their own version of these institutions and outlets—to create what Nancy Fraser calls a "counterpublic" (1990). For example, whereas those activists operating under the first approach would try to shape the content of public school curricula to better channel their views, those following the second approach would create a parallel educational system that satisfies the same needs as public schools, but that is saturated with their message. And whereas the first approach attempts to build political sympathy among the general populace, the second aims to build a parallel society capable of wielding political influence.

The *Nouvelle Droite's* will to construct a "plurliversum" through metapolitics forms an internal conflict in its program. The school strives toward isolation and expansion simultaneously. Together, these twin drives—this double imperative— would spread to nationalist causes throughout Europe.

The Spread of the *Nouvelle Droite*

Beginning in the late 1980s, anti-immigrant and nationalist movements throughout Europe gradually adopted *Nouvelle Droite*-inspired ideology, methodology, and, most importantly, rhetoric (Ter Wal 2000; Bar-On 2013).[21] This diffusion began with parliamentary activists in France—the French National Front in particular— moving thereafter to political parties and activist groups in Italy, Great Britain, and beyond. Relationships between these organizations and the *Nouvelle Droite* proper have been unstable. Alain de Benoist has frequently disavowed association with leading anti-immigration parties in Europe, who he frequently calls "xenophobes" (Von Beyme 1988; personal communication, Alain de Benoist, July 11, 2012; Bar-On 2013).

Concurrently, few elected politicians in European parliaments admit to having been inspired by the *Nouvelle Droite*, fearing accusations of fascism.[22] Perhaps because of this mutual apprehension, the school's ideas are not always described as such when outside groups assimilate them. As a result, it is difficult to trace with precision its impact on contemporary European politics.

There are two exceptions to this trend, however. The first is the technique of metapolitics, which was adopted in named form by political parties during the 1990s throughout Southern and Western Europe (Bar-On 2013:221). The second is the *Nouvelle Droite*'s program for ethnic separatism, which acquired its own label: "ethnopluralism."[23] This term entered the *Nouvelle Droite* discourse in France and Germany during the 1970s and was used to describe the school's agenda of nonhierarchical segregation of ethnicities to preserve global diversity, or an ethnic "pluriversum." During the 1980s and 1990s, the term spread to nationalist organizations throughout Europe as a way to infiltrate the discourse of liberal multiculturalism—to show that nationalists were friends, rather than enemies, of pluralism.[24] The expansion and impact of this concept led scholar Hans-Georg Betz to declare ethnopluralism "by far the most important and influential [*Nouvelle Droite*] concept" (1999:309; see also Lee 1997:369 and Spektorowski 2002).

Metapolitics and ethnopluralism thus became concepts detachable from wider *Nouvelle Droite* criticisms of modernity and equality. One need not embrace the school's readings of history, the nation, or religion to deem intellectualism and expressive culture the primary domains of ideological contestation or to advocate ethnic diversity through separatism. Further, tendencies to separate these agendas from the wider school, and from each other, may derive from their mutual opposition. By emphasizing either the *Nouvelle Droite*'s integrative or disintegrative drive, activists may resolve the school's double imperative.

But while many nationalists throughout Europe assimilate *Nouvelle Droite* ideals in piecemeal fashion, some pursued a more comprehensive embrace of its teachings. Following the turn of the twenty-first century, a score of small-scale extraparliamentary activist groups openly espousing the school's ideals—as well as the teachings of its traditionalist forebears, like Julius Evola and René Guénon— arose throughout the continent. Populated primarily with youths, they devoted themselves to metapolitical activism, staging dramatic public demonstrations, producing expressive culture, and disseminating literature. Rather than calling themselves members of the *Nouvelle Droite*, many coalesced under the heading "identitarianism" (Fr. *identitaire*, Sw. *identitär*)—a term further aimed at contrasting these activists, who fight for regional and continental identities in step with *Nouvelle Droite* teaching, with their counterpart anti-immigrant activists who seek to purify national communities.[25]

The first groups calling themselves "identitarians" emerged in France, and include Jeunesses Identitaires founded in 2002 and Bloc Identitaire founded in 2003. The latter group gained notoriety for distributing soup to the homeless throughout France, and adding pork to deter Jews and Muslims. Shortly after the rise of these French organizations, identitarian groups began emerging throughout Europe—in Portugal, Italy, Serbia, Germany, Austria, Hungary, England, and Ireland. In the mid-2000s, activists at the Nordic Press in Sweden would embrace the school—with both its metapolitics and its pluralism—and use it to ignite their reformist campaign.

Identitarianism in the Nordic Countries

Nordic Press leader Daniel Friberg came in contact with *Nouvelle Droite* literature in 2004.[26] He found English translations of Alain de Benoist's writings online and recalls being particularly impressed with the school's concept of a "right to difference." He says of his first exposure:

> I had this "aha" experience and thought it was totally brilliant, and wondered why these ideas weren't better known. It was the logical construction, the intellectual caliber. It was on a totally different level than I was used to reading—texts from the right, that is. It was radical, but appropriately so. It dismissed egalitarianism, for example. That is a vital position in today's left-wing liberal society. It was so encompassing and well argued. (Interview, Daniel Friberg, June 6, 2014)

Though Friberg had long been committed to intellectualism as a tool of reform, the *Nouvelle Droite* offered him a grounded, comprehensive means to advance that agenda. As he and Lennart Berg continued to read works by Alain de Benoist and Guillaume Faye, they grew convinced that their efforts to create a more upstanding, intelligent, and literate nationalist cause in the North ought to proceed from this continental school. Beginning in 2004, the Press started highlighting the writings of *Nouvelle Droite* authors and traditionalists like Julius Evola.

As identitarianism spread into the Nordic Press, leaders also began to expand their methods of activism, forging avenues for metapolitics—now in named form and with reference to the *Nouvelle Droite*—beyond publishing and retail. In 2004, after the Press had acquired a tabloid and founded a magazine, leaders decided to create a new umbrella organization to house their growing number of projects: the Nordic League (*Nordiska förbundet*). The founding of the Nordic League presented leaders a new opportunity to specify their mission and distinguish themselves within the wider scene. Whereas nationalism in Sweden, Norway, and Denmark had often split into either parliamentary or revolutionary forms, the Nordic League criticized this two-part model in its online opening statement and specified a third path. Leaders explained:

> It is irrational to plan for a nationalist majority, or even advantage in the nearest parliamentary elections. And for every election that goes, the ethnically Swedish voting block shrinks. . . . For every election that passes, we approach the day when the demographic clock tolls and it is actually impossible for us to vote ourselves into power. It is even more irrational to plan for a successful armed revolution or coup in the foreseeable future. No efforts in that direction have led anywhere. They have not done anything to improve our prospects for a real solution. Time and time again, physical struggle that looks beyond the fight for streets and town squares leads to an impasse. Both the parliamentary fight and the physical struggle must be seen as smaller parts or accessories of a much broader ethnic and political pursuit. We need a wide-ranging and more long-term approach, a long-term Nordic survival strategy. We need a strategy that moves forward and reinforces our positions in many different areas, that deals constructively with the here and now, but that has its sights on the horizon—that has its sights secured on our own Nordic, healthy, and viable society.[27]

With this statement, the Nordic League officially rejected prevailing methodologies in the nationalist scene, deeming both the democratic process and revolution ineffectual. They instead outlined a strategy that would spread nationalist values in "many different areas"—that is, multiple arenas of social behavior and communication—to make future parliamentary or militant campaigning productive. Rather than politicians or revolutionaries, these activists declared themselves intellectuals participating in a battle of ideas.

While calling for reform, the Nordic League initially remained entwined with the ethnonationalist establishment. Within its projects, the agendas of Melander on the one hand and Friberg/Berg on the other—of phantom white-power National Socialism and New Rightist identitarianism, of an old and a new nationalism—coexisted. As such, the League was operating in step with the wave of nationalist organizations throughout Europe and the emerging Alt-Right movement in the United States who used methodologies resembling *Nouvelle Droite* metapolitics to propagate a variety of ideologies. This hybridity allowed the League to more easily cooperate and collaborate with National Socialist organizations. From 2005 until

2007, for example, the National Socialist Front participated in the League's annual Nordic Festival. In return, the League joined both the National Socialist Front and the Nordic (formerly Swedish) Resistance Movement for the annual People's March in Stockholm.[28] However, the bulk of the League's growth from 2004 and onward moved away from music and Nazism and toward the production of texts and innovative metapolitics.

Starting in 2006, the League initiated three major online projects. The first of these was the blog portal Motpol (*motpol* = "polar opposite"). Blog posts on the site ranged from media critique to academic-style book reviews and essays. Motpol marketed itself as politically unaffiliated, save for purportedly shared "foundational values based on the defense of Nordic culture and tradition" (*The People's News*, November 7, 2006). However, its most influential writers—bloggers "Oskorei" and "Solguru"—eventually presented themselves as identitarian. Further, starting in 2008, the blog portal began sponsoring the seminar series Identitarian Ideas, which is today the only major annual identitarian gathering in the Nordic countries. Likely for these reasons, insiders have tended tend to speak about Motpol as an identitarian organization despite the fact that the portal has made no such declaration.

Shortly after founding this blog portal, the League established the Wikipedia-style online encyclopedia Metapedia, which officially opened on October 24, 2006. Like Wikipedia, Metapedia contains articles—occasionally grouped into larger series or portals—written by select volunteer editors. In an interview in *The People's News*, Daniel Friberg (under the pseudonym "Martin Brandt") described the motivation behind the project:

> A few friends and I were discussing how important it is for the nationalist cultural campaign that we present our own interpretations of concepts, phenomena, and historic events for a broader public. It is especially important these days, since many concepts are distorted and have lost their original meaning, which you can see as an outcome of our political opponents' successful culture campaign. . . . Just look at how the Frankfurt School and their ideological heirs have succeeded in declaring as sick and stigmatizing what previously were completely natural values by introducing concepts like "xenophobia," "homophobia," and so on. (2006, no. 10)

Metapedia was thus conceived based on an agenda of *Nouvelle Droite*/Gramscian metapolitics; it was an effort to counteract the intellectual domination of liberalism in the west. As such, it did not make its own rendition of every article on Wikipedia, but rather focused only on those topics deemed crucial in shaping discussion of key nationalist concerns. The site issued articles on topics ranging from nationalist organizations, music groups, and prominent activists to multicultural-ism, immigration policy, Islam, and World War II.

Shortly following the debut of Motpol and Metapedia, the Nordic League founded an online community called Nordisk.nu ("Nordisk" = Nordic), which marketed itself as a "portal for Nordic identity, culture, and tradition." The page opened on April 18, 2007, and its mission was to provide a nationalist alternative to social networking sites. Participants on Nordisk.nu would create user accounts, select a screen name, and fill out a profile. They could then make their own webpage and blog, view access-restricted material like photo and graphics galleries and online games, and participate in discussion threads. Threads were not all devoted to politics and activism; some dealt with helping other users with their homework, shar-ing home and garden maintenance tips, and discussing cars. A thread titled "Birka" (named after the ancient Viking-era trade post outside of present-day Stockholm) functioned as a sort of Ebay—an arena for users to buy, sell, and trade goods. The most popular discussion threads, however, focused on politics, media, and music.

The Nordic League's online initiatives filled the social and commercial gap left by white power music culture—a culture that relied on mail orders or congregating in the nonvirtual world. The online initiatives not only survived; they flourished. Metapedia quickly spread throughout Europe and North America, acquiring pages in English, German, Spanish, French, Hungarian, Romanian, Estonian, Croatian, Slovenian, Greek, Czech, Portuguese, Norwegian, Danish, and Dutch.[29] Combined, these pages produced nearly 300,000 articles.[30] The social networking site Nordisk.nu likewise grew rapidly, reaching 20,000 registered users from throughout Sweden, Norway, and Denmark by 2011.[31] As such, the site became one of the largest online venues for Nordic nationalists to interact, publicize events, and exchange ideas at the time.[32] Finally, Motpol, while falling short of the other sites' international reach and number of participants, still experienced steady growth in readership. And given that Motpol provided an alternative to liberal intellectualism and worked to edu-cate nationalists, Daniel Friberg and Lennart Berg considered it the League's greatest success.

The rise of the Nordic League's online initiatives was followed by a series of intense but transformative conflicts within the organization's leadership. Cofounder Peter Melander objected to the influx of identitarianism in the League's projects, and was even suspected of attempting to sabotage Motpol. At the same time, Friberg and Berg disapproved of his continued investment in Nazism and white power music. Outnumbered among the leadership and facing the advance of his opponents' initia-tives, Melander left the League in 2007. Having been the League's primary opponent of the *Nouvelle Droite*, Melander's departure allowed the remaining leaders to accel-erate their embrace of identitarianism.[33]

The first step in this transition came on August 30, 2008, when the Nordic League declared itself identitarian by publishing the booklet *Identity and Metapolitics.* This new statement of purpose—marketed as an "identitarian manifesto"—makes no overtures to skinheadism or Nazism, does not disparage any minority group, and does not voice populist rage against immigration. Instead, and in the distanced, intellectualist style of de Benoist and Faye, it trains its criticisms on modernity by advocating a premodern social form, where

> foundational identity was a given due to our position and function in society, the family, and our heritage, as well as the religion and culture we belonged to and practiced. Identity was, for most in the North, organically linked to what we were born into, and was for the most part unchanged during our lifetimes.... We never questioned our being or existence, but instead saw ourselves as a part of a greater whole, built of parts from what is local and personal—like family, home region, and local tradition—to what is larger— like the fatherland, European cultural tradition, tribe, king, and aristocracy, God or Gods.[34]

The League's declaration of identitarianism completed a trajectory. What began as a jumble of various nationalist ideological and cultural currents in its projects was gradually distilled into a more concentrated and enduring *Nouvelle Droite* profile. Traces of skinheadism and neo-Nazism were not wholly extinguished following Friberg's takeover, however. The Nordic Press continued to sell white power music and literature sympathetic to the Third Reich. However, nearly all growth from this point forward would be devoted to identitarianism, and the League's relations with other ethnonationalist organizations deteriorated in step with this process.

During the summer of 2008—the same summer the Nordic League declared itself identitarian—it and the National Socialist establishment stopped participating in each other's events. This breakdown grew in part from a series of violent conflicts among members of each faction, in part from the growing ideological and cultural rift between the two communities. The public discourse that ensued focused on these latter factors, however, and framed identitarians and National Socialists as irreconcilably different. In a fiery speech at the 2008 People's March,[35] Magnus Söderman of the Nordic Resistance Movement argued this very point:

> People have said that the national movement is divided. But I can promise you, the national movement is not divided.... However, there is a split between us in the national movement, and those who, through different methods—like black propaganda, obscure terminology, ideologies hostile

to our people—tried for their own aims to lead good nationalists astray. But these people are not, nor have they ever been, nationalists. Put clearly comrades, people who call themselves "national anarchists," the "*Nouvelle Droite*," "nihilists," "left-wing nationalists," or the collective term for this nonsense, "identitarians"—they are not nationalists, and they are not a part of the national movement [applause].

Söderman continued with a direct attack on Friberg and his collaborators:

How have they planned to save Sweden? By sitting in [online] forums, coming up with new ideologies, or through the implementation of a—and listen carefully now—"national-anarchist-traditionalist-Catholic-rightwing-nihilism?" Please! ... The Resistance Movement warned you about these forces, and unfortunately we have seen how a tiny, tiny fragment of the national movement worked, not to advance the national struggle, but instead for the sake of their own secret agenda.... A little clique of intellectuals has emerged, and they've gone off the tracks completely. But we, dear comrades, we can handle them. Because if the system with all its economic resources hasn't destroyed the national movement thus far, then these identitarians won't be able to do it either!

National Socialists' hostility toward identitarians was mutual. Motpol blogger Solguru, for example, has been one of the identitarian voices most forward in contrasting his ideal political engagement with the supposed hooliganism and ideological bankruptcy of neo-Nazis (Lundquist 2010). In the song "Your Own Fault" (*Ditt eget fel*), Solguru—rapping under the name Zyklon Boom (see chapter 3)—says:

You skinhead, sitting there with your nose stuffed with speed, then howling about nation and *Volk*—for fuck's sake what nonsense. Head in to town and a fight breaks out, an exercise in violence. With enough liquor and cheap beer, you can make a rock into a communist! Then—in truly Germanic style—you go home and beat the shit out of your girlfriend. But perhaps it's not only because of "the Jew" that your life sucks.

With expressions like these, Solguru attempts to contrast himself with National Socialist skinheads, characterized here as simple-minded, intoxicated, and violent. In contrast, activists like himself are well read, upstanding, and nuanced in their understanding of identity politics. Further, Solguru claims that these qualities make identitarians more formidable political players. In his blog posting "0% Hate" from 2008, he writes of mainstream liberals and leftists:

> [T]hey do not want to see an authentic, traditional Right that can argue without losing its cool. They want to see a stupid, brutal, bellowing, imbecile Right—a Right they can hate. We will not give it to them.[36]

Undeterred by the raging conflict within the nationalist scene, Friberg continued his promotion of *Nouvelle Droite* ideas. His ability to do so strengthened further as the remaining cofounders turned over sole leadership of the Nordic League to him. Feeling that the organization bore a permanent stain of National Socialism from its early years, he dissolved it in 2009 and began to rebrand his initiatives in the image of the thoroughly identitarian Motpol. That same year, he created Motpol Ltd. to house this blog portal as well as Metapedia and Nordisk.nu. He had other plans for the Nordic Press. In October 2009, Friberg met in Århus, Denmark with Norwegian Tord Morsund and two Danish activists. The Danes were founders of Integral Traditions Publishing (ITP), which specialized in the production and resale of traditionalist and antimodern literature—writings by authors like Julius Evola and René Guénon, who provided inspiration to the *Nouvelle Droite* but who were comparatively less political. The pan-Scandinavian group that met in Århus envisioned a publishing house that would combine offerings in traditionalism with *Nouvelle Droite* publications. The following year, Friberg dissolved the Nordic Press and founded a new publisher called Arktos. Arktos would in turn absorb ITP. This new company increased its productivity and reduced its costs by adopting new print-on-demand procedures, and by moving its operation, along with person-nel, to India (Interview, Daniel Friberg, June 26, 2014; Interview, John Morgan, June 23, 2014). Since its founding in 2010, Arktos has grown steadily, and today it is the uncontested global leader in the publication of English-language *Nouvelle Droite* literature.

Unity in New Nationalism

It may appear that the transformations I have detailed thus far exacerbated division within Nordic radical nationalism. The three major camps of the scene—race revolutionaries, identitarians, and cultural nationalists—would seem to have entrenched positions against each other. Race revolutionaries—whether National Socialists or white nationalists—criticize identitarians for relativizing the white/Aryan race, making that race only one among many that needs respect and protection.

Such organizations may also condemn identitarians for exhibiting an intellectualist remove from political struggle. Followers of the *Nouvelle Droite*, in turn, reject Nazism for seeking to impose a hierarchy among ethnic groups, for disregarding all groups' equal rights to life and difference. While voicing this latter charge, identitarians may also condemn National Socialism as a modernist, imperialist cause. Finally, cultural nationalists reject the other camps since both supposedly rest on the proposition that national identity derives from inherited biological traits.[37]

But as was the case throughout the 1980s and 1990s, the appearance of schematic oppositions among nationalists in the twenty-first century belied underlying commonality and interconnectedness. While skinhead subculture once linked warring wings of radical nationalism, diversity talk, metapolitics, and stylized intellectualism would replace skinheadism as nationalists' body of shared behavioral tendencies.

As New Nationalist models spread, however, actors throughout the scene adjusted them to their own values and agendas, just as they had done earlier with skinheadism. Cultural nationalists produced their own version of ethnopluralism and diversity talk, framing their activism as part of an effort to maintain cultural rather than ethnic difference. In the years surrounding the turn of the twenty-first century, the Sweden Democrats began defending their preservationist agenda by describing its benefits to global cultural diversity. This reasoning likely had its roots in the writings of Richard McCulloch, given the fact that some party members were covertly involved in the dissemination of the American theorist's works in Sweden. It first emerged in the Sweden Democrats' party program in May 4, 2003:

> Cultural diversity is as necessary for humankind as biodiversity is for nature. The separate cultures are humankind's collective heritage and should be recognized and protected for the good of all.

Nearly a decade later, party spokesperson Chang Frick was particularly fervent in his use of this rhetoric. His argumentation is exemplified in an exchange during one of our interviews:

> Sweden has to be Swedish if we are going to contribute anything to global diversity. Think, if you want to learn about the pyramids and that stuff, then you should go to Egypt, not Greenland. It's different if we are talking about snowball fights. (Interview, Chang Frick, January 22, 2011)

Aside from their use of diversity rhetoric, many leading Sweden Democrats today also read and occasionally endorse *Nouvelle Droite* theories. Chief ideologue and former Thule skin Mattias Karlsson has followed postings on Motpol. He was initially enthusiastic about identitarianism and slogans featured on Motpol like "100% identity—0% hate," but he objected to the anti-Semitic undertones in much of the site's writings. Nonetheless, it was here where he first came into contact with the notion of metapolitics and rightist readings of Antonio Gramsci. He recalls of his exposure to this body of thought:

> When I became interested in Gramsci, and to look at society a little—and above all the Frankfurt School, the 68-Left—in part I was full of amazement by how [the Left] had succeeded, and taken over institutions that were actually opposed to them, the Church, the Local Heritage Federation, the folk music movement.... Institutions that I don't think should belong to them. (Interview, Mattias Karlsson, February 11, 2011)

Following *Nouvelle Droite* thinking, Karlsson now aims to employ the same tactics used by leftists to gain power. He says of the institutions now apparently dominated by the left, "If we use our resources wisely, we should be able to retake quite a few that haven't been lost, but that have fallen into the opponents' hands" (ibid.). Indeed, much of Karlsson's plans for the future involve pursuing this agenda, which he and a handful of other party leaders openly refer to as "metapolitics."

While identitarian language and methodology gradually entrenched itself at the highest levels of the cultural nationalist Sweden Democrats, diversity rhetoric also spread throughout the ethnonationalist sphere, first among parliamentary ethnonationalists. In 2001, former members of the Sweden Democrats—having resigned or been expelled for ethnonationalism, anti-Semitism, or interpersonal conflicts—formed the National Democrats (*Nationaldemokraterna*). Though former Sweden Democrats composed the bulk of this new party, the National Democrats also recruited apostates and outcasts from the increasingly militant neo-Nazi organization, the Nordic Resistance Movement. Whereas individuals coming from the Sweden Democrats were deemed too extreme for their former party, those coming from the Nordic Resistance Movement were often ejected because they did not appear fully committed to National Socialist ideals. Reflecting the twin ideological purges that produced the party, the National Democrats filled an ideological space in between the rigidly race-centered and supremacist Nordic Resistance Movement and the race-blind, cultural nationalist Sweden Democrats. They would assert that being Swedish meant being ethnically Swedish. But the party formally rejected ideologies of racial supremacy. Instead, they sought to base their ideology on Richard McCulloch's separatist vision (personal communication, Vávra Suk, March 24, 2012).

Omar Filmersson—who translated and published McCulloch's *The Racial Compact*—and former Sweden Democrat Vávra Suk wrote the National Democrats' party program. Though it never mentions him by name, the program holds closely to McCulloch's ideas and rhetoric (Fleischer 2003:20–21). The same held true for early writings in the party's newspaper, *National Today* (*Nationell Idag*). In the first issue of the paper, National Democrats cofounder Tor Paulsson made his case for the party's ideological stance thusly:

> You don't save the panda bear because it is better than other animals. You save
> a species because it is a part of creation and has a place in the fantastic diversity
> of life. In the same way, every nationality and ethnic group has a moral right to
> live, to live freely and to create their own future without the risk of integration
> with another nationality. A principle of live and let live. (2002, no. 1)

Paulsson and others thus adopted McCulloch's internationalism and diversity rhetoric to make their case for ethnic separatism.

But party members were reluctant to explicitly tie their ideology to McCulloch and his "Racial Golden Rule." As former party ideologue Vávra Suk explains, the absence of direct reference to McCulloch and his work has to do with language:

> In Sweden, "race" . . . has a strongly negative connotation. It makes you think
> of skull-measuring and gas chambers. Were you to use that word, you would
> communicate the exact opposite of what we want—while we talk about all
> peoples' right to life, the word "race" makes you think of genocide. (electronic
> message, Vávra Suk, March 24, 2012)

The National Democrats found terminology more suited to their local political climate. Starting in 2006, the party imported the *Nouvelle Droite* term "ethnopluralism" to describe their ideology.

McCulloch's ideas and ethnopluralism would be altered in the hands of the National Democrats, however. The transformations in these concepts concerned the ideal populations and boundaries for separatism and preservation. In contrast with McCulloch, as well as many *Nouvelle Droite* thinkers, the National Democrats declared their commitment to the nation as the target unit for political activism. And when they began to self-apply the label "ethnopluralism," they did so fusing it with the nation-centered agenda central to Nordic activism. They wrote in an overview of their platform:

> Within ethnopluralism, it is obvious that every nation has a right to its members'
> love and care. The nation is like a big family, and cannot function well if those

who belong to it do not care about it. That you place much value on your own nation is no more strange than the fact that you like your own family most.[38]

By maintaining a nation-centered approach in their ethnopluralism, the National Democrats part with identitarian thinkers who see the nation as a modernist entity seldom corresponding to the boundaries of organic ethnocultural communities. The party similarly diverges with McCulloch, who champions transnational racial communities rather than nationalities.[39]

Just as metapolitics and diversity talk surfaced among various parliamentary activists, so too have these streams appeared in revolutionary race nationalism. Norway's semimilitant National Socialist political party Vigrid began presenting its agenda as one of "metapolitics and politics" in late 2009,[40] and it began describing itself as sympathetic to identitarianism and the writings of Guilliaume Faye and Alain de Benoist by early 2012.[41] Swedish National Socialists would be comparatively inconspicuous in their engagement with *Nouvelle Droite* teachings, likely as a result of years of interpersonal conflicts with the Nordic League. Though the Nordic Resistance Movement disassociated itself from the *Nouvelle Droite*, its members began showing less enthusiasm for ideologies of racial supremacy toward the end of the 2000s. Instead of expounding the primacy of the Aryan race, much of their commentary has come to involve disavowing hatred while celebrating pluralism. This shift necessitated commentary on historical Nazism. Resistance Movement member Jakob Haskå, for example, attempted to distance Adolf Hitler from racial supremacy in the organization's newspaper *National Resistance (Nationell motstånd)*. He wrote of Hitler's activism:

> [F]or him it was the simple, decisive fact that he belonged to the Germanic race which solidified his position as fanatically race conscious. Based on that—the actuality of his ethnic belonging—an unyielding loyalty towards the German people emerged. A loyalty that compelled him to see the construction of a worldview that concerned and pursued the interests of only his own races' interests as his mission. (August 14, 2008)

In Haskå's history, Hitler was not motivated by an outward-looking belief in the Aryan people's inherent superiority to others, but rather by inward-looking concern for Aryans' well-being. This reading then enables Haskå to proceed to the following statement without compromising his commitment to National Socialism:

> The project of proving or demonstrating that we Aryans are the crown of an evolutionary progression, by trying to show evidence of superiority in our character, beauty, or "objectively" high marks in intelligence, is now dead.

Efforts to rebrand National Socialism are paralleled by public rhetoric that seems ethnopluralist in character. For example, Magnus Söderman, said the following in the same speech from the 2008 People's March where he condemned identitarians:

As a National Socialist, I love my people. I respect other people, and I have the deepest respect for those natural laws that guide all of us. That is the foundation, love and respect.

It is likely due to the steady proliferation of such statements that Metapedia claims, "Today, National Socialists in Sweden are most often ethnopluralists."[42]

In sum, the rise of the Nordic League's online initiatives—their success in replacing the white power music industry as the scene's venue for socialization—accompanies the expansion of identitarian rhetoric and methodology across Nordic radical nationalism's internal fault lines. As this transition proceeded, activists also drew expressive forms and aesthetic tendencies from throughout Nordic and continental European identitarianism. In 2014, the Sweden Democrats youth wing produced the online video "Salute to the European Youth," which featured eight activists voicing statements of national pride and contempt for multiculturalism in different European languages. Though the Sweden Democrats' production lacked references to race and ethnicity, its rhetoric and visual character otherwise mimicked a video released the previous year by the French identitarian organization Generation Identity (Fr. *Génération Identitaire*)—an organization frequently publicized on Motpol. Both videos consist of close-up, grayscale images of actors, epic and urgent-sounding background music, and calls—dotted with "We are the generation" statements—promising to rebel against regimes of multiculturalism (see Figure 2.1).[43] For the video's producer, William Hahne—who once described skinhead festivals to me as "nothing but meeting places for white trash dregs" (interview, May 24, 2011)—identitarian activist forms offer culturally and socially palatable means to engage with the wider nationalist community.

As nationalists adopt and mold isolated expressions from the identitarian world, a far more pervasive, though still emerging, stream of cultural influence is manifest in their online imagery. On blogs, media sites, and social networking pages, increasing numbers of nationalists are creating profile images of themselves framed with visual emblems of intellectualism, most often books. This trend is most prominent among bloggers at Motpol who depict themselves sitting in libraries, reading books, or in front of enlarged background images of book covers. However, actors in Nationalist Socialist organizations are also embracing an iconography of

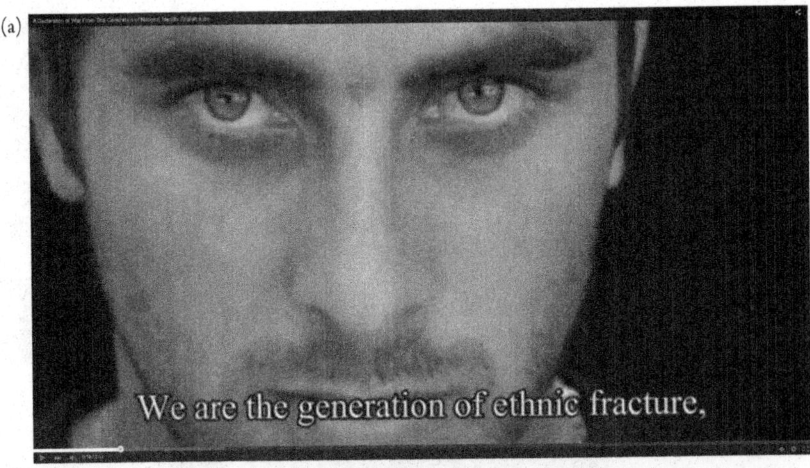

FIGURE 2.1 a) Still from Generation Identity's video *A Declaration of War from the Youth of France* (available online, accessed July 1, 2014, https://www.youtube.com/watch?v=ypIt2kJRO3w). b) Still from the Young Sweden Democrats' video *Salute to the European Youth* (available online, accessed July 1, 2014, https://www.youtube.com/watch?v=VR-lAGj_dlQ).

learnedness. One example of this comes from Magnus Söderman who, when he left the Nordic Resistance Movement and founded an online think tank in 2011, debuted a new profile image of himself standing before shelves of books. Images like this, or that on Daniel Friberg's Motpol blog, both shown in Figure 2.2, seek to reframe the image of a nationalist from the hypermasculine, violent skinhead music consumer, to the cool-headed, erudite scholar—to say that being a nationalist consists in being an intellectual. The embellished nature of these images paints New Nationalists as a type of intellectual nouveau riche anxious to demonstrate distance form their unlettered origins and position themselves in a new community of political thinkers.

FIGURE 2.2 a) Daniel Friberg's online banner from his blog on Motpol (available online, accessed July 17, 2014, https://www.motpol.nu). b) Magnus Söderman's profile image from the webpage for his think tank Nordengruppen (available online, accessed June 4, 2012, https://www.nordengruppen.se).

Intoning New Nationalism

Nationalists would not rely solely on rhetoric or visual representation to stylize and perform their new identities. As we will see, activists' efforts to experience themselves as intellectual, professional, self-loving nonaggressors inspired a wave of new musical practices. But insiders disagree as to how music should participate in this project. The conflict between *Nouvelle Droite* metapolitics and visions for the construction of a "pluriversum"—or the New Nationalist double imperative—drives the vibrancy of musical practices in the contemporary scene.

Metapolitics encourages nationalist activism to seep into all expressive, communicative, and knowledge-producing domains, including musical expression. This agenda assumes that the media transmitting a political message lack inherent political or cultural connotations. It assumes, for example, that nationalist ideals and values can be spread through various clothing styles, various institutions, and various music genres without appreciable mutation or loss of integrity. However, all but the most rigidly race-focused ideologues regard cultural expression as contributing to a people's difference. Virtually all nationalists recognize particular clothing styles, social institutions, or music as constituting the stuff of identity. In such cases, mediums of expression may not only be marked but also exist among the very objects of nationalist protectionism.

New Nationalism, in other words, presents music-makers with a dilemma, framing music as a tool both to integrate with the mainstream and to demonstrate national distinctiveness. The tensions between expansionism and withdrawal into the Self, between those voices who think expressive genres do or do not bear essential political associations and those who think music is and is not part of the difference the New Nationalism seeks, shape the phenomena I detail in the following chapters.

3

....

WHITE PRIDE/BLACK MUSIC

Nordic Nationalist Rap and Reggae

IN 2005 AN identitarian young man from northern Sweden began uploading rap songs for free download online.[1] "Zyklon Boom" was his artist name, a reference to the Zyklon B gas used during the Holocaust. Two years later, another young man from Stockholm calling himself "Juice" began producing and disseminating rap songs that demonized nonwhites and celebrated ethnic Swedes. And in 2010, just after Zyklon Boom released his first full album, the pan-Scandinavian ethnopluralist activist group Nordic Youth released a reggae song that called for ethnic separatism and criticized immigrants.

These projects account for a relatively small body of music—less than thirty songs to date. However, they stirred intense controversy among Nordic nationalists and inspired more internal discussion of cultural expression in the scene than any productions before or since. Nationalists have traditionally reviled reggae and rap music due to its association with leftism and blackness. This is not to say that the genres have been altogether absent from European radical nationalism. Before the British skinhead scene aligned itself with white activism, it borrowed openly from Jamaican and African American–inspired fashion, dance, and music, including rocksteady, reggae, and ska (Hebdige 1988; Mercer 1990, 1994; Marshall 1991:99; Griffiths 1995; Back 2002). Further, organized ethnonationalist and identitarian activists in Europe have been producing rap music since the late 1990s. But the overwhelming majority of nationalist music-making has been rock and punk—music that, despite its roots in Afro-diasporic styles, is often discursively framed as white.

The recent rap and reggae projects in the Nordic countries appear groundbreaking against this historical backdrop. Zyklon Boom and Juice have been the first Nordic nationalists to produce rap, and Nordic Youth's musicians were likely the first worldwide to produce European or white nationalist reggae. And while some insiders condemned these projects, others celebrated them as innovative and profoundly appropriate for the nationalist cause.

In this chapter I examine both the emerging nationalist rap and reggae projects and their reception in the greater scene, showing how these musical and discursive phenomena perpetuate and contest New Nationalism. My investigation of Zyklon Boom's, Juice's, and Nordic Youth's music highlights how these artists mold the symbolic forms of rap and reggae to portray themselves variously as intellectuals, victims, or champions of justice rather than hooliganistic hate-mongers. Similarly, I show how public conversations about these works—whether driven by advocates or critics—allowed insiders to position themselves in relation to the reformist cause and its internal tensions. These conversations have often coalesced around two questions: (1) whether or not these genres belong to particular racial or ethnic communities; and (2) whether or not rap and reggae offer a useful vessel for spreading nationalist values. Put another way, the discussions at their core have been about New Nationalism's double imperative to pluralism and metapolitics.

Insiders' responses to these questions vary. Some see rap and reggae as ethnically neutral. Others regard the genres as inherently black, and a small number even think of them as inherently Nordic, European, or white.[2] Such determinations seldom correlate with general favorability or opposition to the new music projects. Indeed, New Nationalist ideological transformations are allowing activists to embrace as their own music they deem white, racially and ethnically unaffiliated, or even black.

Nationalist Rap and Reggae in Sweden

VOICE 1: He's not a nationalist at all, not at all. He's a coward!

VOICE 2: I know. He reads like Evola and stuff like that.

VOICE 1: Who the fuck is Evola?

VOICE 3: I mean, he's kind of funny, but that name is offensive as hell.

VOICE 4: It's so damn unsettling.

VOICE 3: Yes, exactly, I mean you just don't know how people are thinking.
He is surely, surely a Nazi—like a Sweden Democrat!
But he's not some skinhead. He's a well-read integectual [*sic*].

VOICE 4: Totally, and those ones are the most dangerous.

These conversations—the first involving establishment nationalists, the second left-ists—take place at the beginning of the song "Shut Up" ("*Håll käften*")! by Zyklon Boom. The voices discuss the artist himself who, after these lines, explodes into the soundscape. Set to a computerized backing with a syncopated beat, punchy bass line, and short riff played with a musical saw effect, Zyklon Boom delivers a wide-reaching and ferocious polemic, one focused on demeaning an unnamed opponent who he refers to variously as a "worthless person," "not even gay," and "discolored vaginal fluid." In contrast, the rapper asserts his ability to consume large amounts of alcohol and baffle his intellectual inferiors, adding that he is "crazy, with an immigrant gang's regard for women."

Zyklon Boom's music is not only rapped text, set to a beat. It also builds from core hip-hop rhetorical forms that often accompany rap as it spreads to socially and politically distant actors worldwide. The Swedish artist channels what Craig Watkins calls rap's "oppositional ethos" (2006). This ethos, more so than the genre's association with the Afro-diasporic experience, permeates understandings and uses of rap throughout the globe,[3] encompassing Native Americans (Ullestad 1999), North African minorities in France (Prévos 2001), Muslim minorities in Germany (Elflein 1998), Japanese youth (Condry 2006), Basque separatists (Urla 2001:175), and the Maori (Mitchell 2001b). Global rap communities have fitted the ethos to a variety of local causes, in forms that may be broadly ethnic (Mitchell 2001a), generational (Brown 2006), or gendered in nature.

Zyklon Boom belongs to that prominent class of hip-hop oppositionalism centered on voicing what Keeler calls "fantasies of masculine power" (2009:9). His are works whose self-aggrandizing defamation of the other traffics in standards of manhood. More specifically, he furthers an entrenched tendency whereby white men turn to Afro-diasporic music to forge an alternative masculinity. And just as whites have historically been selective when drawing elements of black manhood through music (Lott 1993; White 2011), so too does Zyklon Boom construct a hip-hop masculinity molded to his particular political agenda as a New Nationalist.

"Zyklon Boom" is one of many projects and personas created by a young man from Umeå in northern Sweden. This same individual started the little-known electronica act Green Army Faction and the online Norse-themed fashion company WotanKlan.net—a play on the American hip-hop group the Wu-Tang Clan. He is best known in Nordic nationalism, however, as Motpol blogger Solguru. Like many activists associated with identitarianism, he has advanced academic training, having studied the history of religions at Umeå University, and he worked for a brief period with Arktos Publishing in India. He is slender and tall with a long blond ponytail, sharp features, a characteristic voice with a thick Norrland accent, and a quick, humorous, and eccentric wit.

This young man's multiple projects and personas—which combined constitute something of a metapolitical tour de force—bear common features. As blogger Solguru, he describes himself as

> [taking] a starting place in perennialism and tradition, and in a politically reactionary foundation ... discussing and criticizing different aspects of modernity, from secularism and humanism, to cultural diversity and feminism.[4]

With its parade of "isms," its esoteric topics, and its broad targeting of modernity, Solguru here seeks to cast his project as intellectual. A similar drive distinguishes Zyklon Boom from other rap projects as well as the nationalist music status quo. For while the rapper's masculinity builds from features common in hip-hop polemics—misogyny, ultraviolence, command of libations, political dissidence, and homophobia (Rose 2008)—it also contains an unusual measure: bookish intelligence.

Claims to a masculinity of superior learnedness emerge in Zyklon Boom's tirades against his unnamed listener. Most of his lyrics center on his ability to overpower, outdrink, and outsmart this opponent, the "you" he disses in his polemic. Though this implied opponent takes many forms, he is typically not part of an ethnic or religious minority, but instead a white male—sometimes a postmodern progressive contemptuous of his own majority status, and sometimes an overzealous political activist from either the far left or the far right. But he is always cowardly, insufficiently virile, and insufficiently read. As Zyklon Boom raps in "Shut Up" (*"Håll käften"*):

> I've been reading Nietzsche since I was thirteen.
> You heard of him before?
> So shut your face, pussy,
> who the hell do you think you are?

While battles over this particular masculinity form the focal point of Zyklon Boom's lyrics, subtext reveals the artist's identity as a nationalist, albeit of an emerging kind. The rapper's claim to a hypermasculinity of intellectualism allows him to wage two assaults. The first targets liberalism, whose adherents are portrayed as hypocritical, self-righteous, and naïve. As he raps to a "modern guy" in a song by the same name, "You have problematized every aspect of existence, except all the nonsense you get from your own political sect." And while highlighting what he sees as a lack of self-criticism and ideological nuance among the left, Zyklon Boom also attempts to undermine liberals' claims to be dissidents or radicals, portraying them instead as darlings of a progressive media and public finance establishment. Addressing Sweden's left-wing hip-hop scene in his song "Hip Hop Is Trash" (*Hip hop är skräp*), he raps,

> Like a radical you fight against "the media's ideals"
> but your filthy face appears on every cover and channel.
> When you talk about your "struggle" nobody boos you—
> Don't you get it? If you are a threat, no one will interview you.
> I apologize for disturbing you in the middle of your meal,
> but the state doesn't pay for you to threaten it.
> To mold people's ideas—that's how they use tax money.
> So just who paid for your course in gender-sensitive mathematics?
> If you threatened "the system" with your "conscious music"
> you'd be locked up or arrested for crimes against the rich.

Impugning the oppositionalism of unnamed leftist rappers, Zyklon Boom frames himself and other antiliberals as the true radicals, the true free thinkers, and the true dissidents.

The identitarian artist's critiques of liberalism extend to assaults on immigration and multiculturalism. His opposition to these forces is far less blatant and vulgar than what is found in white power music, giving his texts a comparatively apolitical quality.[5] For instance, though criticism of Jews and association with organized race activism is an omnipresent element in his lyrics, he sidelines this commentary by confining it to metaphor or irony. He claims to be "a Marxist, so long as we look past the Jewish question," and accuses his unnamed opponent of having an unfaithful girlfriend who sleeps with former Israeli Prime Minister Ariel Sharon.

In those instances when he articulates a political agenda, he follows identitarian tendencies of avoiding direct criticism of immigration. Instead, he often attacks broader socialpolitical movements that allegedly encompass immigration and inter-racialism. In the track "Tiger Ride," (*Tigerrytt*)[6] he raps:

> We will skip egalitarianism and crush humanism.
> And I'm not talking about a street fight, but there will be a change.
> And it may take a thousand years, but in the end we will win.
> You call me a right-wing extremist, I call you a queer with eczema.

Zyklon Boom's identitarianism also surfaces in his second stream of political polemic. His texts target neo-Nazi skinheads almost as often as liberals. His frequent references to National Socialists—particularly given their minuscule representation in Sweden relative to self-identified liberals—are testimony to the artist's pressing need to distinguish himself from these actors. The standard of learnedness cultivated throughout his repertoire again allows him to draw this contrast. Once more in "Hip Hop Is Trash" (*Hip hop är skräp*):

> Now someone is calling me a good old Nazi.
> Yeah—that could be true, were I a biologicist,
> an atheist, an amphetaminist, and a race materialist,
> and liked hanging out with people who fight like crazy,
> and listened to shitty punk, and read like a half a book.

Zyklon Boom here paints skinheads as intoxicated, violent anti-intellectuals with excessive ideological investment in race and depraved musical tastes. In instances like these, the rapper implies how he would like to be perceived; as a refined intellectual whose opposition to immigration belongs to a larger critique of secular, democratic modernism.

Zyklon Boom thus takes hip-hop's transcendent oppositional ethos and crafts it to voice a New Nationalist agenda. In his music he creates and vies for a masculine ideal distinguished by its erudition, and by achieving this identity he is able to condemn both leftism and neo-Nazi skinheadism. His diatribes still contain notable omissions. Race and ethnicity, for example, are marginalized topics in his polemics. His relative silence on these issues is remarkable given that some nationalist audiences would later dwell upon his music's racial and ethnic connotations—on whether a "white" nationalist ought to produce "black" music. Though Zyklon Boom targets immigrants and Jews, his standards for manhood do not rely on belonging to an ethnic group or asserting ethnic pride. Such standards may be unavailable to him: his status as a white Swede seems to deny him access to hip-hop's archetypical forms of racial oppositionalism—forms that gain their charge as retaliation against alleged racial or ethnic disenfranchisement (Mitchell 2001a).

Not all white rappers have been doomed to this fate, however. Following the turn of the twenty-first century, the mainstream rap scene in the United States became a venue for articulating white racial identity. This emerging trend centered on leading American rapper Eminem. Whereas early generations of white rappers in the United States attempted to establish authenticity and credibility by either immersing themselves in black society or by projecting racial ambiguity (Hess 2007), Eminem used hip-hop to assert himself as white. His would not be a whiteness of privilege and normativity. Instead, the rap artist would associate himself with poverty and a shattered family life—as well as unflattering features of white male anatomy— all while distancing himself from emblems of the white mainstream. The product of this positioning, as Loren Kajikawa explains, is a type of "underdog" whiteness (2015:125), one where class identity supplants race and allows its members to claim a downtrodden, outsider status in American society.

While Eminem never voices explicit white nationalism, his minoritized racial identity is poised to resonate with European radical nationalists who conceptualize themselves as victims of discrimination and injustice.[7] Zyklon Boom would not be the artist to exploit this potential, however. At times he seems to embrace a working-class identity, remarking that he works as a janitor, that he lives in an area with neighbors who steal "hens and watermelons," and that he gave up any chance of social advance for "cheep beer, religion, and pure intolerance." Despite these references, the bulk of his texts flaunt the fruits of his access to formal higher education. He belongs to an intellectual elite, and this aspect of his identity hinders him from claiming structural oppression or discrimination. But a second nationalist rap artist would cite Eminem while cultivating a form of underdog, working-class ethnic Swedish identity and corresponding statements of defiant ethnic pride.

Stockholm-based rapper Juice is a young man named Rasmus who began producing music in 2006. Like Zyklon Boom, he most often raps solo and releases single tracks online, uploading his first song in 2007. His output has been small, consisting only of four songs to date. These tracks have been popular in the Nordic scene, however, in particular his song "Now You Know" (Nu vet ni). "Now You Know" is included in Nordisk.nu's online radio player, and uploads of the song on YouTube have been viewed by over 200,000 users. The track is an assault on the rap group the Kings of Alby (Albys kungar)—a group composed in part of immigrants from former Yugoslavia living in the southern Stockholm suburb of Alby. Though they have not experienced any significant commercial success, the Kings of Alby gained attention in nationalist circles by crudely insulting ethnic Swedes in their songs. Juice released "Now You Know" as a response to these songs, targeting the group's front man, Abel, in particular. The track won Juice widespread adoration in nationalist circles—even among individuals who otherwise oppose the use of rap in the scene. Set to a beat from Eminem's song "Lose Yourself," enhanced with chorus effects, and rapped slowly with an unapologetic, unwavering inflection, the sonic character of "Now You Know" matches the aggressive nature of the lyrics:

> You don't understand how fucking terrible you are,
> but it's all your fault because you shouldn't be here.
> You insult the *Svenne*, but you must be joking,
> since your greatest wish is to speak Swedish.
> You think being a Swede is bad even though you yourself moved here?
> Abel—he's a queer, and he'll be slaughtered.

(chorus)
So now you know, that you'll be slaughtered again.
So now you know, that it's time to go back home.
Because now you know, that everyone hates you,
so cut the shit because nobody can take it anymore.

In contrast with Zyklon Boom, Juice's dissing focuses on ethnic politics. But the Swedish identity he asserts in lyrics like these is not one of structural privilege. Instead, it is an identity under assault. He repeatedly self-applies the semiderogatory term for an ethnic Swede, *Svenne*—a move that references African American rappers' embrace of the term "nigga" and enables Juice's posture as resisting Swedish ethnic oppression.

As the song proceeds, Juice claims an authentic urban, working-class identity, rapping, "You're so fucking hated, both you and your friend, what the hell do you know about the street?" In cases like these, Juice mimics the identity construction exhibited in Eminem's music by painting a ridiculed and underprivileged Swedishness. However, and in contrast with Eminem, the artist's corresponding polemics do not target an ethnic Swedish elite. Instead he attacks minority groups, characterizing their nonassimilation as a product of hate-filled anti-Swedishness. These assaults occur as the rapper relishes his underdog position and never declares an agenda to gain elite status, thus separating his rhetoric from that of standard nationalist music. Juice's lack of grandiose, revolutionary visions does not stop him from attacking minorities in ways any less vulgar and demeaning than what is found in white power. At the conclusion of the song he impersonates his opponent, rapping,

"Hi, my name is Abel and I'm twenty years old.
Don't have a foreskin, but pubic hair is cool.
Don't get any girls, so I fucked a camel.
Hate Sweden, but there's nothing wrong with that."

Zyklon Boom and Juice remain novelties in Nordic radical nationalism's musical landscape. However, three years after Juice's debut, a new project would shake the scene further. In a move that to the best of my and my consultants' knowledge is unprecedented in European and white American radical nationalism, activists from the ethnopluralist organization Nordic Youth produced a nationalist reggae song. Nordic Youth is a political action group founded by disaffected members of the National Democrats' (see chapter 2) youth wing in Sweden. The now pan-Scandinavian group gained recognition in nationalist circles for carrying out a string of high-profile demonstrations and acts of vandalism, including egging refugee housing, casting pig's blood on Holocaust memorials, spraying graffiti in major Swedish cities, and destroying what they consider to be decadent art. But before any of these events occurred, Nordic Youth attracted nationalist and non-nationalist attention by releasing the reggae song "Imagine" (*Tänk*) at their founding on January 30, 2010.

"Imagine" features a standard reggae accompaniment with brass, guitar, bass, trap set, and bongo drums, and is sung in Swedish with a Jamaican accent. A single individual from western Sweden recorded all of the tracks for the song, and the lyrics were written by a group of Nordic Youth members from Gothenburg. The song begins:

> Imagine living in a country populated only with your own kind.
> Imagine if my dreams were to come true, in a land where my forefathers
> toiled,
> that one nation shall be one nation,
> one nation where people take each other by the hand.
> So now's the time to fight back, my friend,
> against their sickly lies and distortions.
>
> Losing your country is terrible indeed, so rise up, ethnopluralist!
>   (refrain)
> All have a right to their own homeland, indeed,
> so dear neighbor take me by the hand.
> Stand tall, grow up secure,
> because together we can solve the problems.
>
> Imagine living in a land, a land without buildings ablaze.
> I promise, there is potential, but our government doesn't want to bother.
> Imagine saying what you want, reacting,
> no longer having to sit still.
> Imagine seeing your children grow up
> without being robbed by an immigrant mob.

"Imagine" likely gained more attention in nationalist online forums, as well as in the mainstream media, than any other piece of contemporary or historic nationalist music in the Nordic countries. Journalist Fredrik Strage even offered what amounted to a compliment for the song's producers:

> [W]hile so-called white-power rock is in general much worse than regular rock, "Imagine" is just a little worse than the Swedish reggae that has been produced during the last decade. (*Dagens Nyheter*, February 26, 2010)

Strage also noted that the song's lyrics "evoke a bizarre 'One Love' feeling," referencing Bob Marley's reconciliation and forgiveness-themed hit by that name. Indeed, though the lyrics of "Imagine" scold the Swedish government, speak disparagingly about "immigrant mobs," and foreshadow "losing [one's] country," the overall tone of the text is positive. Themes of unity, fellowship, and resistance fill the refrains and many of the verses, with lines like "dear neighbor take me by the hand" and "together we can solve the problems."

A nationalist reggae song with a "One Love feeling" may seem bizarre to an outsider like Strage. But Nordic Youth's lyrics and choice of genre becomes intelligible in light of ongoing shifts in global reggae culture on the one hand, and Nordic nationalist ideology and rhetoric on the other. Just as artists throughout globe adapted rap's original brand of Afro-diasporic oppositionalism, so too have reggae's core associations been broadened as it spread from its origins. Initially voicing values and protests of Jamaicans at home and abroad, the commercialization of reggae in the 1970s drove broad changes in the music's ideological content. In some instances, reggae lyrics began highlighting the causes of black liberation outside of Jamaica, particularly in Zimbabwe and South Africa. Other times, reggae's protest statements were generalized, such that cries for redemption, oppression, and resistance ceased to address a particular people or political context—thus allowing diverse audiences to embrace and repurpose the genre (Ahkell 1981:15; Jones 1988; King 2002:95–97).

Nordic Youth pushed the generalization and repurposing of reggae to unprecedented limits. "Imagine" uses the genre's rhetoric and language not only to argue that governmental elites oppress ethnic Nordics but also to frame explicit Nordic ethnocentrism as virtuous, just, and oppositional. "Imagine" coauthor Andreas Nyberg explained the link he sees between his activism and reggae during an interview with me:

We see nationalism as an ideology of love, not as a hate ideology that many others see it as. It is about love for your own people, but also love for there being many different cultures that can be experienced. . . . [Reggae is a genre] with an eye towards the Self, but even love for the Other, but not at the same time—from a distance quite simply. But nonetheless love, I mean, reggae is very—it is like the music genre of love. (Interview, Andreas Nyberg, July 4, 2011)

I believe that Nyberg's assessment of the link between his nationalism and reggae is genuinely felt. While on the recording the singer's exaggerated Jamaican accent gives the song a parodical character, Nordic Youth's songwriters consistently spoke of the song to me with reverence and seriousness.

Like Zyklon Boom and Juice, Nordic Youth provided an example of how Nordic nationalists could use music to portray themselves as a new breed of activist. These musicians attempt to frame themselves as intellectuals, victims, or champions of a defiant self-love and the right to difference. Further, all of their projects—via associations connected to musical genre and lyrics—disassociate the artists from skinhead subculture. But these projects' main impact on nationalist reformism came, not from the songs themselves, but from the discussions about them—from the expansive and heated conversations among insiders about the meaning, potential, and appropriateness of nationalist rap and reggae.

Looking Abroad

There is no such thing as "White Nationalist Hip Hop." Such a thing is not possible. It's only mongrelized wigger crap. Race and culture go hand in hand, one cannot exist without the other.[8]

Swedish activists were likely the first to introduce reggae into European and American white nationalist music-making. However, by the time Zyklon Boom and Juice began producing songs, rap had already penetrated nationalist scenes in France, Germany, and elsewhere. These projects ignited a fierce, wide-ranging debate throughout the greater white nationalist world, at times drawing strong criticisms like that above from user "45ACP" on the American white nationalist online forum Stormfront.

Rap advocating solidarity, sovereignty, and pride among white European populations likely originated in France with the group Basic Celtos. Classified as part of the French Identitarian Rock Movement (Rock Identitaire Français) by the online French nationalist forum le coq gaulois, Basic Celtos's lyrics frequently denounce the United States, NATO, immigration, and "finance cosmopolitans" (likely a reference to Jews) while calling for pan-European solidarity and the autonomy of subnational regions. Debuting in 1998, their music blends distorted guitars with rap vocals—a style approximating that of American band Rage Against the Machine—along with infusions of Breton folk instruments. Early in their career, Basic Celtos believed themselves to be the only radical nationalist rap group in Western Europe, noting that they had contact with similar acts in Serbia (Batson 2009:75).

By the turn of the twenty-first century, however, Germany would replace France as the center of rap in radical nationalist Western Europe. German nationalists today can claim more rap groups and greater penetration into the mainstream music market than can their counterparts in any other Western European country. The dynamic nature of German nationalist rap derives from the fact that the country's mainstream scene has long been socially and ideologically differentiated. Since the 1990s, German rap encompassed multiple, often competing political causes. Initially, the scene divided between a multiethnic faction, looking to reject American domination of global popular music and assert a specifically German rap, and a predominately Turkish immigrant faction using rap to reject German national identity, however conceived.[9] Despite the first faction's diversity, its perceived embrace of a still-exclusive national identity, combined with the rise of anti-German hip-hop, served to ethnicize the country's rap scene—making rap not the voice of one ethnicity, nor the site of cross-cultural, cross-ethnic fusion, but instead an arena within which ethnic groups could mobilize against each other (Elflein 1998; Brown 2006; Teitelbaum 2013).

As these transformations took place, artists in the scene's underground were introducing and normalizing the language of racial chauvinism. This was particularly true within subgenres built around improvised lyrics, like freestyle and battle rap. Toward the end of the 1990s, freestyle and battle rappers began using the word "nigga" more frequently and forming analogies in their polemics that referred to World War II and the Holocaust, such as "I'll burn you like a synagogue," or "I will gas you like the Jews" (Güngör and Loh 2002:298–300).

By the turn of the century, high-selling, mainstream German rap artists like Fler and Bushido also began incorporating statements of ethnonationalistic pride into their lyrics, music videos, and album covers. Though many of these artists condemned Nazism in their music, they nonetheless shook a public uneasy with expressions of German nationalism. For example, East German artist Disziplin raps "Scheiß auf dein Hackenkreuz" (Fuck Your Swastika) in his track "Ich bin Deutschland." But he continues:

> I am Germany, and I stand for that.
> I am a German, look how the flag sways in the wind.
> This is black-red-gold.
> This is my blood, my pride, my people.

Commercial rap artists like Fler, Bushido, and Disziplin attracted the adoration of radical nationalist groups in Germany. Skinheads began attending Fler and Bushido concerts (*Süddeutsche*, June 27, 2005); the ultranationalist National Democratic Party of Germany endorsed Fler; and white nationalist online organizations abroad, from the American Stormfront to Sweden's Nordisk.nu, promoted Fler and Disziplin while remaining silent on Bushido—probably due to the latter rapper's Tunisian roots.[10]

The ethnic differentiation in the country's rap scene, the frequent use of anti-Semitic and racially chauvinistic lyrics in underground freestyle, and the normalization of ethnicized national pride in mainstream productions eventually cultivated explicitly white nationalist and National Socialist rap artists in Germany. The rap group Dissau Crime was one of the first such groups, releasing their album *Zyklon D* in 2003. A wave of similar, self-declared neo-Nazi rap artists surfaced toward the end of the first decade of the twenty-first century, including Sprachgesang zum Untergang, N' Socialist Soundsystem, and solo rapper Makss Damage (Staud and Radke 2012).

These pioneers of nationalist rap in France and Germany faced intense criticism. Though Basic Celtos earned the support of identitarian and ethnopluralist groups in France like Nouvelle Résistance and later Unité Radicale (Bales 2002:42), the black origins of their music stirred controversy in other radical nationalist circles. When asked in interviews to justify their use of rap, Basic Celtos members used two strategies. On the one hand, they stressed the metapolitical importance of their project:

> The rap scene in France is the second in the world behind the United States. Twenty percent of music sales go to rap music . . . we can't bear the thought that such a large proportion of the French people only hear the complaints of immigrants or attacks against nationalists.[11]

Here they claim that, because of rap's popularity, French nationalists cannot afford to surrender the genre to liberal voices. If rap is the preferred music of a large portion of the French public, acts like Basic Celtos are needed to spread the nationalist message and expand the nationalist movement. Basic Celtos also responded to critical voices by qualifying their engagement with rap and rap culture:

> We do a certain kind of rap, but we are not "rappers." We rap in the sense that we don't sing, but we don't wear baggy pants and we don't smoke marijuana all day.[12]

Here group members claim that they adopted a musical technique associated with rap—chanted vocals, or "not singing." But they refuse to identify as "rappers" on sociocultural grounds.

German artists used similar argumentative tactics when discussing the appropriateness of their genre in European nationalism. Like Basic Celtos, the German rap duo N' Socialist Soundsystem described the rap scene in their country as overwhelmingly antinationalist—this despite the presence of voices like Fler, Bushido, and Dissziplin. Accordingly, N' Socialist Soundsystem aimed to neutralize this threat to the movement by offering a nationalist alternative to standard, antinationalist rap. In further parallel with Basic Celtos, they disavow any genuine love for rap; a position illustrated most clearly in their song "Scheiss auf Hip Hop" (Fuck Hip Hop). Similarly, in their name, the German group Sprachgesang zum Untergang mimics Basic Celtos's attempts to redefine their music as in some way not being rap. Sprachgesang zum Untergang, or "Speech-Song to the Down-Fall," frames the group's vocal technique as "speech-song"—a style of recitative singing common in Romantic-era German opera—rather than rap.

Hating Rap, Hating Reggae

Advocates of nationalist rap and reggae in the Nordic countries would face challenges different than those of their counterparts in France and Germany. Zyklon Boom, Juice, and Nordic Youth released their music into a local radical nationalism that had for decades treated rap and reggae as its musical antitheses. Throughout the 1980s, 1990s, and 2000s, Nordic activists scorned these genres for their alleged associations with leftism, domestic immigrant activism, debauchery, and blackness.

Antagonisms between nationalism and Sweden's, Norway's, and Denmark's rap scenes have been most pronounced. This is likely due to the fact that, compared to reggae, Nordic rap scenes are older, larger, and more exposed in mainstream media and popular culture. The initial wave of Nordic mainstream rappers in the late 1980s and early 1990s was dominated by ethnic Swedes, Norwegians, and Danes whose lyrics were not obviously political and who strived toward a deracialized party-boy aesthetic comparable to that of the Beastie Boys in the United States. The commercial successes of early groups like Sweden's Just D, however, paved the way for a more politicized music performed by artists outside the sociocultural norm. Throughout the 1990s and early 2000s, headlining groups like Infinite Mass and the Latin Kings in Sweden, Karpe Diem and Madcon in Norway, and Outlandish in Denmark— each predominately made up of non-European immigrants—used hip-hop music to deliver scathing critiques of Nordic society and its treatment of minorities. Some of these projects sought to reject Nordic national identities outright (Sernhede 2002), while others used hip-hop to carve out a place for themselves in the national community (Bjurström 1997:51; Skyum-Nielsen 2006; Knudsen 2010, 2011).

Although explicitly political rap in the Nordic countries has provided a voice for immigrants throughout the past twenty years, the scene also contains multiple acts espousing leftism. These two political threads—leftism and immigrant advocacy— often overlap. But some Swedish rap groups like T-Röd and Ray Marx, as well as reggae groups like Kapten Röd, devote themselves almost exclusively to championing communism.[13] Leftist, anarchist, and syndicalist youth groups, in turn, often choose politically sympathetic rap or reggae music to profile themselves in public. For example, as I was observing nationalist demonstrations and marches throughout Sweden, counterdemonstrators from the socialist Justice Party (*Rättvisepartiet*) routinely played songs by Swedish communist act Konkret Konspiration through loudspeakers at their information tents.

Nordic rap thus lacked the intense internal political oppositions featured in German scenes. And given its link with immigrant activism and leftism, rap became a voice for explicit antinationalism during the 1990s (Peterson 1995:58). This was especially true of the Swedish rap group the Latin Kings. The act, whose members have roots in Latin America, hails from immigrant communities in Stockholm's southern suburbs. Their often crude and misogynistic lyrics also tend to advocate minority rights and criticize Sweden's treatment of its immigrant populations. An anonymous nationalist recalls:

> During high school [*gymnasiet*] in the early 1990s, when I was in high school, I heard that everyone in school who didn't like blacks and immigrants listened to Ultima Thule, and everyone who liked blacks listened to the Latin Kings. And so I thought, fine, then I don't like the Latin Kings. (Interview, anonymous, July 14, 2011)

Attitudes and associations like these helped render hip-hop in general, and the Latin Kings in particular, a target for nationalist ideologues and musicians.[14] For example, the Trollhättan-based white-power punk band Brigad Wotan (later known as Somalia Kickers) targeted the rap group on the cover of their 1995 album *Sweden Ablaze* (*Sverige i brand*), shown in Figure 3.1. In this image, they attribute

FIGURE 3.1 Cover to Brigad Wotan's 1994 album *Sweden Ablaze* (*Sverige i brand*) on Svea Musik.

what they see as the destruction of Swedish society to the Latin Kings and the sub-culture they inspire.

In parallel with the efforts of white power bands, 1990s nationalist political parties painted rap and hip-hop music as being at variance with their cause and Nordic culture in general. We find examples of this in an unattributed article in the 1993 issue of the Sweden Democrats' newspaper *SD-Kuriren*. The article, which attempted to provide guidelines for developing the party's cultural policy, argued:

> Afro-American music's global expansion constitutes a setback of thousands and thousands of years. The lyrics typically encourage only sentimentalism, shallowness, immorality, and low living ideals. A positive counterweight to this is the popular music containing nationalistic lyrics that today is poised to make nationalism fashionable. Primitive elements are still no less influential even in these cases. Music has degenerated such that it mainly consists of only rhythm. An immense decline, unfit for the Nordic person. (*SD-Kuriren* 1993)

Here, the authors argue that Afro-American musics—likely conceived as hip-hop given the article's reference to rhythm—conflict with a healthy Nordicness in both their lyrical content and their musical structure. The National Democrats also assailed expressive forms like hip-hop music in the cultural policy section of their official 2001 party platform. There they described their goal to

> [l]imit the influence of foreign cultures in Sweden, especially those whose aim conflicts with what is traditionally Swedish. Prioritize healthy causes in public places that expose life-affirming qualities worthy of pursuit. Limit public display of divisive or degenerative elements, such as the glorification of perversion, disgusting art, and manifestations of American ghetto culture.

Nationalist audiences encountering Zyklon Boom and Juice, as well as Nordic Youth's reggae track, thus had to consider whether they could embrace musics long celebrated by their foes and demonized by their friends. But their attitudes toward these projects would be conditioned, not only by the past, but also by emerging ideological and cultural agendas in the scene.

Rap, Reggae, and the New Nationalism

Most discussions of Zyklon Boom, Juice, and "Imagine" took place online. Combined, they encompassed more than a thousand blog posts, articles, and chatroom and article comment entries. The online forums Nordisk.nu and Frihet.nu, as well as the comment fields for the online newspaper Nationell.nu, hosted the largest discussions. The bulk of those participating wrote in Swedish, though a handful of statements came from Danish and Norwegian speakers. These individuals rarely operated under complete anonymity. Rather, most wrote under well-known pseudonyms, their true identities apparent to other insiders as well as to me. Virtually all came from ethnonationalist ideological circles—some identitarian, some National Socialist—and to the best of my knowledge no active Sweden Democrats participated, though a handful of party members have told me they followed the discussions.

Nationalists' conversations about the emerging rap and reggae projects can be divided into two categories: those considering whether rap and reggae bear immutable ethnic or cultural associations, and those considering whether the genres offer legitimate avenues for spreading nationalist messages. These two categories overlap and interact. For example, many voices who regard rap and reggae as essentially black also deny that these genres can legitimately perpetuate metapolitics. Alternately, those denying that rap and reggae hold inherent associations tend to view these styles as suitable tools for expansion. There are few thoroughly consistent patterns in insiders' responses, however, and constellations of positions abound. Instead, commentary is distinguished by its agenda—by whether it seeks a musical demonstration of Nordic distinctiveness or musical vessels to spread the nationalist message.

Sounds of the Pluriversum

The first category of commentary encompassed both supporters and opponents of Zyklon Boom, Juice, and "Imagine." Though these participants might disagree as to whether rap and reggae projects are appropriate for the Nordic scene, their standards for judgment are the same. They all desire musical styles that inherently reinforce Nordic particularlisms. As such, these discussions of Zyklon Boom, Juice, and Nordic Youth rarely consider lyrics and the possibility that different reggae or rap performances could express different sentiments. Their focus lies instead on determining and assessing these genres' transcendent identities.

Most opponents of Zyklon Boom, Juice, and "Imagine" motivated their positions by describing rap and reggae as essentially black musics. These voices have the benefit of aligning with established discourses in Nordic radical nationalism, and for that reason escape the burden of explaining their position in detail. Rarely did they elaborate as to how they assign a racial identity to the genres. Some traced rap's (but never reggae's) blackness to musical features—to rap's showcasing of rhythm over melody and thereby its distance from European musical instincts. Most frequently, however, insiders highlighted the genre's origins. Nordisk.nu user "Nils" provides an example of the latter:

> Nationalist hip hop? . . . If you are Swedish and proud of your country and want the best for it, then you shouldn't sink so low as to make such music. Just think about where hip hop comes from. It isn't in our history, and it shouldn't be there anyway since it was the blacks who came up with that shit. Therefore I have a question for those of you who listen to this shit and for those of you who want to produce it. How the fuck can you call yourselves nationalists?[15]

While a plurality of opponents accused nationalist rap and reggae artists and fans of trafficking in black music, some tied these genres to other non-Nordic peoples. Sanna Hill—a high-profile female activist and former journalist for the ethnopluralist National Democrats' newspaper *National Today*—described reggae as a genre saturated with antiwhite, Jewish propaganda. In a Nationell.nu post criticizing Nordic Youth's decision to debut with the song "Imagine," Hill wrote:

> Since the 1970s practitioners of the 'Rastafari' religion used reggae music as a form of religious expression, and if you read about that very "interesting" religion you'll see that certain words appear consistently, "Africa," "Israel," "Zion" and "Holocaust." Undeniably a zesty choice of music genre to start an organization with.[16]

Hill here attempts to link Rastafarian concepts of Israel and Zion—as well as the far less common use of the term "Holocaust" in reggae texts—to Jewish activism. With her critical posture toward Nordic Youth, Hill implies further that Rastafarian terminology derives from a foundational ideological character that is left intact in "Imagine" despite that song's lack of explicit reference to topics she finds so troubling.

A portion of critical voices based their opposition, not on rap's and reggae's ethnic essences, but rather on the genres' association with allegedly non-Nordic behaviors and cultures. Nordisk.nu user "Fester" addresses supporters of nationalist rap:

> I don't understand how you are thinking. All nationalists' object of hatred today is decadent skinhead culture. And now that it is about to disappear, you want to go for a new, equally, if not more despicable, subculture? Because fuck if that's going to end at "the music."[17]

"Fester" implies that rap music is not his concern. Apparently, were nationalist use of the genre to "end at the music," little harm to the movement would have been done.

But he argues that use of rap music will lead activists to a destructive lifestyle. And it is that lifestyle, rather than the music per se, that most concerns him.

Though statements like those by "Nils," Sanna Hill, and "Fester" were standard, they do not account for all commentary positing a racial or cultural essence for rap and reggae. Some of Nordic Youth's apologists defended "Imagine" by asserting, rather than denying, reggae's blackness. These voices argued that, as distinctly black music, reggae demonstrates the reality of ethnic particularity. For them, even though reggae does not itself project the distinctly Nordic, it nonetheless contributes to global pluralism in ways that rootless, unmarked, cosmopolitan genres do not, and therefore merits celebration and promotion by nationalists in the North.

One example of this reasoning comes from DN.se user "Dennis," who argued that Europeans' use of black nationalist music resonated with ethnopluralism. He writes:

> [O]ne of the cornerstones in the Rastafari movement is ethnic nationalism and the desire to see all blacks return to their motherland. That is to say, that blacks belong where they ethnically descend from, exactly like ethnopluralism means that you believe Europe should be European, etc. If you look at Nordic Youth's homepage and their anti-imperialist position on the Palestinian question and the Afghanistan question, then it is also a crystal-clear statement for ethnopluralism considering the text "All have a right to their own homeland."[18]

"Dennis" claims that, viewed through the prism of ethnopluralism, black nationalism is equally desirable to white nationalism. Therefore, reggae—with its Rastafari-inspired calls for black nationalism—is a legitimate object of praise for organizations like Nordic Youth.

Nordic Youth activist Petrus Grafström likewise suggests that reggae has essential associations—both cultural and racial—that white nationalists can champion. Though he did not participate in the production of "Imagine," he does listen to reggae regularly, and I asked him during an interview to explain his and his organization's interest in the genre. He replied:

> PETRUS GRAFSTRÖM (PG): My activism has to do with traditional values against modern [values], and that is something I share with large parts of the reggae movement. Their music is also about traditional values.
>
> BT: How so?
>
> PG: If we look past the slackness-scene and look at the conscious-scene, then it only deals with religion—black Rastafarianism, criticism of modern, white

society—Babylon, on black women—"Mama," the inner and the outer flame—fyah bun [condemnation of unrighteousness] and so on. In general, it is the same values we have, just a different color.

BT: Yes, yes, some have even said that reggae is ethnopluralistic.

PG: No, it's black, plain and simple, but in its form it is an expression for ethnopluralism, like Nordic folk music.

BT: How is Nordic folk music an expression of ethnopluralism?

PG: It is a manifestation of the soul of the Nordic people. (Interview, Petrus Grafström, August 10, 2011)

Grafström begins by naming points of ideological resonance between his cause and that of Rastafarians. Distinguishing between more and less pious types of reggae culture—"conscious" and "slackness" scenes, respectively—he sees in "conscious" reggae an antimodern movement built from values he shares. Reggae's blackness does not corrupt these values, nor does it render them unavailable to activists like himself. As our conversation proceeded to consider the genre's ethnic associations, he said that reggae can be an "expression for ethnopluralism." Nordic folk music is also an expression for the ideology in his mind because it is a "manifestation of the soul of the Nordic people." Likewise, he implied that reggae is a manifestation of the soul of black people. And later he would clarify his thinking to me: that as expressions of separate peoples' separate souls, musics like Nordic folk music and reggae reinforce ethnopluralistic conceptions of humanity—that peoples are irreducibly different, and beautifully so.

Like "Dennis" and Grafström, some apologists for Zyklon Boom and Juice also defended rap by linking the genre to particular racial and ethnic identities. However, these essentialisms differed from those of reggae advocates. With highly eccentric reasoning, some nationalists argue that rap is appropriate for the scene, not in spite of its blackness but because of its inherent whiteness. One individual who used this indigenizing arguement is Nordisk.nu user "Bockas"—a well-known nationalist figure affiliated with identitarianism and the Nordic League. His reasoning assails the alleged whiteness of radical nationalism's favored musical style—rock—and dissects the notion that commercial rap today should be classified as black. "Bockas" attempts to whiten rap by referencing American artist Eminem and by tying the genre to musical and poetic techniques used in Old Norse society. He wrote:

Rock music is also "negro music," and most other music builds from rock music. All metal, for example, is built on rock music, and, following that same logic, all "freedom rock" [white power rock] is also negro music.

And to mix things up: Perhaps the biggest rapper in the world is white? And he says specifically that he is not a "wigger," and that he is: "a piece of white trash and proud of it."

Further you can draw pretty strong parallels between creating rap and old ancient Nordic balladry, and if you have heard rímur (which I doubt), that is exactly what you hear—Icelandic old men who "rap," even without music, or by sitting and stamping the beat (that can be compared to "beatbox" if we would like to). Another phenomenon in the world of hip hop, that also interestingly enough is represented in the Nordic culture, is "battles"; that is, that you—without preparing and in verse—shall taunt each other in the cleverest way possible in front of an audience. There are many examples of these insult-songs [*nidvisor*], for example, Lokasenna in the Poetic Edda is one big display of "battle skills" from Loki's side.[19]

After highlighting the black roots of rock and expounding upon Eminem's unrestrained whiteness, "Bockas" moves to his most daring claim: he attempts to provide a Nordic precedent for elements of rap music structure and practice. He finds such precedent in the Icelandic chanted poetry tradition rímur, and with the Old Norse/British tradition of *flyting* where individuals exchange improvised insults in verse—here referred to in the mythological poem "Lokasenna," which features a rhymed insult war among the gods of the Old Norse pantheon.

"Bockas" is only one of many in these discussions who attempted to trace rap to white, European populations. Motpol user "Oliver" responded to an article defending Zyklon Boom by adding:

[Zyklon Boom] is not "rap," but instead rhyming poetry, which according to European tradition emerged among British poets during the Middle Ages.[20]

This approach parallels not only that of "Bockas" but also argumentative methods used by French identitarian hip-hop group Basic Celtos. "Oliver" denies that Zyklon Boom's music is rap, choosing instead to define the music as generic "rhyming poetry," much like Basic Celtos describes their style as "not singing." These arguments rely on overlooking the many musical and rhetorical qualities in Zyklon Boom's and Juice's works that channel standard hip-hop style—such as the Swedish artists' use of syncopated rhythms and sample loops, as well as their claims to oppositional class, gender, and ethnic identities.

The most ambitious effort to link rap to European sources comes from an author named "Alexis," writing for the anti-multiculturalist Swedish Nihilist Underground

Society. In an online article about the black roots of jazz and hip-hop music, the author makes the following statement:

> We are all too familiar with the prevailing climate in Sweden, where immigrant youths play up a "gangster role" based on African American rappers. What is interesting in this case is not that they look past their own original culture, but that they think that hip hop is "black music" that rebels against white, European society. Surprisingly, even that is a modern, multicultural myth. Hip hop and rap were not discovered by blacks at all, but were instead discovered by the Germanic synthesizer pop band, Kraftwerk, which basically laid the foundation for modern hip hop as the youth today know it.[21]

Though not directed at the debate over nationalist rap, this article was nonetheless circulated widely in discussion threads on Nordisk.nu and other online nationalist forums. With this approach, activists were able to suggest not only that Zyklon Boom and Juice were not making black music but also that rappers like 50 Cent, Snoop Dogg, or the Latin Kings were in fact producing white music.[22]

In sum, these discussions show how a broad section of nationalists appear committed to the notion that their scene's music ought to manifest or promote distinguishing features of the national people. These individuals nonetheless disagreed as to whether rap and reggae can serve such a purpose. Many regarded these genres as inherently and irreversibly non-Nordic and thereby unfit to promote national distinctiveness. However, a smaller number of insiders countered that reggae's and rap's immutable associations resonated with the nationalist cause. Activists who defended these musics on account of their allegedly fixed associations did so in different ways depending on whether they spoke of reggae or rap. Apologists for Nordic Youth quoted above accepted the notion that reggae was essentially black, but they suggested that campaigns for black and white nationalisms were complementary. Reformist ideologies and values enable this way of thinking. In parallel with ethnopluralism and the *Nouvelle Droite* creed that "[o]ne is only justified in defending one's difference from others if one is also able to defend the difference of others" (De Benoist and Champetier 1999:133–34), these nationalists redefine their cause as one advancing global ethnic distinctiveness. And they hope to reinforce the boundaries between peoples by promoting reggae as a vessel for black separatism.

The arrival of reggae on the Nordic scene thus coincides with the rise of a New Nationalist argumentative model for justifying the use of foreign musics. This way of thinking and speaking about music would have been far less intuitive for nationalists of previous decades, as well as for contemporary activists who reject reformism.

Indeed, I have never heard insiders justify their celebration of rock, punk, or metal by showcasing these genres' Afro-diasporic roots.

Advocates of rap did not replicate the justifications of their reggae-advocate counterparts. Instead, they denied the blackness of Zyklon Boom's and Juice's music. Their strategies resonate with scholarly claims by Paul Gilroy (1994) and Tony Mitchell (2001a) that rap is not always received as black music as it travels throughout the globe. However, nationalists' subsequent claim that the music might be inherently white suggests that, while rap may not always be seen as black music, disparate social actors tend to regard it as race music. Further, with the exception of author "Alexis," those attempting to provide an alternate history and lineage for rap appear to have been aided by their ability to reduce Zyklon Boom's and Juice's music to its abstract structural and sonic elements. Having conceptualized this music as simply chanted text, relocating it in other traditions becomes uncomplicated. Chanted text, after all, is no more endemic to African American hip-hop than it is to Icelandic rímur.

While defenses of reggae may seem eccentric, nationalists' domestication of rap recalls similar argumentative techniques used by early advocates of rock and metal. White power rock musicians were rarely forced to defend the racial credentials of their genre, but when facing critics, some activists sought to extract isolated elements of heavy metal sound that they could then replant in Nordic music soil. For example, Canadian white-power artist George Burdi offered the following defense of heavy metal in 1995 on the American white nationalist radio program, *American Dissident Voices*:

[The white race has] had many different styles of music during the last three or four thousand years, many of which these same critics would not like very much. For instance, the ancient Vikings used to make as large a racket as possible: banging on drums, smashing things to make as much noise as they could. This was a form of ritual dance and music that was intended to summon the gods. They believed that they would waken the gods by creating this thunder. In many ways, if you compare that to the modern skinhead culture and even the wider culture of pro-white music, you have a lot of it that sounds very noisy, that sounds very heavy, and very loud. And it is meant to be played loud. It is warrior music. It is the new Viking music.[23]

While Nordic nationalists redefined and defended Zyklon Boom and Juice as European chanted text music, Burdi characterized metal as noise making—a move that allowed him to place the genre in a tradition of musical cacophony leading back to the Vikings.

The very strain of such arguments—the amount of musical and social material they must dismiss to produce their alternative histories—is itself testament to the enduring importance of music in nationalists' drive toward racial, ethnic, and cultural purity. By laboring to explain how rap and rock could derive from Nordic society, these activists affirm the notion that the music they consume ought to exhibit their national uniqueness.

Music for Metapolitics

As the debate about music and ethnic identity raged, nationalists initiated a parallel, at times overlapping discussion about rap's and reggae's ability to spread their message. Two issues were at stake in this second exchange: whether the community listening to rap and reggae was a legitimate target for nationalist outreach, and whether these genres could faithfully convey nationalist values. The debate over rap, reggae, and metapolitics focused on Nordic Youth's "Imagine," largely because Nordic Youth debuted the song with a press release describing the need to change "the forms" but not "the message" of nationalist expression.[24] A statement by Frihet. nu user "Robert" provides an example of those opposing this position:

> As far as I'm concerned niggers can have a monopoly on their drug abuse and Rastafari music. Because these are the people, and their sympathizers, who make this music, not society at large. The fight over reggae may be your fight, but it's not mine.[25]

According to "Robert," reggae's alleged nonwhite audience makes the genre an invalid site for metapolitics. By creating nationalist reggae, Nordic Youth injected their message into black society, not Nordic ethnic society. Nationalists like singer–guitar player Viktor Sjölund (writing under the name "Viktor" in the Frihet.nu forum) extended this line of attack by claiming that attempted metapolitics through reggae was not only ineffective and wasteful, it could also harm agendas of ethnic purity. He wrote:

> [T]here are other, less attached, music genres to expand through. The ultimate goal for nationalist political, cultural, and social structures cannot be to acclimatize people to prevailing multiculturalist norms. We must organize around the identity we see as healthy and productive for the people. Normalizing reggae culture does us a disservice in that regard. . . . I think it will be hard to say that you stand for ethnic-conscious politics if you simultaneously pump out culture marked with multiculturalism.[26]

Reggae, for Sjölund, is culture automatically "marked" as non-Swedish. Therefore, even though the lyrics of "Imagine" might voice genuine nationalism, those values are mangled beyond redemption by the medium of expression. Nordic Youth's actions thus appear to Sjölund, not as an instance of cleaver subversion, but rather as a concession and testament to multiculturalism's continued dominance of Swedish cultural life.[27]

Still, while positions like those of Viktor Sjölund or "Robert" were not rare, most commentary on musical metapolitics was favorable toward nationalist rap and reggae. For example, Frihet.nu user "Frigörelse" offered the following defense of "Imagine":

> If you can win over a lot of youths and hinder them from falling into destructiveness by instead offering a desirable, healthy, national Swedish identity, then I don't understand why one medium would be forbidden, and others allowed. For me, it is the content that matters.[28]

This claim from "Frigörelse" and those like it assume that music genres do not have fixed and contagious political or ethnic connotations—that rap and reggae could transmit nationalist messages accurately in their lyrics, or their "content." Insiders defended such assumptions in various ways. In a reversed verision of Viktor Sjölund's argument, some participants argued that rap and reggae belonged to a limited class of music styles that lacked inherent associations, and could therefore be imbued with diverse meanings. User "Peace," writing on the forum Frihet.nu, provided one of the more dynamic expositions of this stance:

> I don't think that pitches have values. That is, I don't think that a certain type of music can really be "Swedish" or "Nordic" or "multicultural." There are of course different, particular styles that have historically been played in different countries, like our folk music, Irish folk music, or the Middle East's yalla yalla music. These music styles . . . have rooted themselves in cultures for hundreds of years. I would have understood the strong reactions, and reacted just as strongly myself, had [Nordic Youth's song] been of the yalla yalla type, like howling Arabs from the Middle East. But there is a big difference between these classic cultural music styles and today's. Modern music styles, like rock, pop, reggae, etc., that have existed a few decades don't have the same anchoring. Instead they are quite open.[29]

As an "open," rootless genre, reggae can channel diverse cultural and political impulses. While such classifications would make the music undesirable to nationalists seeking musical demonstration of ethnic difference, it frames reggae as ideal for metapolitics.

Voices like "Peace" argued from what appears to be a more moderate position in the nationalist scene. They call upon their fellow activists to abandon dogmatic commitments to Nordicness and engage with culturally, ethnically, and politically neutral forms of expression. However, apologists for nationalist rap and reggae occasionally paired a liberal stance in cultural matters with a rigid investment in race or ethnicity. Their willingness to deconstruct notions of cultural purity relied on asserting the fixedness of blood identity. In these cases, if expressive forms like music provide the neutral realm for expansion and cosmopolitanism, activists look to race and ethnicity to confer particularity to themselves and their behaviors.

Following this model, Nordic Youth member Andreas Johansson paired cultural and musical nihilism with ethnic essentialism. Johansson, writing under the name "Talemannen" in the forum Frihet.nu, defended "Imagine" thusly:

Culture is never static, and it isn't possible to control it. Swedish culture according to me is whatever Swedes do. That is, if many listen to reggae in Sweden then it is a part of Swedish culture, assuming that it is ethnic Swedes who are listening. Were ethnic Swedes to start Thai boxing, then it would be a part of Swedish culture.[30]

Johansson here defended "Imagine" by arguing that reggae could in fact be Swedish. But while some apologists for Zyklon Boom and Juice argued that the Nordicness of rap was rooted in musical sound, Johansson traces reggae's potential Swedishness to the ethnicity of its practitioners. According to his thinking, music and other expressive forms bear no inherent ethnic associations, but are shaped by the identities of people who perpetuate them. Music is therefore a site for ethnic conquest.

Johansson's claim, that ethnic Swedes transfer a Swedish identity to whatever phenomenon or activity they favor, was guaranteed to receive criticism from other nationalists. This way of thinking could render any type of culture or behavior Swedish, thereby stripping nationalists of one of their core criticisms of mainstream Swedish society—that ethnic Swedes' prevailing behaviors and values are fundamentally and dangerously un-Swedish. Unsurprisingly, Johansson's stance received swift rebuke, including the following response from Frihet.nu user "Folkbildare":

If Thai boxing becomes Swedish culture because Swedes do it, well, then the Jewish mass media becomes Swedish culture when Swedes read it.[31]

Neither Johansson nor any other user responded to this statement by "Folkbildare."

When I asked Johansson about the exchange over a year later, he maintained his initial stance, but quickly retreated to a more standard metapolitical argument. He said:

> Reggae isn't a part of Swedish culture, but it is becoming [a part], and because we live in a multicultural society. What we did was, simply, to use a music genre that is very politically correct, and fill it with politically incorrect messages, just to create this internal conflict in people. I think that, if you work in this way, you reach those—I usually call them free thinkers—people who manage to think for themselves. (Interview, Andreas Johansson, May 29, 2011)

Multiculturalism is making reggae a part of Swedish culture, Johansson still contended. However, in concert with Nordic Youth's official statement on the song, he retreated to suggest that his organization's actions were based more on a desire to inject the nationalist message into a place where it previously was absent. His argumentative tendencies remind us that, of all methods of advocating for nationalist reggae, that citing the need to expand the scope of nationalist activism—to perpetuate metapolitics—is most likely to receive sympathy within the scene.

Rap, Reggae, and Reform

The rise of nationalist rap and reggae exposes conflicts inherent to the New Nationalist project. It lays bare the potential irreconcilability of efforts to cultivate difference while embracing new mediums of expression. For these musical phenomena force the question: Can metapolitics occur if national identity consists of certain expressive forms, and if mediums are the stuff of difference?

Insiders may have felt compelled to comment on this new music because it reveals formidable conceptual challenges facing reform. The legitimacy of New Nationalism hinges upon activists' ability to effectively defend or reject innovative projects like these. And if the advent of nationalist rap and reggae makes insiders apprehensive about trajectories of change, such feelings can only be exacerbated by the scene's inability to formulate a coherent, unified response. As this chapter has shown, reactions to Zyklon Boom, Juice, and Nordic Youth varied widely. Insiders disagreed as to whether musical sound could possess inherent political, cultural, or ethnic associations, and what—if any—associations were essential to rap and reggae. Likewise, opinions scattered as to whether and under what circumstances these genres offered nationalists a useful means of engaging outsiders. Consensus in these discussions existed only in implied assumptions that the scene's music ought to promote national distinctiveness or perpetuate metapolitics more broadly. This itself is testament to the spread of New Nationalism in the scene today.

Public discourses about Zyklon Boom, Juice, and Nordic Youth were nonetheless productive. Diverse activists used these exchanges to profile themselves as new kinds of nationalists. Apologists coupled their statements of support with declarations of self-love, anti-imperialism, and the universality of the right to difference. Others made impassioned, almost desperate attempts to align rap and reggae with the promotion of Nordic identities. Further, these discussions provided virtually all apologists a platform to announce their general will to see the nationalist scene break from its staid forms.

The social positioning that took place during the production and reception of nationalist rap and reggae has been enduring. Antireformist voices from the National Socialist establishment continue to reference these events while justifying their opposition to other nationalist actors. For example, Richard Langéen—creator of the Internet magazine Nationell.nu and frequent critic of the Sweden Democrats and identitarians—routinely dismisses Nordic Youth as an organization that produced "nigger music." These voices treat the creation of rap and reggae as evidence that reformist forces in the nationalist scene are anything but true nationalists.

It is unclear whether and to what extent the commentary of other rap and reggae opponents derives from an antireformist agenda. It is unclear, for example, if their rejection of these genres was part of a broader effort to make the nationalist scene more Nordic or metapolitically formidable than it used to be. Some of those arguing against the inclusion of rap and reagge in online forums, like musician Viktor Sjölund, are producers of 1990s white power music. These voices may criticize Zyklon Boom, Juice, and "Imagine" in order to defend the status quo in nationalist music-making and thereby the older nationalist scene more generally. But for others, their rejection of rap and reggae seemed to ignite new efforts to cleanse the scene of both recent and entrenched foreign contamination. User "Palnatoke," writing in a Nordisk.nu discussion thread on Zyklon Boom, is one such insider:

Our music would have been developed more properly, and become better and more original without major intrusions from jazz, rock, or other foreign music. To repeat this mistake with a music that is much more foreign than any of those ever were is pure craziness.

We need to reconquer our own culture, not willfully replace it with someone else's! We need, in other words, nationalist folk music.[32]

INHERENT NORDICNESS, INHERENT GOODNESS

Renewing Nationalist Folk Music

IN AN INTERVIEW with the newspaper *Sydsvenskan* on October 3, 2010, the Sweden Democrats' chief ideologue Mattias Karlsson claimed that state sponsorship of traditional Swedish culture was declining. The reason for this, he argued, was that national and local governments were diverting arts funding to projects that promoted foreign culture. Asked by the reporter to defend his claim, he replied:

> When public music conservatories give more resources to teaching foreign folk music, then there are simply fewer spaces and resources available for Swedish folk music. I think it is pretty obvious, as long as you don't assume that resources are unlimited, and they aren't.

The interview came just weeks after the 2010 elections and the Sweden Democrats' entry into parliament. With media scrutiny at a frenzied pitch, party members found themselves struggling to clarify key elements of their political program. Attempting to distance themselves from their ethnonationalist past, the Sweden Democrats asserted that they were fighting for a national community that would be culturally, rather than ethnically, homogeneous. They claimed to champion a Swedish identity that was available to any individual regardless of her or his ethnic background, an identity not ascribed but achieved by assimilating particular traits. Having proclaimed cultural nationalism, party members were compelled to identify the values, practices, and traditions that comprised Swedishness and that needed protection and promotion. In his statement to *Sydsvenskan*, Karlsson aimed to provide such clarity: to strengthen Swedish identity, he said, one must strengthen Swedish folk music.

Public intellectuals and leaders of opposing parties—all jostling for the politically advantageous position of chief adversary to the Sweden Democrats—responded to Karlsson's thinking, as they had so often in the past, by questioning the existence or value of the distinctly Swedish. Then Minister of Culture Lena Adelsohn Liljeroth, for example, challenged the Sweden Democrats directly by declaring, "there is no specifically Swedish culture" (*Dagens Nyheter*, October 6, 2010).

I was in Helsinki at the time for a gathering with Nordic folk musicians. Leading Swedish folk fiddler Sven Ahlbäck arrived in Helsinki incensed by what was taking place in Sweden. As we spoke late at night in the lobby of Hotel Helka, he decried both the Sweden Democrats' advances on Swedish folk music and the responses that, as he saw it, either surrendered the genre to nationalists or denied its existence. Moreover, he objected to the fact that this public debate had been taking place without the involvement of any actual folk musicians. But, he assured me, measures were underway to change that.

Before traveling to Helsinki, Ahlbäck and a group of younger Swedish folk musicians met in Stockholm to form a political action group. Fiddler Bridget Marsden initiated contact with the other participants (Interview, Bridget Marsden, November 22, 2010). These individuals eventually adopted the name "Folk Musicians Against Xenophobia" (Folkmusiker mot främlingsfientlighet), drafted a manifesto, and began planning a public debate and demonstration outside of Sweden's parliament to take place on October 19, 2010. Their efforts inspired groups throughout the country, such that, when this Stockholm contingent gathered in Mynttorget on that rainy October afternoon, folk musicians in Malmö, Gothenburg, Arvika, and elsewhere staged simultaneous demonstrations in their home cities. These events brought Swedish folk music unprecedented levels of media exposure, briefly shifting media scrutiny of the Sweden Democrats from the topic of immigration to cultural policy. Moreover, they helped alert the wider folk music community to nationalists' desire to engage with their music, an interest that was growing throughout the nationalist scene with various goals.

This chapter explores Nordic nationalists' interest in folk music. Theirs is an emerging interest, and much of it responds to values and developments surrounding reformism. Here, we will see how they use folk music to express their love of self and diversity as well as to demonstrate that their worldview is within the mainstream. Their overarching goal, however, is to show that they are unlike the nationalists of the past whose activism was brutish, uninformed, and foreign in its expressive forms and ideology.

Nationalist organizations throughout the west—particularly Hungary's Jobbik and the British National Party (Spracklen 2015)—have long showcased folk music in their activities (Sweers 2004; LaChapelle 2011). However, Sweden has been the northern epicenter for contemporary nationalist interest in the genre. The overall disinclination toward romanticized nationalism in the country's mainstream (see chapter 1) imbues folk music with a political charge absent in Norway, Denmark, and Finland. Given that public celebrations of national identity are comparatively less common in Sweden, folk music offers nationalists there an avenue through which to antagonize. Further, while broader sociocultural trends in Sweden politicize folk music, so too does the community producing it. Folk music practitioners in Sweden have been far more inclined than their Nordic counterparts to incorporate foreign styles in their projects. And like similar music scenes throughout the west, Sweden's folk music community is politically left-leaning. These features make folk music a site where nationalists can champion a wholesome domesticity against alleged foreign intrusion.

Folk and Folk

Nationalist and non-nationalist Swedes often use the term *folkmusik* to describe fiddle and nyckelharpa dance music traditions, which were common in rural Sweden from the 1700s through the 1900s, as well as ancient herding music created using pipes, cow horns, and the vocal style *kulning*.[1] The term can also refer to a genre of dance music called *gammeldans* ("old dance") that emerged during the late 1800s and early 1900s. This genre typically features the accordion and semi-choreographed dances like the schottische, waltz, and hambo. Finally, Swedes—often those less engaged with the genres just mentioned—may apply the label *folkmusik* to various types of twentieth-century popular music like dansband and singer-songwriter. Dansband music is a style drawn from German schlager, American country, and occasionally gammaldans forms, and it acquires a label as "folk music" by virtue of its association with older, rural demographics. Popular Swedish singer-songwriters of the 1950s, 60s, and 70s—like Evert Taube and Cornelis Vreeswijk—are today spoken of as folk musicians in much the same sense that John Denver or Bob Dylan are in the United States.

Whether they refer to rural fiddlers' music, herding forms, gammaldans, dansband, or singer-songwriter styles, nationalists think of "folk music" as music that is essentially local, Swedish, or Nordic via its instrumental musical structure, the community surrounding it, or the methods of its production. Though contemporary discourses may refer to various genres using the term "folk music," they tend to focus on those styles that may be regarded as traditional, whose roots appear to stretch back to premodern Sweden. That is to say, the rising nationalist interest in folk music tends to focus on fiddle and nyckelharpa dance music, herding calls, and gammaldans (with the assumption that gammaldans is indeed an older artform unique to Sweden).[2] When I refer to folk music in this chapter, unless otherwise indicated, I too refer to these genres.

A Forgotten Past

Ultraconservative forces in Sweden have a history of rallying behind folk music. The genre's associations with premodern, rural Swedish society rendered it attractive to those late-1800s and early-1900s actors who sought to counter cosmopolitan social, political, and cultural changes. Sweden's anti-Marxist elite, for instance, promoted rural culture among the newly urbanized in part to reinforce workers' allegiances to nation instead of class (Klein 2000; Sundin 1999). Some of the country's major folk music organizations would likewise mobilize against what they saw as an influx of foreign musics and foreign musicians. The leadership of Sweden's largest folk music organization during the war years, the Swedish Folk Dance Ring (*Svenska folkdansringen*), was home to multiple Nazi sympathizers (Ling 1980:33); the organization's journal, *Hembygden*, published articles decrying jazz and shimmy as loathsome musical products of "wild races" and the accordion as an instrument brought to Sweden by Jews and Italians (1922, 6–7).[3] But as anti-Semitic activists and race ideologues grew increasingly marginalized following World War II, their interest in folk music became less visible.

Only a handful of contemporary radical nationalists seem aware of this history. David Eljas—former member of the Nordic Resistance Movement—frequently wrote articles celebrating prewar connections between folk culture and ultraconservatives. Eljas typically finished his historical vignettes with a call to action, writing, for example:

In the future we will hopefully get to see a growing nationalist folk music movement. For who is best suited to carry folk music forward if not we, the true patriots? (*Nationellt Motstånd*, August 1, 2004)

Eljas's call reveals that during the time he wrote, in 2004, there was no "folk music movement" within nationalism that could compare with the scene's investment in punk and metal. Eljas was not the first contemporary nationalist to find this lack of interest in folk music problematic. In 1998, the Swedish white power music magazine

Nordland published an article on one of the few acoustic singer-songwriters, or what they called "folk music acts," in the international scene: American Eric Owens. In the introduction to the piece, author Peter Andersson writes:

> A big part of patriotic music is obviously aggressive due to the simple reason that we *are* aggressive.[4] . . . Obviously there should be plenty of patriots who play folk music. But there aren't. (*Nordland*, no. 12 (1998); emphasis in original)

If troubadour folk-music artists like Eric Owens and his Swedish counterparts like Odalmannen, Ferox, and later the project Svensk Ungdom are rare in the nationalist scene, insiders who perform traditional dance music—the type Eljas called for in 2004—are almost unheard of. The few activists who engage with traditional folk music are scattered throughout the nationalist scene. Fiddler Nils Blomberg, who performs solo and in the nationalist bands Ferox and Tors Vrede, is a member of the Nordic Resistance Movement. The highly active folk dancer and former committee member of Umeå Folk Music Union, Erik Alhem, has written for the National Democrats–affiliated newspaper *Nationell Idag* and later *Nya Tider*. And renowned fiddler Marie Stensby became a member and spokesperson for the Sweden Democrats in 2010, much to the shock of the broader folk music community. This is nearly an exhaustive list of activist nationalists who frequently participate in traditional folk music and dance.[5]

To the extent that nationalist music-making has incorporated folk music themes, it has typically done so through Viking rock. Though Viking rock bands almost never include fiddles, nyckelharpas, flutes, or bagpipes,[6] they do perform renditions of well-known folk tunes with their standard, hard rock format. More commonly, groups will base solo guitar lines on common Swedish folk melodic idioms rather than specific tunes.[7] Alternately, white power and Viking rock may cite folk music in lyrics rather than instrumental lines, such as in the chorus to Enhärjarna's track "Gryningssol" (Early Sunrise)":

> With sorrow in his chest, anger in his sights, he plays, though it is forbidden.
> He begins yet another tribute song with a melancholy sound.
> He does not turn; he plays on, with the bow in his hand.
> From moonlight to sunrise, he plays for his country.

This text depicts folk music as an expression of nationalism, and a subversive, "forbidden" practice for that reason.

Contemporary nationalists appear broadly uninterested not only in performing folk music but also in listening to it. Marie Stensby recalls an anticlimactic reception she received when she performed for fellow Sweden Democrats at a party convention:

> MARIE STENSBY (MS): It was really just one of those lousy gigs, like when people aren't really listening—just, like, mingling. I spoke with a few afterwards, they came up and talked. I spoke with Mattias [Karlsson] a bit. But as a gig, gigs like that are not that much fun of course.
>
> BT: Because they haven't been that engaged with folk music?
>
> MS: No, no. They are not that knowledgeable in that area.... There I have a bit of teaching to do if I am going to teach them to say the right things.... They don't have the "inside" so to say. (Interview, Marie Stensby, November 19, 2010)

The guests' apparent disinterest in Stensby's music fits with a pattern we see throughout the broader scene. Folk music has been almost entirely absent from nationalists' formal avenues for disseminating music, and it is scarcely represented among online retailers.[8] It is, however, included in online streaming radio from nationalist websites. The now-dormant white nationalist portal Info14.com offered a "folk music" channel in its radio player. Nationalist singer-songwriter acts like American Eric Owens and the Swedish group Ferox, as well as non-nationalist folk-rock groups like Garmarna, dominated this channel, and there was no acoustic instrumental dance music. The identitarian site Nordisk.nu also has a streaming radio function, and like Info14.com, they too offer a folk music channel. Of the eighty-one tracks in the folk music channel's playlist, most are fusions of rock and folk music, typically consisting of a standard rock ensemble with a single folk instrument playing solo lines. The bulk of the tracks that are not folk rock—that could qualify as being more traditional—either come from Icelandic singing traditions or are renditions of Swedish folk music using eccentric playing styles or instruments, such as the bagpipe. Only one track, "Wedding March from Dalarna in Sweden" (original title in English), includes what I consider to be traditional fiddling.

Folk music's scarceness in these venues could stem from retailers' efforts to promote nationalist musicians. The fact that virtually no outspoken nationalists have recorded traditional folk music would therefore exclude the genre from these settings. As nationalist folk dancer Erik Alhem said:

> I think that [retailers] want to sell music that cannot be found anywhere else. And then we are talking first and foremost about music that is explicitly political. (Interview, Erik Alhem, February 28, 2011)

However, nationalist radio stations and retailers showcase music that is not produced by nationalists, does not articulate a clear political message, and is widely available and appreciated outside of nationalist circles: Sverigebutiken.se, Arminius.se, and the radio station on Nordisk.nu sell and stream western art music. The absence of traditional folk music recordings, in other words, cannot be attributed to any commitment to nationalist musicians or music with an explicitly nationalist message, nor is it due to music appreciated only in nationalist circles.

The absence of folk music in these venues is unproblematic for some insiders. Certain ethnonationalists, for example, claim that by championing Nordic traditions, activists may unwittingly obscure the importance of race and ethnicity in national identity. Thorgrim Bredesen—former co-leader of the Norwegian party Vigrid and a frequent collaborator with the Nordic Resistance Movement—argued this point as we sat at a bar at Aker Brygge in Oslo. He said:

> I get so sick of this shit when they put niggers in folk costumes and have them dancing around, down here at the castle [in Oslo], thinking that if you do that then they're Norwegian. No, the basic—the most important thing is that the country be white again. If you bring that back, the culture will follow. These music and dance traditions, they come from the real Norwegian society, and that society is a white society. (Interview, Thorgrim Bredesen, July 6, 2011)

Bredesen depicts music and expressive culture not as instruments for promoting the national people as a unique population, but rather as a barometer of that people's racial integrity. His thinking—which exhibits the characteristics of what some insiders call "race materialism"—frames race as the ultimate foundation of social life such that other behaviors like musical practice derive from it. Accordingly, activism in the realm of race's by-products, in its superstructure, will be ineffectual.

Nationalists less interested in race may nonetheless argue that folk traditions do not belong to the body of culture they fight to defend. Identitarians in particular tend to omit vernacular European culture in their discourses and aesthetics, showcasing instead either classical high art or futurism. As eccentric Frenchman and leading identitarian Guillaume Faye argues,

> The soul of European artistic culture lies not in small pyramidal objects of baked clay, painted furniture from Schleswig-Holstein, Breton bonnets or the naïve wooden sculptures of Scandinavian farmers; rather, it is found in the Reims cathedral, the double-helix Italian stairway in the Château de Chambord, the drawings by Leonardo da Vinci, the comics by Liberatore and the Brussels

school, the design of Ferraris and the German-French-Scandinavian Ariane 5 rockets. By reducing European culture to mere folklore, this is depreciated and dragged down to the level of "primitive art." (2010:35)

By rejecting such "folklore," Faye and likeminded actors seek their own form of reform within the cause, one whereby a self-deprecating posture is exchanged for one unafraid to claim European cultural superiority.

Folk Music and the Sweden Democrats

The majority of nationalists from the 1980s to the present have thus shown apathy, and in some cases opposition, to the consumption and production of folk music. Nonetheless, a growing minority has begun to embrace the genre, and this trend has its foremost base in the Sweden Democrats. The party's interest in folk music, which in 2010 seized the attention of the folk music community and the media, is entwined with earlier transformations in its leadership and ideology. Since establishing themselves as a political party in 1988, the Sweden Democrats have had two major administrative turnovers: first in 1995, when Mikael Jansson unseated former Nordic Reich Party associate Anders Klarström; and second in 2005, when Jimmie Åkesson and a contingent of southern Swedes unseated Jansson. These shifts in leadership were not only major steps in the party's overall moderation process, they also changed its conceptions of Swedishness and cultural policy.

During the past twenty-five years, the party gradually shifted from championing the high Nordic and fine arts to celebrating Swedish folk culture, and with it Swedish folk music. Music was involved at official events and social gatherings early in the Sweden Democrats' history. Sometimes this music appeared fitted to the party's political agenda, sometimes not. At a 1983 meeting of the organization Keep Sweden Swedish (*Bevara Sverige Svensk*)—one of the Sweden Democrats' predecessor organizations—attendees were reported to have sung "national songs [*nationella visor*]" (*BSS-Nytt* 1983, no. 4). The label "national songs" likely describes a repertoire of classic patriotic hymns. In contrast with this early event, a report from a Sweden Democrats party meeting in Gothenburg on April 29, 1989 states that dire and depressing speeches about mass immigration, as well as moments of silence for murdered party members, were interspersed with "fun happy-jazz [*rolig gladjazz*]" to lighten the mood. And after then party leader Anders Klarström gave the final speech, he closed by saying, "Let us Swedish patriots sing the most beautiful song we know, our own [national anthem,] Thou Ancient, Thou Free" (*Sverige Kuriren* 1989, no. 7–8).

Folk music seems to have been absent from these settings. However, isolated writings in the party newspaper *Sverige Kuriren* occasionally celebrated the genre. The first issue of *Sverige Kuriren* in 1988, for example, included a review of nyckelharpa player Åsa Jinder's album *Salute to Life* (*Hyllning till Livet*), praising the album for its glorification of rural life and tradition. But in this first issue, folk music shares space with four other styles. One article calls for the preservation of the mounted military music corps, one criticizes the removal of the patriotic hymn "Church of the Fathers" (*Fädernas Kyrka*) from the state church hymnal, while another celebrates turn-of-the-century art music composer Wilhelm Peterson-Berger. Additionally, the issue included advertisements for Viking rock band Ultima Thule and their latest release *Sverige, Sverige Fosterland*—an album financed in 1985 by the party's predecessor organization Keep Sweden Swedish.

Though the paper initially showcased five different music genres—folk music, military music, Christian hymns, art music, and Viking rock—subsequent numbers of *Sverige Kuriren* abandoned folk, military, and religious music. Writings on culture instead grew to focus on the High Nordic; Swedish art music composers, poets, playwrights, or painters; and the lives of heroic kings and Vikings. An author writing under the name "Balder," for example, filled early editions of the newspaper with articles on painter Carl Larsson (1988, no. 2), poet Verner von Heidenstam (1988, no. 3–4), novelist Selma Lagerlöf (1988, no. 5–6), early-nineteenth-century nationalist writers group the Gothic League, and King Charles XII (1989, no. 7–8). Though no articles focused on Viking rock throughout these years, advertisements for Ultima Thule were omnipresent. The contrasting representations of music in articles and advertisements may shed light on readers' musical practices. The paper's editors seemed most interested in teaching readers about the high arts, but readers seem to have been more likely to consume skinhead music.[9]

The Sweden Democrats would also discuss music and expressive culture in their early party platforms. These declarations of policy agendas—adopted via party vote—routinely devoted sections to cultural policy and, occasionally, music. Initially, platforms gave few details as to which types of culture the party preferred. The platform from 1989, for example, includes the following section on culture:

The Sweden Democrats want to fight for the standing of Swedish culture and promote its development on both national and local levels. The Swedes have a rich cultural heritage that cannot be lost for future generations. That cultural heritage is seriously threatened by poor instruction in culture in schools, rising non-European immigration, as well as commercialized, USA-inspired "trash culture." Therefore, Swedish primary school education must give students increased knowledge of cultural expressions in the local community, Swedish and Nordic cultural heritage. The Sweden Democrats want to work for a new, living Swedish culture that is an alternative to today's cultural darkness.[10]

The authors juxtapose "creations [that] shape expressions of [Swedish] national and cultural identity" with "commercialized, USA-inspired 'trash culture,'" but they offer no clarification as to the content of these categories.

The 1989 party platform maintained its endorsement until 1999. Though the 1999 version retained some elements from the previous edition, the sections on cultural policy were expanded. Changes in cultural policy stemmed from Mikael Jansson's successful bid to replace Anders Klarström as party leader in 1995. Jansson's group of supporters—a circle known to this day as "the bunker"—came to include multiple reformist voices who sought to distance the party from ethnonationalism and skinheadism. One reformer, Johan Rinderheim, was elected to serve as vice president in 1998. And in an interview with the party newspaper following his election, Rinderheim said that one of his first tasks as vice president would be to

work with the party's ideological profile. There needs to be more literature so that the party can be more rooted. The importance of culture and national identity will be emphasized a bit, even though my ambition is that the Sweden Democrats will be a broad party, with strong positions in every area of politics. (1998, no. 34).

Indeed, the cultural policy statement in the 1999 party platform began to specify organizations and expressive forms that the party wanted to support, offering a more nuanced presentation of Swedish culture than the previous program:

The country's different local heritage organizations must receive increased support. Swedish folk dance and folk music shall be supported and through state direction be disseminated to the people.... Public places in society shall be adorned with statues and paintings that describe our history and our cultural heritage.[11]

The statement calls for support to both "low" and "high" culture, advocating local heritage organizations and folk music and dance on the one hand, and statues and murals on the other.

As the Jansson administration modified the Sweden Democrats' official cultural policy, informal statements—as well as social practices in the party—continued to favor Nordic high culture. Throughout the 1990s, the party continued to use Viking iconography in its promotional material. Likewise, the party paper maintained its focus on poets, composers, and military leaders, and party members frequently commemorated historical Swedish kings in street marches. The focus on high culture and military history received an additional impulse when Torbjörn Kastell rose in the ranks of the Jansson administration, becoming editor of the party newspaper in 1996. Since his youth, Kastell was deeply interested in Swedish military and political history (Interview, Torbjörn Kastell, March 29, 2011), and he focused on these topics during his tenure as editor.

Toward the end of the Jansson administration, however, internal voices began critiquing the party's stance on cultural issues. One instance of this came in 2004 when then high-ranking party member Jimmy Windeskog wrote in the party paper,

> If you look back at [the Sweden Democrats'] work, especially in newspapers, imagery, and demonstrations, you can see a clear, and probably unhealthy fixation on statues and poetry rooted in Sweden's age as a great power. Only occasionally is that image supplemented, and then often with farmer romanticism [*bonderomatik*] from the beginning of the last century. (*SD-Kuriren* 2004, no. 58)

Despite voicing these criticisms, he did not specify why he considered the party's cultural profile problematic. He provides some insight into his thinking, however, when he proceeds to celebrate ice hockey in the province of Dalarna. He suggests that ice hockey is a cultural phenomenon the party could support on the grounds that it

> creates contact between people in society where we to a greater and greater extent keep to ourselves. That is exactly what culture should do. (ibid.)

The reader is left to assume that Windeskog opposed the party's fixation on statues, poetry, and "farmer romanticism" (read traditional folk culture) on the grounds that these cultural forms are less effective at fostering interaction among Swedes. His praise for ice hockey, alternately, indicates a desire to see the party consider supporting types of culture that may be more relevant to contemporary life and society in Sweden.

Windeskog would not get a chance to enact these changes, however. As part of the political circle surrounding party leader Mikael Jansson, he was stripped of his posts following Jansson's loss to Jimmie Åkesson in the party leader elections on May 7, 2005. That same year, Windeskog was thrown out of the Sweden Democrats completely for criticizing fellow party member Tony Wiklander's decision to adopt a non-European daughter.

A Music for the People

The 2005 party leadership elections swept not only Windeskog but also Rinderheim and Kastell from power. Mattias Karlsson, a member of the so-called fantastic four faction surrounding incoming party leader Jimmie Åkesson, then became the central force driving the party's cultural policy. Karlsson shared Windeskog's overarching goal for an approach that would cultivate contact and solidarity among Swedes. The culture Karlsson considered best suited for this task, however, contained some of the very symbolic and expressive forms Windeskog sought to scrub from the Sweden Democrats' profile. Karlsson aimed to focus his party's cultural policy on the promotion of folk culture. When I interviewed him about his rise to power in 2005, he recalled of his agenda:

> Many of those who wrote about culture in the [party] newspaper at the time had an almost exclusive focus on the High Swedish. A lot of conservative poets, Carolean soldiers, Sweden's era as a great power, and Vikings, etc. And I felt that, while that was interesting, the era as a great power is also politically sensitive. And then I thought that, if you are going to find something to build a cultural renaissance around, it should be something that unites as many as possible. Many of these traditions and holidays that they highlighted, connected to the Royal Family and the era as a great power, were ultimately just something that the aristocracy were involved in and cared about. And I thought now, the type of voter we had, I felt that it could be difficult to get them to identify with that. But this folk culture—that comes from the Swedish peasant tradition, that is something most Swedes have just two generations back. (Interview, Mattias Karlsson, February 11, 2011)

Karlsson's conception of folk culture encompasses clothing, architecture, holiday celebrations, and Swedish folk music and dance. This understanding is based on his own life story. He describes folk music as a sidelined, yet constant feature of his early upbringing. Though not a musician himself, various family members played instruments and danced. His father played fiddle and flute, his grandfather played accordion, and older members in his family danced common Swedish folk dances like the schottis and hambo (Interview, Mattias Karlsson, December 3, 2010; Teitelbaum 2013). He nonetheless recognizes today that there is a difference between the type of folk music he had in his family and "older," ostensibly more authentic variants. He says of the music in his childhood home:

> You can call that type of music folk music, but it's a little younger. . . . But it was much more accordion music and a lot of Evert Taube songs, some singing.

That is perhaps the folk music of today. But this older tradition, with a lot of fiddles, nyckelharpas, certain types of flutes, Swedish bagpipes, I didn't have any knowledge of that. (Interview, Mattias Karlsson, February 11, 2011)

This "older tradition" was one that Karlsson today privileges within his conception of Swedish cultural heritage, naming the nyckelharpa, for instance, as an icon of Swedish culture (*Aftonbladet*, January 27, 2011). His interest in older traditional music began when he started listening to folk rock groups as an adult during the late 1990s:

A few bands came out at that time that started playing modern folk music, popularized, like Garmarna, Hedningarna, and Nordman. And it was kind of natural that you started looking at it. And we went to a few concerts. It was ultimately via modernized folk music that I started paying attention to folk music in general. Of course you know that it existed, but you didn't have any relation to it at all. You had heard the modernized variants, and then you get interested in the authentic tradition that they built upon. (Interview, Mattias Karlsson, February 11, 2011)

Karlsson and his first wife Gabriella Hedarv would later include a song by Garmarna at their wedding in 2006.

Karlsson's activities outside of the party reflect his interest in both folk culture and the High Nordic. In 2009, together with fellow Sweden Democrat Erik Almquist, he founded the party-unaffiliated cultural organization Gimle. The two conceived of Gimle as an avenue to promote Swedish and Nordic culture among social conservatives and nationalists, and to provide these individuals a forum to engage with this culture as practitioners. Gimle maintains a website with articles written almost exclusively by Karlsson on topics ranging from folk music to regional holiday celebrations. The organization also sponsored a festival in 2009, complete with feat-of-strength games, Viking food and drinks, folk dancing, and motocross bike racing (the latter on the grounds that it has become a part of contemporary Swedish culture). The festival concluded with a visit to a folk music festival in nearby Borås.

At the Gimle festival and other Sweden Democrats party events, Karlsson and Almquist typically perform the *oxdans* folkdance ("ox dance") shown in Figure 4.1—a dance Karlsson learned by watching YouTube videos. The ox dance is a choreographed dance-fight between two men that originated in a secondary school in Karlstad during the early 1800s (Andersson 2001 [1964]:78). Karlsson considers the dance ideal because of the overrepresentation of men in Gimle and his party.

FIGURE 4.1 Erik Almquist (left) and Mattias Karlsson (right) teaching attendees at Gimle Festival in 2009 to dance the *oxdans*.

In public statements nearer to the 2010 elections, Karlsson began describing the Sweden Democrats' cultural policy as focusing more on folk music and dance than official presentations of the party platform imply. Whereas the party's election manifesto called—in most general terms—for culture that "gratifies, beautifies, and creates community," Karlsson clarified in newspaper and radio interviews that folk music and dance, as well as local heritage organizations, constituted that culture.[12] And in their 2011 spring budget, they proposed the establishment of a "state cultural heritage fund where individuals and organizations . . . can turn to in order to receive support for their operations and projects."[13]

But despite his focus on the genre, folk music is not an obvious choice for Karlsson's agenda to "unite as many as possible." As David Kaminsky writes, virtually no folk musicians in Sweden "would argue that folk music, in any real way, is today a 'music of the people' in the sense that it might have been in the eighteenth and nineteenth centuries" (2012a:76). While folk music enjoys relatively frequent exposure in Norway, only a small portion of Sweden's population performs or listens to the genre regularly, and this is especially true of the "older folk music"—esoteric in its sounds and difficult to perform—that Karlsson idealizes. Practitioners of this particular style are largely urban, educated, young, and left-leaning, much like their counterparts in folk music communities elsewhere. These features led critical commentators to dismiss the Sweden Democrats' overtures to folk music as illogical. For example, folk musician and educator at Malmö Academy of Music, Pär Moberg, rejected the notion that the genre could be seen as "music of the people" today, and added:

> I would say that there are significantly more Swedes today—if we are talking about ethnic Swedes in case there is such a thing—who are interested in tango, and popular music above all else. And similarly, in their budget the Sweden Democrats talk about how elitist culture should have less money. If there is something that is elitist today, it is Swedish folk music.[14]

But Karlsson's concerns go beyond the popularity of cultural products. He finds folk music suited to his agenda because of what it signifies. We discussed the issue in greater depth:

> BT: I understand that you want music that everybody can gather around, but is folk music the best music for that? Dansband, psalms—if there is something more obviously appreciated by the majority of Swedes?
>
> MATTIAS KARLSSON (MK): I don't think that one prohibits the other, we haven't really deemed folk music more important than psalms. But I think nonetheless that many Swedes have—there are certain symbols, mental images connected with Swedishness. There, I think that specifically folk music and folk musicians and such are a very central symbol. And I actually think many Swedes, even if they are not nationalistically inclined, get a certain feeling when they hear Swedish folk music, but perhaps not other music. As regards dansband, it doesn't really have that—there isn't that seriousness, there aren't those roots back in history that folk music has that could rouse strength. . . . In those contexts that incorporate folk music today, for example in Swedish TV, or in other contexts, folk music accompanies descriptions of Swedish holidays and traditions, moments of positive fellowship, or pictures of Swedish landscapes that are very important for Swedes and the Swedish self-image and the Swedish identity. That is something very significant for the Swedish self-image, that it is closely tied to nature—more perhaps to nature than to people and habits, and holidays, really. Folk music is seen as connected to nature, there is a sound in Swedish folk music that developed in some form of symbiosis with the Swedish landscape. Kulning, for example, which uses the Swedish landscape to send its sound between two points. Or herding music [*fädbodsmusiken*] in general. (Interview, Mattias Karlsson, December 3, 2010)

Folk music's appeal thus goes beyond its potential to serve as a musical common denominator for Swedes. Karlsson links the art form with wholesome community life, and claims that this association is formed in part by the entertainment industry. Additionally, he associates folk music—herding music in particular—with Sweden's landscape, and he sees this association coded within the musical sounds themselves. Given longstanding tendencies to associate nation with nature in the country (see Löfgren 1979; Berggren and Trägårdh 2009), his ideological investment in folk music seems intuitive. Karlsson says that the art form's link with landscape gives it potential to inspire Swedes on an emotional plane, connecting them with Sweden and Swedish identity in ways other musics cannot.

Other voices linked to the Sweden Democrats, however, contend that such focus on folk culture is solely an act of political strategizing. Torbjörn Kastell, former vice party leader whose faction was ousted in 2005, says of the current administration:

> They are vote-maximizers above all else. There we have a conflict between the factions regarding tactics and strategy, basically. The [new] faction placed significantly more emphasis on maximizing votes, while my side held onto ideology more tightly whether it helped or hurt us. . . . But I think that, as soon as the Sweden Democrats become a more "mainstream" party, they can go back a bit and emphasize high culture and history. I know that it is still there, deep down in them. (Interview, Torbjörn Kastell, March 29, 2011)

Torbjörn Kastell argued that, though the current leaders of the Sweden Democrats feel passionately about high culture and history, they hide their interest in public. Leaders do this, Kastell suggests, because it renders the party less controversial to potential voters. Karlsson's statements to me appear to endorse this interpretation. He calls the history of Sweden's age as a great power "politically sensitive," and his personal interest in Swedish military and Viking history is absent from much of the public communication and official party literature he produces. Alternately, both Karlsson and Kastell describe folk culture as inherently less offensive to the Swedish mainstream. Whereas references to Vikings and kings associate the Sweden Democrats with militarism, aggression, and even Nazism, party leaders think that folk culture will soften their image and counteract entrenched perceptions of nationalism in Sweden.

The party's embrace of folk music, in other words, parallels the campaign of reform sweeping throughout the wider nationalist scene. A trickle of nationalists beyond the Sweden Democrats began celebrating folk music at roughly the same time as Karlsson—treating their interest in the genre as an emblem of their cause's positive nature. One such individual is Vávra Suk—a Czech national who immigrated to Sweden as a child and became a nationalist during his youth. Once a Sweden

Democrat, Suk belonged to a faction in the organization that was pushed out for alleged ties to extremism, and which thereafter founded the National Democrats party (see Chapter 2). He would continue to serve as editor of the National Democrats' newspaper *Nationell Idag*. Throughout his tenure as editor, Suk routinely published articles on folk music written by others in his staff, and during an interview I asked him to explain his paper's focus on the genre:

Sometimes we are criticized for only focusing on multiculturalism's problems or immigration and immigrants, etc. And [in articles on folk music] we show that isn't true at all. Here we take up genuine Swedish culture, things that aren't multiculture, but instead part of the Swedish tradition, of European tradition. . . . Other papers, what they write about—the news is crime, crises, and different sorts of problems. Multiculture is often involved in those problems, we think. And the difference is that we write that, they don't. But at the same time, unlike them, we also look at real Swedish culture, both folk culture and national events—Swedish Christmas celebrations, culture articles that delve into tradition more broadly. . . . So really, we have less multiculture, less immigration, than the big papers. (Interview, Vávra Suk, April 1, 2011)

According to Suk, these writings on folk music—on "real Swedish culture"—provide evidence that his newspaper is not consumed with negative reporting. With their celebration of folk music, they show that they are for, not just against something. Such qualities are essential to Suk's sense of nationalism. He explains, beginning with a reference to activists from previous decades:

Many of those who reacted earlier, to the problems, were not nationalists. Instead, they saw a problem that dealt with immigration and crime, cultural conflicts and such—they were against that. But they didn't have much of their own. If you are a nationalist, you build out from the Self—what you *want* to create, how you *want* society to work. (ibid.; emphasis in spoken original)

Andreas Nyberg, leading member of the ethnopluralist and National Democrats–derived action group Nordic Youth, arrived at a similar point when we discussed the relative absence of folk music among nationalists.

BT: Why isn't [folk music] bigger in nationalist organizations, why aren't there more people investing in it?

ANDREAS NYBERG (AN): I think I know part of the answer, and that is that nationalists have been so incredibly bad at emphasizing, and recruiting people who have any type of quality. They have tried—they have attracted a completely different type of people who sometimes have not been so positive for nationalism, people who maybe like to drink, people who don't have very high morals, and that has been very negative. (Interview, Andreas Nyberg, July 4, 2011)

Just as Suk regards the presence of folk music in his paper as a sign of the positive, upstanding nature of nationalist activism, Nyberg traces folk music's absence to hooliganism.

In sum, different nationalists—moving in or near the Sweden Democrats—treat folk music as an uncontroversial and essentially good cultural practice. This understanding, in turn, makes folk music a dynamic tool for perpetuating New Nationalism. By associating themselves with folk music, nationalists hope to both highlight Swedish particularity and render themselves less offensive to the mainstream. But while activists may champion folk music because of what the music represents, they also celebrate the genre because of the people it attracts.

Folk Music and Implicit Whiteness

They want to promote a very strong culture, but it is the type of culture that only a certain kind of people like, and those are Swedes.
ANDREAS NYBERG

During my interview with him on July 4, 2011, I asked Nordic Youth leader Andreas Nyberg to define nationalism. Like most activists outside of the Sweden Democrats, he said that to be a nationalist one must be principally concerned with preserving the ethnic purity of Swedes. In his mind, cultural nationalists—those who engaged on behalf of a national culture rather than a national ethnicity—were phonies. As we continued talking, however, his opposition to groups like the Sweden Democrats softened, and he managed to briefly reconcile the party's cultural nationalism with his own commitment to ethnic solidarity. Yes, he said, the party championed culture, but their efforts might still constitute a form of phantom ethnonationalist activism, for this culture was consumed first and foremost by ethnic Swedes.

For decades, nationalists have observed—as have I—that Swedish folk musicians, dancers, and enthusiasts are overwhelmingly white. Nationalists react to the whiteness of the folk music community in different ways. Some cultural nationalist Sweden Democrats interpret the ethnic homogeneity of folk music as an undesirable product of multiculturalism and Swedish self-contempt—illustration of the fact that Sweden's immigrants are not assimilating into the national culture (see the quote on the subject from Marie Stensby in chapter 1). In contrast, some ethnonationalists celebrate folk music gatherings as oases of ethnic camaraderie in a society otherwise plagued by diversity. Despite these divergences, nationalists commonly hold that the genre's whiteness confirms one of their foundational claims: that a Swedish people exists and that its inner solidarity offends prevailing social agendas.

When contemporary nationalists talk about the ethnic composition of contemporary Swedish folk music, some do so explicitly referencing the concept of "implicit whiteness." Psychology professor at California State University, Long Beach and outspoken white nationalist and American Alt-Right figure Kevin MacDonald coined this term to describe patterns of tacit white ethnocentrism in multiethnic democracies. He describes the concept:

> [W]hite people are gradually coalescing into implicit white communities that reflect their ethnocentrism but "cannot tell their name." They are doing so because of the operation of various mechanisms that operate implicitly, below the level of conscious awareness. These white communities cannot assert explicit white identities because the explicit cultural space is deeply committed to an ideology in which any form of white identity is anathema. (2006–2007:23)

Discourses prevalent in the public sphere, in "explicit cultural space," discourage whites from behaving ethnocentrically, a behavior MacDonald claims is essential to our psychology, and thereby a virtue. In his other writings (1994, 1998a, 1998b), MacDonald argues that Jews perpetuate such discourses in an effort to undermine white solidarity. Accordingly, he interprets the phenomenon of implicit whiteness as a symptom of defeat in this struggle:

> Because there is no mainstream attempt by whites to shape the explicit culture in ways that would legitimize white identity and the pursuit of white ethnic interests, implicit white communities become enclaves of retreating whites rather than communities able to consciously pursue white interests. (2006–2007:24)

MacDonald's writings have been translated and distributed in the Nordic countries by the identitarian Arktos and white nationalist Arminius.se. But long before MacDonald had written about implicit whiteness, Swedish nationalists were observing the same phenomenon. And whereas MacDonald claims that implicit whiteness in the United States appears in stock car racing (NASCAR), evangelical Christianity, Republican voter registration, and country music, his Swedish counterparts saw tacit white collectivities forming around Swedish folk music.

Early Sweden Democrat Ola Sundberg encountered such a collectivity at Stockholm's Mälarsalen dance hall in 1990. During this time, the Sweden Democrats were generally an ethnonationalist organization, and Sundberg described his experience in an issue of the Sweden Democrats' newspaper *Sverige-Kuriren* (1990, no. 9). On this particular evening, attendees were dancing to dansband music—a German schlager–styled genre that can include gammaldans dance forms, and thereby occasionally acquires the label of folk music. Sundberg writes:

> You might think that because of the atmosphere you were somewhere in Blekinge, Dalarna, Östergötland or Jämtland. . .but the fact was that I was in Mälarsalen in the heart of our capital Stockholm. That evening . . . the dansband Lill-Nickes from Halmstad was playing, full with enthusiastic and skillful dancers on the floor and pleasant people with a nice, clean, and harmonious atmosphere all around. The number of attendees that night was about 700, which is pretty representative for a dance on Sunday evenings.
>
> Who were these attendees, what kind of people were they? Well, all ages from 18 up to 75, and only Swedes and Scandinavians—at least that evening. In fact I didn't see a single person with non-European ancestry. It is truly a pleasure to see that Swedes and Scandinavians see the need to carry on with our traditions.
>
> . . .
>
> Hans Ryberg [the venue's owner] says also that Mälarsalen has become an obvious choice for nationalistically-minded Swedes, just like Skansen.[15] Flashy headlines are not needed–people just know where they feel at home.

In the center of a multiethnic city, an event featuring what Sundberg considers Swedish traditional dance drew ethnically homogeneous patrons. But the key statement comes in the final sentence quoted above: "Flashy headlines are not needed–people just know where they feel at home." For here Sundberg says that without being told, Swedes sought out ethnically homogeneous collectivities where they can feel at home, and they did so without explicit encouragement or direction.[16]

More than twenty years later, nationalists continued to have experiences like Sundberg's. A man I am here calling "Mr. X"—an unaffiliated activist and musician who has been involved in both ethnopluralist and identitarian circles—is one such individual. During a conversation we had in 2011, he disagreed with my suggestion that folk fusion projects and nonwestern music were popular in Sweden. As evidence for his contention, he described his visit the previous summer to an outdoor concert at Vitabergsparken in Stockholm featuring folk singer Sofia Karlsson. Karlsson's style draws from older rural traditions as well as classic popular Swedish singer-songwriter repertories, and her popularity has been growing in mainstream music scenes and among nationalists. Mr. X described his arrival at the concert that evening in Stockholm:

> I was very surprised. There was free admission, true, but I was still very surprised by "the turn out." It so happened that this very concert had the public attendance record. There were 6,000 people there. And there was an unbelievable, ah, it's kind of a political term, but, feeling of a people's community [Sw. *folkgemenskap*, Grm. *volksgemeinschaft*]. There were 6,000. I struggled to get pictures, there were people everywhere, absolutely everywhere. . . . But of those 6,000, who were really engaged in the concert—there was a lot of Swedish music—and of those 6,000 there wasn't one—not one—from, like, Somalia. There might have been one who looked like you [referring to author]. 6,000, and unbelievable fellowship, and enthusiasm, and people sang along at times, and it was quite telling in a way. And it was mostly Swedish music, both older, from the early twentieth and nineteenth centuries, but there was also a little—she had guests from other EU countries, England, so there was that kind of folk music as well—a little "cross over." But nonetheless unbelievable enthusiasm, a genuine, ah, there was something in the air. So, if you think of all these projects to bring Congolese musicians here—you just cannot compare the enthusiasm for that. (Interview, Mr. X, March 4, 2011)

In addition to describing the crowd's ethnic characteristics, Mr. X also comments on the Swedishness of the music and what he experienced as attendees' passion for the event. He juxtaposes this passion—exemplified in part by the size of the crowd— with ethnic Swedes' alleged lack of equivalent passion for foreign musics. Mr. X was thus referring to the concert as an example of the fact that ethnic Swedes prefer participating in Swedish culture more than they do in multiculture.

Mr. X, like most activists, claims the Swedish political establishment and the media seek to convince ethnic Swedes that they need cultural importation—specifically culture from the nonwestern world—to be a well-functioning society. Further, virtually all nationalists claim that public criticism of this sentiment is stigmatized, such that in official discourses, in what Kevin MacDonald would call "explicit cultural space," Swedes must express approval of cultural importation. Against this backdrop, the enthusiasm for Swedish music and the ethnic fellowship on display at Sofia Karlsson's concert constitutes subversion of official agendas and discourses. It constitutes, in the nationalist worldview, silent rebellion.

Vávra Suk elaborated on this same theme in his analysis of Sweden's folk music community. As we discussed that community's ethnic homogeneity, I mentioned to him that, in my experience, its participants are also generally left-leaning, and that most would likely say they support multiculturalism if questioned. Just as Mr. X contested my suggestion that Swedes on the whole seemed enthusiastic about foreign musics, so too did Suk question whether the scene's leftism was genuine. He responded:

> I think that it is somewhat hypocritical also. Because, were there a lot of multiculture, they would probably go looking for a new group . . . another group where there isn't so much multiculture. That is my guess. They say, "yes, we want to take in these other cultures" and so on. But, to start with, these other cultures have different ways of looking at things, another way to socialize where there are other rules as to how you should relate to each other, between men and women that is. It creates a greater insecurity as to how you should act, they don't really know what to expect from the others. And that's what is so great about the folk music scene, you understand everybody else, you don't have to be worried. I think that Somalis who go to their cultural organizations, they feel exactly the same way. You know how people work. (Interview, Vávra Suk, April 1, 2011)

Thus, Suk extends his assertion that the folk music community is disobeying the directives they receive from political elites: Members of this community, he suggests, may even act against their own stated convictions. Though they may claim to support and appreciate cultural diversity, their actions speak otherwise.

Whether true or not, the belief that everyday Swedes live out tacit ethnocentric drives in folk music addresses a key concern facing nationalists as they justify their continued activism. Despite claiming to fight on behalf of a majority population, nationalist organizations in Sweden are unpopular when compared with mainstream political groups.[17] Nationalists thus need to explain why they are often disliked by the people they champion, and their commentary on the folk music community quoted above can resolve this dilemma. It allows nationalists to claim that everyday Swedes in fact support their ideals. However, this people expresses its support, consciously or unconsciously, with its feet rather than its votes. Nationalist ideals may fail at the ballot box, but according to the voices quoted above, those ideals reign supreme in music consumption.

Kevin MacDonald occasionally describes a link between the implicitly white collectivity and the activity or practice that attracts it. He claims, for example, that whites coalesce within the Republican Party in the United States because this party best advances white interests (2006–2007:19–20). Most of the Swedish activists quoted above, in contrast, do not mention any fundamental connection between Swedish folk music and the demographic that surrounds it. But Mr. X attempts to establish such a link. As he spoke about the concert in Vitabergsparken, he twice broke his narrative flow to remind me that the music being played was Swedish. When I asked him to clarify the role of music in the event, he said:

> I thought that it spoke its own language, so to say, it spoke for itself through the event and atmosphere. It was satisfactory in an artistic sense, but since I am not really for the politicizing of art, I think that one can draw his or her own conclusions. But I've given you a few hints. But still, I think there is a term often called "implicit whiteness." (Interview, Mr. X, March 4, 2011)

I later pressed him on the point, and he replied:

> [The event created] a sort of belonging and a community built on something that doesn't need to be verbalized. So in a way it is the power of music, even though it wasn't instrumental [music]—that music picks up where words run out and says that which perhaps cannot be said. I can't imagine that anyone who left the concert, after a couple of hours, all encores and such, was dissatisfied. But at the same time it wasn't in any way an exclusive event. It was rather the opposite of exclusive, but still there was a certain pattern among these 6000 everyday Stockholmers. . . . They themselves can explain why they were there, but all the same, it was a very enjoyable event (ibid).

Though he did not state it outright, Mr. X carefully suggests that Sofia Karlsson's music was the non-offensive, uncontroversial medium for transmitting "that which cannot be said," that which "doesn't need to be verbalized"—the call to and continued existence of Swedish ethnic fellowship.

A Tradition Under Siege

Thus far we have seen how activists use folk music to illustrate the existence of distinctly Nordic national peoples. Whether regarded as an echo of a shared history or a present-day beacon for ethnic gathering, nationalists describe folk music as an embodiment—and existential demonstration—of the populations they fight for. The associations between their conceptions of folk music and Nordic national peoples at large run deeper yet, however. Just as nationalists strive to define native Nordics as threatened by liberalism or foreigners, they argue that the region's folk music traditions are similarly besieged.

Contemporary folk musicians, especially those in Sweden, are politically left leaning, and the community acquired this profile during a 1960s and 1970s folk revival. Like their counterparts in France, Britain, and the United States, anti-war Swedish youths at the time began embracing folk music as a means of challenging western cultural imperialism and global capitalism (see Ling 1980; Ramsten 1992; Kaminsky 2012a). Individuals from this generation founded and assumed leadership roles in music conservatory folk music departments, major record labels, and local and national folk music organizations. Smaller circles of hardline communists and Maoists also joined this movement as performers and commentators, seeing in folk music a refuge from Anglo-American cultural expansion and commercialization.[18]

The history of leftist, and at times explicitly communist involvement in Sweden's folk music scene provides an opening for nationalists to dismiss contemporary resistance to their agenda and advance their narratives of social and political change in the west more generally. Fixating on the political transformations that took place during the folk revival, nationalists identify what they see as an additional site of a broad Marxist campaign to infiltrate and transform emblems of national identity. This account is especially intuitive for nationalists familiar with identitarian and *Nouvelle Droite* accounts of liberalism's triumphs in the west (see Chapter 2). For these individuals, to trace the recent history of folk music in Sweden is to rearticulate their established theories of how cultural or ethnic solidarity in the country was undone, and why calls for nationalism are so marginalized today. Sweden Democrat Mattias Karlsson, whose agenda to promote folk music drew negative reactions from musicians themselves, referred to post-war leftist movements and the folk music revival when offering an explanation.

BT: How is it that you are supporting people who don't want your support?

MK: . . . There is a historical explanation for that, as I see it. During the '68-wave in Sweden, which was very strong . . . they ultimately were inspired by Antonio Gramsci's ideas about power through the institutions, that it is important to break down the traditional bourgeoisie culture, even more important than taking power in parliament – that is how you can realize a socialist society. They sought out different forms of cultural expression for their socialist ideas. . . . To find an alternative to the imperialist American culture, many turned to folk music, in part because it was anti-hierarchical in such a way that anybody could join and play. Everyone stands together at folk music festivals. They were against all forms of hierarchy, and they didn't like it when one artist stood up there on a stage, and everyone else sits passively. Because of that, the Swedish far left embraced the music. And suddenly thousands of youths began showing up at folk music festivals in Dalarna and Härjedalen that earlier were almost only for older people. And those people who got involved did it mostly for political reasons. They later came to take over the folk music organizations (Interview, Mattias Karlsson, December 3, 2010).

Karlsson's response to me, which mimics responses he has given in newspaper interviews,[19] frames his most vocal opponents in the folk music community as agents in cultural Marxist activism. This impugns the authenticity of anti-nationalist folk musicians today—who in Karlsson's statement are placed opposite the ostensibly less politicized "older" generation of folk musicians—and signals that he considers folk music an ongoing site for political struggle.

While cultural nationalist voices like Karlsson describe folk music's recent history as one of liberal infiltration, some ethnonationalists voice a similar historiography where Jews rather than liberals at large are named as the forces of corruption. Their commentary on folk music belongs to wide-reaching theories of Jewish involvement in cultural politics that circulate in race revolutionary and, to a lesser extent, identitarian circles. These theories, articulated with the most fervor by ideologues like American Kevin MacDonald (1994, 1998b) or Swede Magnus Söderman (2011), claim that Jews conspire to achieve power by undermining competing ethnic groups' self-consciousness. Jews allegedly attempt this by dismantling traditions and creative expressions testifying to other's distinct history, culture, and unity. And while their actions promote a rootless cosmopolitanism among global populations at large, Jews fiercely guard the integrity and boundaries of their own ethnoreligious community, the end goal being that they—and they alone—can act with collective self-interest.

Conspiracy theories of this kind encourage nationalists to view Jews as likely saboteurs of folk music's political potential. If folk music is a powerful living symbol of ethnic identity, the reasoning goes, then Jews will attempt to undermine it by obscuring knowledge of its essence or transforming the music such that it no longer could be regarded as belonging to a particular people. Few Jews are active in Nordic folk music scenes today, however, and for that reason theories of Jewish infiltration are less common among nationalists than theories of leftist/Marxist conspiracy. But a handful of Jewish folk music enthusiasts have been targeted in nationalist media and online forums, including American expatriate and folklorist Israel (Izzy) Young, myself, and most especially folk dancer and organizer Lars Farago.

Lars Farago emerged as a central target among nationalists on account of his leftism, his Jewishness, and his drive to participate in public discussion of folk music and politics. Originally from Hungary, he immigrated to Sweden in 1958 with his parents when he was ten years old and learned folk dance as a teenager. He went on to help found the National Union for Folk Music and Dance (*Riksföreningen för folkmusik och dans*), an organization distinguished within Sweden by its promotion of global traditions rather than the Swedish alone. Farago would serve as the Union's president in 1994, and he wrote for its magazine through the early 2010s. A former member of the Left Party, he publicly condemned the Sweden Democrats' cultural policy and anti-immigrant nationalism more generally, organizing a nationwide seminar series and publishing articles where he criticized romantic nationalism and advocated cultural diversity.

Surfacing in public debates as an influential, leftist Jew promoting foreign folk traditions within Sweden, Farago appeared to align with nationalists' visions of Jewish infiltration and manipulation. But reactions to him grew most heated when he made public statements interrogating the relationship between folk music and national identity. During a live, prime-time television debate with Mattias Karlsson on October 21, 2010, he argued that traditional music in certain parts of Sweden more resembled styles from across, rather than within, the country's borders. Accordingly, he argued that the term "Swedish folk music" might be misleading and that "Nordic folk music" would be a more accurate label. In subsequent media appearances Farago appeared less equivocal in dismissing the Swedishness of Swedish folk music. A local newspaper covering one of his public seminars reported:

> Farago emphasized that there is no folk music or folk dance that originates only in Sweden, so he rejected purity terms like "genuine Swedish" and "specifically Swedish." (*Piteå Tidning*, November 19, 2010)

Nationalists interpreted commentary like this as part of an effort to conceal folk music's Swedish essence, and thereby deprive ethnic Swedes of a means to identify themselves as a distinct group. Impressions that Farago was fulfilling conspiracist prophesy sharpened when nationalist media—the former National Democrats' newspaper *Nationell Idag* (National Today) in particular—reported on his engagement with the international organization Limmud, an organization that in its own words strives to "strengthen and develop" Jewish identity, albeit while maintaining a commitment to "inclusiveness" and political neutrality.[20] Though Farago only participated in Limmud events as a guest speaker, nationalist media described him as an official member.

Piecing together these various observations, nationalists were able to portray Farago as a leftist Jew bent on diluting local folk traditions and notions of distinct Swedishness, all while working to strengthen Jewish identity. *Nationell Idag*'s former editor Vávra Suk pushed this account during an interview with me:

> [Farago] is a hypocrite of the worst kind. Because he says that, "Yes, but Swedish culture, there really isn't anything that is genuinely Swedish. Instead

it was influenced from abroad," and so on. But at the same time he is a member of the Jewish cultural organization Limmud. If you go in to their home page it is like, "Oh the fantastic ethnic, genuine culture and klezmer dances." Because then, all of a sudden, it is completely acceptable, there you'll find not a word about multiculture. It isn't like "Yes, but klezmer comes from a bunch of outside influences, you can't really say that it is really Jewish." "What is Jewish culture, really?" Nobody says that, right? And how can he, on the one hand, give lectures for Limmud, and talk about how fantastic—they have their own traditions, and then go to the Swedes and say, "But you don't have any. What do you have to be proud of? Everything came from abroad." Isn't that hypocritical? (Interview, Vávra Suk, April 1, 2011)

Suk's newspaper published a series of articles presenting this profile of Farago, after which online nationalist discussion forums erupted with reactions. Most commentary cited Farago as proof that theories of Jewish treachery were true. User "Varnagel," writing on Feburary 22, 2012 in the forum Flashback, channeled the common tenor of these online discussions:

It is the Jews who have destroyed our cultural identity and who actively prevent us from recovering it and building it up. One of many examples is the Jew Lars Farago, who for some fucking reason is president of the Swedish folk music organization (!) or whatever it is. There, he claims that Swedish folk music doesn't have to be Swedish, and a ton of other shit. At the same time, he is a member of Limmud, which is an explicitly ethnic Jewish society that promotes what is Jewish.[21]

Discussion threads devoted to Farago emerged on Nordisk.nu and Frihet.nu in addition to Flashback, and by mid-2012 Metapedia had produced Swedish-language articles presenting accounts of his professional activities and political stances.

Viewed within the broader context of the debates over folk music that emerged following the Sweden Democrats' rise, the intense reactions to Farago appear peculiar. Farago's positions and ideas are far less dogmatic than his opponents imply, and in many cases his stances position him closer to nationalists than many other prominent liberal voices in public conversation. In interviews and publications, for instance, he has emerged as a critic of those questioning the existence of Swedish culture.[22] He explained his position in more detail to me during an interview:

We've seen the effect that, some culture journalists and some politicians deny that Swedish music exists, and that there are Swedish traditions. And that is a very strange polarization too. So I think it is very unfortunate that you have to counter the Sweden Democrats by saying that it doesn't exist. At the same time, I think you must see how interwoven it all is, historically, with other parts, other genres. . . . There are completely unique qualities in music cultures that don't exist anywhere else in the world. We must always say that Nordic, Swedish—only exists in Sweden. That needs to be number one, in a way, and it hasn't been. That is a weakness in Sweden—that we don't do a better job of protecting it. (Interview, Lars Farago, January 24, 2011)

Farago thus expressed an understanding of Swedish folk music and Swedish culture in line with that of some nationalists, such as the authors of the cultural policy sections in the Sweden Democrats' party programs, as well as those identitarian voices who claim that cultural and national boundaries do not match. He asserts that cultural phenomena in Sweden arose in exchange with other forms. But despite this history of outside influence, he still claims that there are practices unique to Sweden, even if those practices do not perfectly follow the boundaries of the nation-state.

The demonization of Farago, when considered against the totality of his activism and commentary, suggests that nationalists' focus on him deals more with his ethnic identity than the content of his output. Responses to him therefore remind us that folk music remains a nascent and marginalized interest for nationalists, one that in ethnonationalist circles is far subordinated in importance to campaigns against Jews. Folk music proved relevant for these voices primarily because of the ways it allowed for further exposition of existing beliefs and agendas.

For Diversity's Sake

Whether they blame 1960s youths, Marxists, or Jews, nationalists often claim that outside ideologies, peoples, and sounds have corrupted a once inherently domestic tradition. Nationalists thus see in folk music a manifestation of the social and cultural transformations they most oppose—here growing foreign influence is allegedly threatening the integrity of their difference. In addition to challenging the influence of leftists and non-Nordics, nationalists have injected themselves into debates about innovation and tradition in folk music performance. Though such debates rage in many folk music scenes throughout the world today, folk musicians in Sweden increasingly conceive of innovation as fusion with non-Swedish folk musics (Lundberg, Malm, and Ronström 2000; Kaminsky 2012a). Discussions about innovation and tradition in Swedish folk music therefore provide nationalists an opportunity to demonstrate their commitment to the Swedish in the face of globalization and multiculturalism. Just as New Nationalists see themselves as champions of cultural, ethnic, or racial difference, so too do many claim to seek a more Swedish folk music for the sake of protecting the musical pluriversum.

Sweden Democrats spokeswoman and famed fiddler Marie Stensby devoted much of her public activism to this agenda. During a P2 national radio debate on October 17, 2010, Stensby squared off against fellow folk musicians Ale Möller, Pär Moberg, and Lotta Johansson. The latter three voices all opposed the Sweden Democrats' policies, and advocated both state support for foreign music and the need for diversity and change in the Swedish folk tradition. Stensby responded to these charges with her own celebration of diversity:

> I see things like this, that world music that is so celebrated today, I think that if you look past the musical qualities, and the very competent musicians, then I think that it is a step away from the rich characteristics of every culture, going instead in the direction of a dreary, grey gruel. If it is going to sound the same throughout the world, I think that the music of the world will lose it nuances.

Stensby argues that preserving the purity of Swedish folk music is a necessary step toward maintaining a vibrant musical life throughout the globe. And as she said earlier in the debate, it is the responsibility of the government to assure that this diversity will live on.

Ethnonationalist voices use similar rhetoric when discussing foreign influence in Swedish folk music. Former *Nationell Idag* journalist and folk dancer Erik Alhem spoke to me about music groups showcased at folk music festivals in Sweden. He bemoaned recent tendencies of importing acts from abroad to play their local folk music in Sweden. But he was most incensed by groups that sought to blend separate music traditions—groups like the Ale Möller Band or Ellika and Solo (Interview, Erik Alhem, February 28, 2012). The Ale Möller Band, for instance, intertwines traditional music and instruments from Europe, Latin America, and Africa, seldom playing music from one region without including elements from another. According to Alhem, the "all folk music is the same" or the "let's make a global folk music" ethos underlying such projects constitute an affront to the survival of musical diversity. As he wrote in *Nationell Idag*:

> We Swedes are, like many other nationalities, gifted with a rich and vibrant cultural heritage. All different sorts of music, types of dance and costumes that our people produced, all that diversity we managed to create completely devoid of a vast and encompassing mass-immigration. It is indeed thanks to

the fact that people have been distanced from each other that it was possible to develop everything that is unique for every group of people.... Why do some want to take away all these wonderful differences? (October 23, 2010)[23]

Alhem advocates a pure Swedish folk music and dance with rhetoric that treats cultural diversity as a virtue and a resource rather than a threat. Following the rhetorical techniques of the New Nationalism, Alhem makes this characterization via an extension of the arena for musical diversity, by expanding the forum for difference from a national to an international context where musical homogeneity within one's country constitutes musical heterogeneity from a global perspective.

Alhem's and Stensby's words show how New Nationalistic rhetoric on human exchange can be been transferred to musical domains. The similarities between nationalists' commentary on foreign peoples in Sweden and foreign influence in folk music could suggest that one discourse is a proxy for the other. The sentiments and rhetoric exemplified in the above quotes could be a substitute for more incendiary and controversial commentary on immigration, ethnicity, or race. Criticizing folk fusion is far less inflammatory than criticizing interracial marriage. However, there are other indications that nationalists' condemnation of world music and folk fusion is not always a sublimated discourse, but may at times stem from an alleged link between expressive culture and demographic transformation.

As Mr. X and I were discussing folk fusion and world music, specifically the Ale Möller Band, he mentioned that he avoided such music on both aesthetic and philosophical grounds. I asked him to explain this philosophical distaste, and he replied:

> It can function as propaganda. It markets a sort of problem-free, sterilized, multiculturalism where you can just take in a small portion, like "one more scone." (Interview, Mr. X, March 4, 2011)

After having grouped such music under the larger heading of boutique multiculturalism—a term Stanley Fish uses to describe manifestations of cultural diversity that are inoffensive to majority sensibilities (see Fish 1997)—he specified his criticism:

> This boutique multiculturalism paves the way for mass immigration because it sends out signals that, "but we will be so enriched, we need cultural exchange," bla, bla, bla.... [B]outique multiculturalism masks the other sides of what can be called an exchange of peoples. That is of course the danger, and that is what I mean when I say that it can function as propaganda. (ibid.)

In the scenario Mr. X describes, music can provide a cover for more contentious and dangerous phenomena. Folk fusion and similar emblems of cultural exchange have the potential to popularize social developments that will corrupt Swedes' broader cultural or ethnic integrity. Thus, the plights of a pure Swedish folk music and a pure Swedish population are related. Opposition to cultural expressions like folk fusion is, in embryo, opposition to immigration and multiculturalism.

A Future in Metapolitics

Conceptions of folk music in the nationalist scene, though at times contradictory, also share some common features. As was the case in nineteenth- and twentieth-century romantic nationalist movements, contemporary nationalists treat folk music as a music "of the people," one that is inherently native either in its musical structure or via the population coalescing around it. This is true even for race materialists, who, though they discourage activism that focuses on folk music, nonetheless see the genre as a natural outgrowth of a racially pure population. Furthermore, in these examples, folk music frequently functions as both an instrument and product of the broader reform process in radical nationalism. Mattias Karlsson accentuated folk culture in the Sweden Democrats' public profile in part so that the party could connect with average Swedes. Framing the folk music community as implicitly white enabled activists like Vávra Suk and Mr. X to claim that their observations are shared and acted upon by the greater public. And nationalists of various kinds find in folk music a platform to present their fears of liberal erasure of national difference.

Though they may celebrate it, nationalists seldom practice folk music themselves. Their engagement with the genre often takes place via the performances of others—folk musicians and dancers who are often hostile to the anti-immigrant cause. Nationalists' attempt to embrace folk music thus brings them into increased contact and conflict with their political opponents. This dynamic continues to unfold, and leftist folk music enthusiasts like Lars Farago remain cautious as they look to the future. Farago said of the nationalist interest in folk music:

The danger is that it would split up [the folk music movement] . . . that a "we-are-defending-Swedish-folk-music" organization would emerge that would be friends with the Sweden Democrats, and thereby create a polarization. (Interview, Lars Farago, January 24, 2011)

Of course, such an organization emerged in the form of Mattias Karlsson's and Erik Almqvist's Gimle. But when Karlsson spoke to me about his future plans, he described a metapolitical vision that Farago might find even more unsettling:

> I want to focus more and more on the extraparliamentary. Build associations, and hopefully provoke these existing, larger associations more. We can't just sit and be Internet warriors, and write op-eds and such. Instead we have to join these associations and get involved, join a folk dance team, or a local heritage council, and work actively there, win the members' trust and get elected as a representative at conventions and so forth. And in the beginning, we may not have a chance to take over these associations, but we can at least make sure that the debate moves into their own conventions and meetings. I think that there is an assumption that, once you have started the debate, there are actually a fair number who are active in these associations who lean in our direction. I don't think that the normal, volunteer worker in a local heritage council necessarily agrees with the leaders. But there has never been an alternative. Not for a long time at least. (Interview, Mattias Karlsson, February 11, 2011)

5

LAMENT FOR A PEOPLE

Women Singers and New Nationalist Victimhood

There is nothing I find more discouraging than browsing through a catalogue of white racist CDs and finding NO WOMEN ARTISTS! Sure, racist music is racist music. The message is roughly the same whether a man or women sings the song. But, I like to hear women singing too. And those female voices just aren't out there in racialist music. Women need to harness music's power. . . . It allows more potential concert goers because some women are turned off by ultra-aggressive testosterone-laced performers.[1]

AMERICAN WHITE NATIONALIST Cindy MacDonald issued this statement in a 1997 article on the website *Her Race*. As the name implies, *Her Race* addressed itself to female activists and served as one of the main outlets during the late twentieth century advocating for greater inclusion of women in the otherwise male-dominated American and European race-revolutionary scene. This article, "Aryan Women in Music," likewise called for women to break into the world of white nationalist music, dominated as it was by white power and the sounds of charging punk or metal-based accompaniments, lyrics demonizing nonwhites, and the hollering voices of skinhead men.

As MacDonald wrote her piece, however, there were a handful of female white-power musicians scattered throughout Europe and North America. The singer "Jackie" joined the otherwise all-male neo-Nazi band Lionheart in 1989. The British band Razor's Edge occasionally performed with a female bass player, "Kel," as did Italian band ADL122. And Swede Sunita Ringstad released the solo album *Frihetskamp* under the artist name Sunita in 1994 (Ekman and Poohl 2010:147–48). To varying extents, each of these performers cultivated the so-called skinbyrd persona as musicians—that is, they adopted skinhead-style appearances and an aggressive demeanor. They donned bomber jackets and combat boots, and some wore the semicropped, "feather-cut" hairstyle. The music they played matched that of most white power acts at the time. Their style was Oi! punk or thrash metal, and their lyrics attacked blacks and Jews, calling for the implementation of racial separatism or supremacy through violence. And when the female performers sang—as was the case with Sunita—they employed the semi-screamed vocal techniques common in most white power music.

Even if MacDonald were aware of these musicians when she wrote her piece, they were likely not the women she was seeking. Rather, MacDonald envisioned a female presence that could offer a contrasting, softer character to radical nationalist music, an alternative to the "ultra-aggressive" and "testosterone-laced" as it manifest on stage and in sound.

Today, more than fifteen years after MacDonald wrote her piece, the most celebrated performer in the global white nationalist music scene is a woman from Sweden, Saga. She has been a headlining act in Great Britain, Germany, Finland, Hungary, and the United States for most of the past decade. Saga typically collaborates with race nationalist organizations like the now-disbanded National Socialist Front in Sweden, the white nationalist Resistance Records in the United States, and the anti-Roma, anti-Jewish party Jobbik in Hungary. Her popularity continues to soar: some uploads of her songs on YouTube have more than one million views—numbers that, while small compared to mainstream popular music acts, far surpass those of her white nationalist musician counterparts. Further, her name was thrust into mainstream Scandinavian media in June 2011 following Anders Behring Breivik's terrorist attacks in Oslo and Utøya, Norway, and the discovery that he considered her his chief musical inspiration.

Unlike the female performers active during the 1990s, Saga is no skinbyrd. She almost never appears in combat boots or bomber jackets, and she has never had the cropped, feather-cut hairstyle. She seldom screams her vocals, and her accompaniment has gradually shifted from punk and metal to a light rock style she calls "freedom pop," featuring beats, guitar riffs, synthesizer backgrounds, airy piano accompaniments, and slick, overdubbed vocal harmonies.

Saga's surging popularity parallels both her move toward freedom pop and her cultivation of a new persona in song. Through the themes in her lyrics, her rhetorical modes, and her dynamic musical performances, Saga frames herself as an embodiment of the white race, a figure who endures personal pain because of multiculturalism, immigration, and interracialism, and who relies on outside intervention for deliverance. It is an identity fitted to traditional nationalist gender imaginaries wherein women cradle or constitute national essence, but depend on men to defend that essence in the public sphere.

While previous chapters in this book explored musical practice among identitarians and cultural nationalists, a focus on Saga offers us an opportunity to explore the ways music is changing among race revolutionaries in the Nordic countries and beyond. Here I trace Saga's life and career, exploring the nationalist scene's shifting gender ideologies and analyzing Saga's most famous performance, the song "Ode to a Dying People." I conclude with an investigation of insider reactions to Saga, showing how nationalists use her performances to imagine themselves as defenders of a victimized, threatened population. The discourses surrounding Saga's music, in other words, perpetuate New Nationalists' emerging image of themselves and the people they fight for.

Saga

"Saga" is the stage name of a woman born in 1975 in a city in southern Sweden. Despite her success, she makes relatively little money from her music, and for that reason has pursued other careers, including running a beauty salon and working as a salesperson. Having lived for extended periods of time in both the United States and Great Britain (and given that her German boyfriend and former bodyguard Dennis does not speak Swedish), Saga speaks impeccable English, and in dress and demeanor she reminds me more of an American than a Swede.

I first began contacting Saga in the wake of the Breivik attacks in summer 2011. In the center of his 1,500-page manifesto, the Norwegian terrorist praises her polished musical abilities and her rejection of hard rock and heavy metal instrumental styles. Further, Breivik highlights her as a source of inspiration for his imagined community of followers—the "Justiciar Knights of Europe." In a section of his manifesto devoted to helping individuals maintain their drive while planning and carrying out attacks like his, he writes:

> Saga is a courageous, Swedish, female nationalist-oriented musician who creates pop-music with patriotic texts. She is, as far as I know, the best and most talented patriotic musician in the English speaking [*sic*] world. And for those of you, like myself, who hates [*sic*] "metal," Saga is one of the few sources available that offers quality patriotic pop-music with brilliant texts.... I discovered Saga's music relatively late, in 2008, but have enjoyed it ever since. I have listened to many of the tracks several hundred times and I don't seem to get tired of them. I would HIGHLY recommend that all Justiciar Knights of Europe and other revolutionary conservatives use these tracks for self-motivating purposes. Don't just listen to the tracks but learn the texts as well. It has worked brilliantly for me and it will likely work just as well for you. (2011:847)

After this statement, Breivik lists the lyrics to twelve songs that Saga recorded, seven in English, five in Swedish.[2]

Breivik was attracted to Saga in part because she appeared musically and socially distinct from 1990s neo-Nazism—a scene he claims never to have identified with. However, Saga developed the persona that appealed to fans like Breivik gradually, and her image today can mask her past and present orientation within nationalist activism. Unlike most musicians and ideologues I profiled in previous chapters, Saga has few connections to reformist groups.[3] Instead, her social and professional activities have typically taken place in neo-Nazi skinhead and semimilitant white nationalist circles—circles that are often targets rather than vessels of reform.

Saga became involved with nationalist activism as a youth. She recalls growing critical of immigration and multiculturalism throughout secondary school. However, one experience pushed this critical stance to outright opposition. I asked her about her entry into nationalist activism:

SAGA (S): To begin with, it was just something that happened to me, and I got in a lot of arguments with people from—that are not Swedish. Arguments [laughs]. And then there was one specific event that made me very uncomfortable.

BENJAMIN TEITELBAUM (BT): I take it you don't want to say what the events were?

S: No, that stays with me. It was kind of serious though, it involved a lot of people, it was just a very unpleasant experience. And then, there were some trials, and there were some things like that. And then the outcome of the trial was terrible for me and for the other ones. That was like, what? You know. And then I started looking up some other similar cases, and in every case where there was a non-Swede, the sentence was always milder, always, always, always. In every case, it was a milder sentence. And that makes me go, like, why? Why, if you commit the same crime, in the same country, to the same people, why are there two different sentences, why don't you get convicted for the same—treated equally?

. . .

BT: Before this incident, did you have any connections with the nationalist world?

S: Yes, I had friends. And I had my beliefs. That was not the first incident, that was just the incident that made me see red. . . . That is what made me become Saga, if you know what I mean. I had all the beliefs and stuff before, but that was what made me feel like I really just had to do something. Maybe not for everyone else, but for me. I was going nuts, I had to do something, so my music has always been therapy to me, it has always been like therapy. (Interview, Saga and Dennis, July, 28 2011)

While Saga traces the intensifying of her political sentiments to this traumatic experience involving an immigrant, she describes her entry into the nationalist music scene as having been more coincidental and casual. She recalls:

> At that same time I met a guy who was into the scene. He knew someone who knew the record label Midgård, and then I got in contact with them. We just spoke, talked like friends and then they asked questions about me and I was like, "yeah, I'm a singer," and they were like "hey, do you want to do background vocals for a band that I have." And I was like, "yeah, I can do that." (ibid.)

She recorded background vocals for Swedish white-power punk band Pluton Svea and their 1998 release *88% Unplugged*.[4] Impressed with her performance on this recording, producers at Midgård Records—one of Sweden's largest white power labels—invited Saga to participate in other projects.

> The ball started rolling. [Midgård's producer] asked me if I wanted to be a singer on a project, which was Symphony of Sorrow, and I said "yeah, why not." "It's already recorded, the music's already recorded, it's already done." So I said, "ok send me the music." And they sent me the music and I went like, "hmmm. Yeah, ok, well, I'll do this and nothing else." (ibid.)

Midgård Records paired Saga with National Socialist band Triskelon to create the group Symphony of Sorrow. They released their first album *Paradise Lost* in 2000. Singing at the depths of her register, and accompanied by Triskelon's bassy carpet of sound, this metal project has a dark, heavy tone. Likewise, the themes in the lyrics are severe—unwavering as they describe the threat of multiculturalism, and unequivocal in their glorification of violent rebellion. The title track, "Paradise Lost," offers an example of the album's prevailing character:

> A paralyzed dream and stifled scream.
> Europe torn apart from the seams.
> Preparing for war with a mutant horde.
> Striking at the heart of the system's core.
>> (chorus:)
> Let my fury be known—the seeds of violence be sown.
> Let my hatred be fed—with the body count of the enemy dead.
>
> Hell unleashed like a sacred beast.
>> Vengeance arriving to crush the hated peace.
>> A mighty cost for this paradise lost.

The only response is a holocaust.
…
You've built a lie into a governing state.
So now our force runs its brutal course.
We'll kill you all without remorse.
We'll kill you all without remorse.

Having had little creative liberty during the production of *Paradise Lost*, Saga initially planned to cease work with Symphony of Sorrow. However, she wanted to continue making nationalist music. Again, circumstances presented a new opportunity, this time to perform music by flagship British white-power band Skrewdriver and its legendary deceased leader, Ian Stuart Donaldson. She explains:

Symphony of Sorrow is not my kind of music. However, I did the recording and everything was fine and dandy. And the guy that I was seeing at the time was listening to Skrewdriver a lot, so I'd heard Skrewdriver way before of course, but it's like, I listed to Skrewdriver 24/7 for a long time. And then they asked me if I wanted to make a tribute CD and I went, "Yeah, why not." Because I like some of the songs that Skrewdriver does. . . . So I said, "yeah sure, but I need to do it better, better recordings and stuff like that," because Skrewdriver, they didn't really have the studio equipment that I had access to. (Interview, Saga and Dennis, July 28, 2011)

Almost immediately after singing for Symphony of Sorrow, Saga began recording covers of Skrewdriver songs. This recording effort began with the release of two volumes of tributes, followed by the album *Live and Kicking* recorded at a Midgård-sponsored memorial concert for Ian Stuart Donaldson. These albums were released in 2000, and a third volume of Skrewdriver covers followed in 2002.

The tribute recordings—rather than Symphony of Sorrow—established Saga in the international white nationalist music scene and made her the highest-selling artist at Midgård Records. The production quality of her covers easily exceeds that of the originals. Further, she molded the character of the songs to make them less inflammatory: Saga often selected more moderate versions of Donaldson's lyrics (e.g., "Free My Country"),[5] avoided screamed vocals, and occasionally abandoned the punk rock accompaniment altogether in favor of sparse and soft piano backing (e.g., "Tomorrow Belongs to Me"). I have spoken with nationalists who think her covers strip the Skrewdriver originals of their bite and character. However, by recasting these originals, Saga hoped to carry Donaldson's classics to new audiences—those disinclined to the unpolished, harsh musical character of standard white power punk.

Global demand for Saga increased following her tribute albums, and she began performing at concerts and festivals in Great Britain, Germany, and Finland in addition to Sweden. Her celebrity grew in North America as well—thanks in large part to promotional efforts by the American white nationalist record company Resistance Records—and for a short time she lived in the United States. Saga returned to Sweden in 2005 and, on the grounds that she would be given greater artistic control, recorded another album with Symphony of Sorrow. It was with this second recording, *Symphony of Hatred*, that Saga began developing a new persona that would accompany her rise to even greater heights of popularity.

The group's second recording featured a more complex musical and lyrical model than that of their first release, *Paradise Lost*. Here, the music oscillates from subdued sections to high-speed, explosive passages with screamed vocals. These two musical flavors typically bear contrasting textual themes, with lyrics to subdued sections voicing sorrow, dread, pessimism, and subjugation, and those to more energized and aggressive music calling for resistance, revolution, and even chauvinism and hatred.

Saga often restricts her singing to the former type of passage, leaving the hate lyrics to a screaming chorus composed of the other male band members. In such instances, she performs the role of sufferer; it is in aid of this victim that the chorus issues its call to action. The title track "Symphony of Hatred" offers the clearest example of this format:

Saga: A vortex of madness is torturing my mind,
layer on layer of lies deceiving our kind.
A flickering maze of pictures staring back at me,
people with fabricated smiles gloom in my TV.
My head is filled with sick lies—food for my brain.
No wonder the time's up, no wonder the world's insane!

Male Chorus: Hatred—are [*sic*] nourishing my body as my warrior soul
comes to life!
Hatred—are feeding my mind as I watch our people die!
Hatred—is the essence of survival, we need it to save our kind!
Hatred—don't be scared, hatred is our friend!

Saga: A vortex of madness is torturing my mind,
layer on layer of lies deceiving our kind.
A mouth is murmuring about money, health, and state.
Behind our backs, they're digging our kind's grave.

FIGURE 5.1 Banner for Saga's official website. Available online, accessed April 21, 2012, www.thisis-saga.com.

Here, Saga's artistic persona suffers psychological distress over the deception and betrayal of her kind, enduring mind-torture as the media fills her head with "sick lies." The phenomena she sings about are not external; not the concern of an abstract community. Rather, they manifest inside of her. She withdraws from any type of resistance by declaring "time's up" and calling the world "insane."

The male chorus sings from a different position. The political plight of their kind also inspires in them a personal, emotional response. However, that response is one of hatred rather than sorrow. And it is followed by calls to channel hatred in an effort to resolve the situation. In this sense, the individuals in the chorus do not share Saga's defeatism, nor are they implicated in any surrender on her part. They treat themselves and their listeners as actors in an ongoing, unsettled struggle for the survival of their kind. Saga is not part of the struggle; her suffering is rather evidence for its necessity.

Today, Saga represents many things to her fans. Her status as a sex symbol certainly saturates her own promotional efforts, such as in the slogan for her website shown in Figure 5.1, "Resistance Never Looked This Good." But in the years since her Skrewdriver tribute albums, Saga has enhanced the identity displayed in "Symphony of Hatred"—that of an individual exemplifying the suffering and sorrow of the white race, an individual who cries for help, but who, like an abstract community, must rely on the efforts of activists to survive.

"They Have Been Given a Gift": Gender Ideologies in Radical Nationalism

Saga's new artistic persona relies on conceptions of gender that are enjoying increased currency in radical nationalist Europe as skinheadism declines. This gender ideology is not new. Instead, those involved in producing and consuming Saga's music are embracing ultratraditional conceptions of femininity and masculinity that have shaped the thinking of nationalists in historically, geographically, and culturally diverse settings.

Nationalist imaginaries, in forms mainstream and deviant, often contain a series of conceptual paradoxes. Nationalism simultaneously advocates modernism and tradition, engagement abroad and seclusion at home, materialism and spirituality, rationalism and emotionalism (see chapter 1). These multiple dualisms (Nairn 1998) also tend to be gendered. Anne McClintock argues that gender difference has often been used to illustrate nationalism's temporal dualism, where "[w]omen are represented as the atavistic and authentic body of national tradition (inert, backward-looking, and natural), embodying nationalism's conservative principle of continuity. Men, by contrast, represent the progressive agent of national modernity (forward-thrusting, potent, and historic)" (1997:92). Partha Chatterjee, examining nationalism in colonial India, further emphasizes the role of gender in nationalist conceptions of place: while men roam the "outer," westernized world with its decadence and materialism, women should instead root themselves in the "inner" world of the home, preserving the spirituality and tradition that would define emerging eastern national cultures (1986, 1993). Associations with tradition, the home, spiritualism, and emotionalism have marked women as vessels of national essence in varied historical and geographic contexts.[6]

Radical race nationalists have adapted this table of gender relations to their own cause. Here, men's cosmopolitanism manifests via confrontation with ideological, cultural, or racial opponents in the public sphere, through democratic activism or militancy. Ideal women, on the other hand, are to avoid the public sphere, disengage from media and higher education—both driven by corrupting Marxist or Jewish forces—and commit themselves to building large, politically conscious, white families. Put another way, whereas men fight for the ethnonational people in public, in the "outer" world, women are to wage this battle in their homes and in their wombs.

Manifestations of this ideology vary. Nationalists may vilify women as the source of whites' demographic shrinkage. These discourses predominate both in the international scene and in the Nordic countries.[7] Norwegian Thorgrim Bredesen, cofounder of the paganist, ethnonationalist organization Vigrid, articulated this position to me during an interview:

You know those [white] women who get pregnant with a black guy? They should be thrown in jail. Because it's like, they have been given a gift. They've been given genes that have been passed down from generation to generation, hundreds of years, and they just destroy it. . . . You know how environmentalists talk about "nature is passed down," that we don't own it, and we don't get to, you know, do anything we want with it because it's not ours? I'm not an environmentalist, but it's kind of like that. Those genes belong to a lot of people, so you shouldn't get to just throw them away. They're not yours. (Interview, Thorgrim Bredesen, July 6, 2011)

Ethnonationalists like Bredesen would strip women of any transcendent ownership of the white race while simultaneously holding them responsible for maintaining racial hygiene.

Though at times nationalists think of women as agents of their people's decline, they may alternately regard women as the chief victims of multiculturalism. Typically, these claims center on sexual crimes committed by immigrant men against white Nordic women. Nationalists, from National Socialist militants to the moderate Sweden Democrats, tie Sweden's high rate of reported rapes—among the highest in Europe[8]—to the growth of the country's immigrant population. To support these claims they often cite a 2005 report from *Brottsförebyggande rådet* (the Swedish National Council for Crime Prevention). In the report's data, an individual born abroad is five times as likely to commit a sexual assault than an individual born in Sweden to two non-immigrant parents (2005:42).

Alternately, insiders ascribe a victim status to white women, not because women are under attack from immigrant men, but because political and cultural elites have allegedly engineered a culture that hinders them from maintaining an ultratraditional, race-conscious lifestyle. White nationalists throughout the globe train these criticisms on western society in general, and on Sweden in particular due to its status as a bastion of liberal gender politics. Throughout the late 1900s and early 2000s, Swedes have had more women in their government, a higher percentage of women in education, and more expressed support of gender equality among its wider population than any other country in the world (Inglehart and Norris 2003; Miles 2011). Alongside aspiring to provide women equal access to educational, political, and economic opportunities, Sweden has also been the site for more daring campaigns to disassemble the traditional gender binary. During the early twenty-first century, major toy retailers upended their advertising practices by depicting girls firing play guns and boys combing doll's hair; Stockholm's municipal government installed only gender-neutral bathrooms in public buildings; and leading national newspapers and children's authors began promoting the new Swedish gender-neutral pronoun *hen,* an alternative to the male *han* and the female *hon* (Milles 2008). *Hen* was originally intended for use when the gender of an individual was unknown, but sectors of this latest wave employ the term in place of all gender pronouns.

Though only some nationalists voice opposition to social equality between sexes, virtually all condemn recent attempts to deconstruct notions of "maculine" and "feminine" as fixed, distinct identities. For some activists, the erasing of gender is one manifestation of a broader liberal agenda promoting the notion that humans are essentially alike. Efforts to deny the existence of gender, according to these nationalists, reinforce the idea that all cultural, ethnic, or racial differences are illusory.

Nationalists also link the breakdown of gender identity in the Nordic countries to declining white birth rates. Paulina Forslund, writer and activist for the militant Nordic Resistance Movement, made such a claim when she spoke at one of her organization's meetings in May 2011:

> The union between men and women has always been a precondition to life. Nothing can be more important than that. Without the sexual drive, there will be no children. . . . Our race will die if more don't feel this energy. This vital energy is being gutted by an unnatural society that all, unfortunately, are forced to live in today. You all know what I'm talking about. A crooked society, where men are encouraged to be sensitive and feminine, and women should, from childhood, act more like men. It's not surprising that many women, though foolishly, chose immigrant men. The media depicts the foreign man as exotic, erotic, and masculine.[9]

In contrast with tendencies in American race nationalism (see Hodes 1997), Forslund focuses not on an alleged threat that nonwhite men pose to white women, but rather on progressive politics and the ways its emasculation of white men has led women to choose nonwhite sexual partners.

Despite the prominence of ultratraditional gender ideals in the scene, women have shaped nationalist activism in ways other than family building and home making. Female insiders have also rebelled against those ideologies that emphasize gender difference or restrict them to the private sphere, pursuing instead participation akin to that of their male counterparts. Women in parliamentary nationalist organizations have served as politicians. German-Swede Vera Oredsson, for example, was both a politician and leader of the Nordic Reich Party from 1975 to 1978—the first woman in Sweden to head an official political party. Alternately, women in militant circles have taken up arms alongside male activists. During the 1990s, a group of race nationalist women in Norway even created their own paramilitary unit called Valkyria.[10]

It was skinheadism, however, that offered radical nationalist women the most formalized alternative to ultratraditional gender roles. In the Nordic countries and beyond, men and women in the skinhead subculture adopted similar personas. The relatively gender-blind nature of skinheadism manifests in multiple domains. Like their male counterparts, female skinheads—or "skinbyrds"—donned combat boots, bomber jackets, and cropped or semicropped hairstyles. As mentioned at the beginning of this chapter, female and male skinhead musicians did not produce appreciably different sounds or stage appearances. And skinbyrds also participated in violent confrontation and demonstrations, cultivating an image of themselves as, in the words of Michael S. Kimmel, "kick-ass street-fighting 'women warriors'" (2004:xii).

In sum, two contrasting models of femininity have prevailed in radical race nationalism: the conservative mother-of-the-nation and the fiercely activist skinbyrd. Scholars have suggested that female insiders' ability to gain influence in the scene shifts based on which of these broad personas they align with. Women brandishing a more traditional image typically participate in race nationalist organizations by fostering a family-like ethos and by facilitating positive interaction among insiders and with outsiders—roles that sociologist Kathleen Blee calls "familial" and "social." Though vital to an organization's functioning, activists often conceptualize these as supportive, background roles. In contrast, women embracing skinhead or militaristic identities have had a greater chance of playing an "operative" role. Here, female insiders directly enact an organization's central method of activism and achieve formal and informal leadership positions (Blee 2004).

To the extent that skinheadism offered women in the Nordic countries a pathway toward increased agency, that opportunity diminished with the rise of New Nationalism. Reform targeted skinheadism regardless of its gender. However, agents of change have been generally uninterested in critiquing the mother-of-the-nation persona in nationalist activism, and some women in the scene today are treating this as an opportunity. In a reversal of the system observed by scholars like Blee, they seek influence by rallying behind ultratraditional gender identities—by performing and stylizing their distance from modernity, rationalism, and agency itself.

A Softer Song

> And though it's not your nature
> to stand against the throng, Let the Valkyrie ride
> by the white man's side and sing the racial song.
>
> American white nationalist David Lane

Music serves as a tool for nationalists looking to project ultratraditional gender identities. Though Saga has used music to this effect with the greatest sophistication, her style builds upon the work of other female acts in the scene, particularly those who abandoned punk and heavy metal. Foremost among these acts is the American girl duo Prussian Blue. The now-disbanded Prussian Blue consisted of twins Lamb and Lynx Gaede, who first performed together at the American white nationalist festival Euro-fest in 2001 (Davis 2009:16–18). Releasing three albums between 2004 and 2006, roughly half of their tracks are covers, while the other half are original material, typically backed by Lamb's acoustic guitar and Lynx's fiddle. Though Lamb and Lynx no longer perform, the model they established— that of two sisters singing to a light, acoustic accompaniment—was replicated by the duo Heritage Connection. The Arkansas-based teen sisters Charity and Shelby Pendergraf began playing in 2003, and like Prussian Blue, they play guitar and fiddle.

Europe lacks a major child act like Prussian Blue or Heritage Connection. However, a handful of solo female musicians began performing around the same time as the American girl duos. Italian Francesca Ortolani, also known as "Viking" and "Aufidena," started producing records in 2000 and is still active today. The former Sapienza University of Rome student often identifies as a fascist, and sets anti-Semitic lyrics to either solo acoustic guitar or a synthesized pop/classical accompaniment. While receiving less international and mainstream attention than Ortolani, Annett Müller gained relative fame in her native Germany, thanks in part to her connections with Germany's National Democratic Party. She began recording acoustic singer-songwriter pieces in 2001 with her husband Michael Müller, occasionally under the name Faktor Deutschland (Dornbusch and Raabe 2008:176).

In 1998, before Prussian Blue, Heritage Connection, Francesca Ortolani, or Faktor Deutschland started recording, producers at Midgård Records in Sweden released an album showcasing the solo singer Frigg. The recording was the first in a series called "Pro Patria." The music on *Pro Patria I* was not punk or hard rock, nor the acoustic troubadour style of Francesca Ortolani or Annett Müller; rather, it was light pop, featuring moderate tempos, muffled percussion, diverse instrumentation, and polished, non-screamed vocals. This recording seemed to serve Midgård's overarching goals at the time. As they recall it on their official website, "We wanted to reach more people with music and try new styles. Styles that were non-existent in [radical nationalist music]."[11]

The singer "Frigg"—a woman named Ulrica Pettersson from the Viking rock band Hel—did not produce the album. Despite the fact that her singing formed the project's focal point, she contributed only as a hired studio musician. Pettersson is not even the same woman as that pictured on the album cover shown in Figure 5.2. Instead, Joakim (Jocke) Karlsson and Nigel Brown—both prolific white power musicians—wrote and produced *Pro Patria I*. The album's ten songs speak to and praise male activists, celebrating "the sons of Sweden" and "free Swedish men."

FIGURE 5.2 Album cover for *Pro Patria I*, Midgård Records 1998.

The lyrics also lack the hate rhetoric of standard white power punk, though they do vilify "Zion's men" and borrow lines from writings by 1930s Nazi-sympathizers Per Engldahl and Sven-Olof Lindholm. Pettersson was skeptical of the lyrics when she began to record. The album's coproducer, Jocke Karlsson, described the recording session with Pettersson thusly in the online forum Nordisk.nu:

> She almost refused to sing anything that dealt with the fatherland, etc., so we had to lie about what Zionism is. I don't remember what we said, but I have some memory that we tricked her into thinking it was some kind of mystical spirit. We even had to quickly throw together a lie about who Lindholm and Engdahl were too. Hahaha.[12]

Sonic and visual depictions of femininity, in other words, were more important to the project's producers than actual female authorship. Frigg and *Pro Patria I* were largely the construction of two men. Nonetheless, with its softer sonic profile and milder lyrical content, the project introduced a new model that future female performers would develop.

Saga was one such performer. Her first use of the light pop accompaniment appeared in 2003 when she was featured on the final volume in Midgård's Pro Patria series, *Pro Patria III*. For this album, Saga borrowed the catchy guitar riffs, smooth synthesizer, and gentle lyrics from *Pro Patria I*, adding to this assembly R&B–style beats. She would later call this style "freedom pop."[13] *Pro Patria III* was a great commercial success for Saga and for Midgård. It was the highest-selling volume of the series, and a handful of tracks on the album, including "Valkyrie," "Yttrandefrihet" (Freedom of Speech), and "Drömarnas Stig" (The Path of Dreams) would retain their popularity among Scandinavian radical nationalists throughout the following decade.

Saga would briefly return to her punk and metal backing when she produced her second album with Symphony of Sorrow in 2005. But when she embarked on her first self-produced album in 2007, she embraced freedom pop. This later album, *On My Own*, would combine the instrumental character of the Pro Patria series and the rhetorical model she had cultivated with Symphony of Sorrow—a rhetorical model centered on Saga's personal suffering due to the struggles and declines of white people. The result of this mixture would be what is perhaps international white nationalism's most celebrated musical performance: Saga's recording of the song "Ode to a Dying People."

"Ode to a Dying People"

Eyes shining bright with unspilt tears,
Thinking about all these wasted years.
Everything worth living for is gone.
Brother, I find it hard to keep fighting on.
Falling down towards the abyss, the abyss.
The reaper embraces me with his kiss.
It makes me want to refuse to care (refuse to care).
To watch this all unfold—too much to bear.

(chorus)
If this is the way it ends,
if this is the way my race ends,
if this is the way it ends,
I can't bear to witness.

Disease encroaching on all I hold dear.
Somehow I gotta get my soul out of here.
Heart of agony, faint burning hope.
I'm finding it hard to try to cope.
Because liars own the world with conquering poise (with conquering poise),
in a wasteland of meaningless noise.

We don't stand a chance with dormant pride (with dormant pride).

The heroes of our race have already died.

(chorus)

To imagine it has all come down to this.

Apathy and suicidal bliss.

It's all over except for the crying.

With a whimper instead of the roar of a lion.

The greatest race to ever walk the earth,

dying a slow death with insane mirth.

The tomb has been prepared, our race betrayed (our race betrayed).

White man, fight the flight towards the grave.

(chorus)

Don't let it end this way!

Don't let it end this way!

Don't let it end this way!

I can't bear to witness.

Don't let it end this way!

Don't let it end this way!

Don't let it end this way!

I can't bear to witness.

Saga did not write "Ode to a Dying People." Her recording is a cover of the original written by Canadian George Burdi of the band RaHoWa (short for "racial holy war"). Somewhat the "Summertime" of contemporary white nationalist music, over twenty groups in multiple countries have covered the song. Saga's rendition, however, has been the most popular and is often mistaken to be the original. Her version may be the most listened-to white nationalist recording of any kind in recent history. Counting views of uploaded songs on the online video website YouTube is one of the only available methods for tracking consumption of radical nationalist music. And combined, uploads of Saga's "Ode to a Dying People" on YouTube have passed one and a half million views, a number far beyond not only other covers but also any other white nationalist song on the website.

Fans—mostly men—describe the recording as having been particularly inspirational, claiming that it "changed their life" or that it has "something religious about it."[14] Frequently, these individuals link the track's emotional charge to Saga's gender. Facebook user Matthew Bostdorf, for example, wrote the following on Saga's official fan page on November 4, 2011:

Saga, I heard your version of "Ode To A Dying People" for the first time recently. I caught on to it and played it again. This time it really started to sink in. My throat tightened and eyes started to swell (it's touching!) Then my wife and two boys walked in behind me. She looked at me and asked "honey, what's wrong?" Gabe looks up and asked "daddy why are you sad?" I couldn't speak! I shrugged my shoulders, shook my head and hit play again! Now, my wife thinks she should monitor my listening time. No way[.] You have the power men dread most! The ability to penetrate our chests and pierce our hearts to the core and make us cry. You could conquer the world! All Hail Queen Saga!![15]

Throughout my research, I heard various accounts of the song's provenance. The most common explanation holds that George Burdi, the song's author, wrote the piece after witnessing a romantic relationship between two whites implode due to domestic violence. Subsequently, this event led Burdi to reflect upon the declining birth rates among whites—upon the fact that whites are a "dying people." Burdi, however, offered a different explanation to me during an interview. He instead ties the song to his personal struggles surrounding his conviction and incarceration for assault—experiences that would eventually prompt his exit from white nationalism. He recalled:

I wrote "Ode to Dying People" in the winter of 1995 while in the middle of a legal battle. I got out on appeal after serving a month in jail for an assault charge. At this point I'd been in the movement about seven years. I was alone, it was about 2 a.m., and it was just me and my guitar and a pack of cigarettes.

In many ways it's ironic that the song "Ode to a Dying People" has become as popular as it has because in reality it was my farewell to the movement. It was . . . in many ways my admission that I couldn't continue with my activities of the previous decade, but I was tired and I was ready to leave. (Interview, George Burdi, April 3, 2012)

Burdi's performance of the song is sober, with a slow tempo, solo guitar accompaniment, and vocals sung in the depths of his register. The song maintains this structural profile throughout, thus exemplifying those characteristics Les Back writes of when he likened Burdi and Rahowa to the English rock band Pink Floyd (2002:111). But despite the subdued nature of his performance, Burdi insisted that the song does not express defeat, saying,

the last lyric of the song is "don't let it end this way," which despite all the lamenting and desperation is ultimately a message of hope. (Interview, George Burdi, April 3, 2012)

FIGURE 5.3 Transcription of vocal melody line from the chorus of "Ode to a Dying People." Top line: Saga's version. Bottom line: George Burdi's original version. Burdi's melody has been transposed up a perfect fourth to facilitate comparison.

Saga abandons the sparseness and static dynamics of Burdi's original. Her version combines acoustic guitar, bass, trap set, and synthesizer cellos, and uses these forces to power a large-scale dynamic curve peaking at the lines, "The greatest race to ever walk the Earth," in addition to more localized dynamic shifts. Her alterations to the melody are shown in Figure 5.3. Reflecting the prominence of Saga's recording, most covers of "Ode to a Dying People" after 2007 use her melodic variants.[16] But Saga's expressive rendition of the text—her ability to capitalize on lyrical ambiguities to create alternate meanings—is the most striking difference between her version and all others.

The song's lyrics deal with the alleged impending death of the white race, and in Saga's rendition, they offer little in the way of consolation. The approaching disease, the agony, the liars, the meaningless noise, the dormant pride, the whimpers, the apathy, the flight toward the grave—how does the singer respond to this? "I can't bear to witness." Saga colors this response musically to frame it as an exasperated, defeated nonresponse, one that retreats from potential collective action into solitary escape. The verse melody begins at the bottom of her register. The dynamic level rises with the melody, climaxing at the onset of the chorus, and the line, "If this is the way it ends." The percussion aids this development through diminutions that continue through the first two verses and choruses. These forces build expectation for a statement of resilience in the chorus, a call to resistance, an expression of hope or encouragement. Her alterations to the melody in the chorus, which avoid Burdi's resolving descent to the tonic, reinforce this tension. But with her dynamic level falling and her voice turning thin, she delivers the line, "I can't bear to witness," and the buildup dissolves.

Saga's rendition of "Ode to a Dying People" becomes a performance of emotionality and fragility in ways Burdi's is not. And in a section toward the end of the song, she extends this performance through imitations of crying and by calling directly for outside intervention. She delivers the lines, "Don't let it end this way, I can't bear to witness," in an anxious, urgent tone interspersed with sighs and gasps for air. She pleads for intervention. And on the penultimate statement of the line, "Don't let it end this way," she opens into a sharp, arching melodic flourish suggestive of a shriek. Her rendition of these lyrics does not deliver the "message of hope" that Burdi imagined. Here, Saga sends a cry of pain into nothingness.

The key features of Saga's performance—her musical displays of suffering, alienation, and dependency—have been used to advance nationalist gender ideologies elsewhere. These same musical elements are common in lamentation practice—ritual songs of sorrow sung often at funerals. Among the characteristics of lamentation, scholars like Greg Urban, Steven Feld, and Aaron Fox name (1) imitations of crying and (2) the use of dialogic rhetoric in lament texts without the presence of an actual addressee (Urban 1988:386; Feld and Fox 1994). Singers may imitate crying through vaulted melodic lines, trembling, wavy pitch, and stylized gasps for air. And lament texts may speak directly to the deceased, or they may cry to the community at large, the lack of a response to their pleas and questions marking either the deceased's absence or augmenting the lamenter's display of solitude and despair.

Studies of disparate lamentation traditions have interpreted ritual wailing as a form of resistance, a practice, for example, that allows singers to publicly criticize society and control interpretations of death (Caraveli 1986; Briggs 1992; Wilce 1998). However, the combined emotionality and social detachment exhibited in practices like lamentation has also supported patriarchal gender identities, including gender identities in nationalist movements. In those instances where women typically perform laments, the musical display of emotionality may reinforce ideologies that bar them from rationalism and relegate them to the domain of premodern tradition. Anthropologist Sascha Goluboff, for example, argued that performances of sorrow in funeral laments in the eastern Caucasus helped establish women as emotional rather than rational, as removed from modern society and the public sphere, and that men in turn used these designations to justify women's role as bearers of tradition (2008).

Saga enlists musical features common in lamentation—stylized crying and unanswered dialogical rhetoric—to perform sorrow and dependency. By internalizing and personalizing the impact of large-scale demographic transformations, she positions herself as, if not a manifestation of the white race, then as a being that bears the race's collective fate. As a representative of this population, her pain and fears depict the white race as a people defined by its vulnerability. Putting a stop to her pain entails saving the white race from decline and death.

In further parallel with lament practices in nationalist contexts, Saga's male fans seem to regard the defining features of her performance as distinctly feminine—so much so that they avoid rendering "Ode to a Dying People" as she does. Male nationalists' reluctance to reproduce her interpretation of the song becomes apparent during her concerts. Typically, attendees at radical race nationalist concerts participate by exchanging right-arm *Sieg Heil*! salutes with performers and by singing along with the music. Audience behavior at Saga's shows often follows this same model. However, her fans appear to modify their singing when she performs her more recent material.

At a concert in London on November 8, 2009, Saga sang "Ode to a Dying People" to a small but enthusiastic crowd of nearly a hundred. The predominately male skinhead audience knew the song and her version of it well, and they sang to her melody throughout the performance. Despite this, the crowd and Saga were not singing the same thing, and the divide was particularly evident during choruses. Saga's live performance matched that on her studio recording, where she moves from a full-voiced, loud dynamic and bold character at the beginning of the chorus and the line, "If this is the way it ends," to an abrupt, fading retreat at the onset of the line, "I can't bear to witness." The audience at this concert rendered the chorus in opposite fashion. Shouting as much as singing, their dynamic level is relatively static throughout the chorus. But audience members increase, rather than decrease, their volume at the line, "I can't bear to witness." Further, they deliver that line with emphases on the words "I" and "bear."[17]

Audience members' dynamic rise could be a response to Saga's corresponding dynamic drop—it is an opportune moment for them to showcase their presence. Additionally, their emphases on the words "I" and "bear" could stem from relationships between text and meter in the song. These words fall on beats one and two, whereas the preceding and following words are syncopated and don't fall on beats three or four. But a similar metric and textual relationship occurs at the start of earlier lines in the chorus, and the audience does not perform the same articulation there.

Rather, audience members and Saga have chosen to express different sentiments in their performance of the line, "I can't bear to witness." Whereas Saga articulates defeat and sorrow, the sentiment I hear from the audience is one of anger, of contemptuous disgust with white decline. Similar dynamics between Saga and her audiences occurred during other performances of this song, such as that at the Nordic Festival (*Nordiska festivalen*) in Sweden in 2007. Further, covers of "Ode to a Dying People" with male singers—covers that adopt Saga's melodic variations—also reverse her dynamic progression in the chorus.[18] The ambiguity of the song's lyrics accommodates these dueling renditions, allowing for a (masculine) performance of revulsion and a (feminine) performance of despair.

Sounds of Oppression, Imperatives of Suffering

I do not experience the real-life Saga as a helpless victim; I see her rather as the opposite. She has a bold, assertive personality, and she commands attention both on stage and in private social settings. Her career within radical nationalism has been one of eminence. She has gained creative liberties often denied to female insiders, and her albums almost singlehandedly sustained a major record label. Perhaps with these achievements in mind, Saga claims to be uninterested in portraying herself as weak and victimized. Though she does hear herself as crying at the end of "Ode to a Dying People," she is otherwise ambivalent about my analyses of her songs. Saga claims that the character of her recent work derives simply from her attempts to render all lyrics more expressively, to sing with "feeling" regardless of what message a song delivers. When I asked her whether or not her music had an overriding agenda or concept, she responded:

> What I want is for people to listen to my music and go, "Oh, she feels the same. I'm not alone." My music should be an option for normal people who feel that there is something wrong, but they don't have to go out and get punched in the nose for it. (Interview, Saga, July 28, 2011)

With her music, she wants listeners to be able to identify with her, and further, to give them a means of engaging with nationalist ideas outside of street activism.

Male insiders' experiences of Saga do not always follow her intended program, however. Their commentary on her music tends to frame Saga not as a participant fighting alongside male activists, nor as a voice articulating their unarticulated grievances, but rather as a manifestation of the national people, a symbol whose existence provides inspiration for action.[19] Canadian white nationalist George Burdi, author of the song "Ode to a Dying People," described Saga in these terms:

> For many in the movement, her beauty is the ideal they are fighting for. Being that there is a dearth of women in the movement, Saga's male fans can live vicariously through her music, and she becomes the female urging them on, supporting them through their struggle. She is their Helen of Troy. (Interview, George Burdi, April 2, 2012)

Dennis, Saga's boyfriend and former bodyguard, echoed this same sentiment when he reflected on audiences' reaction to her.

> Everybody says [she is] the Valkyrie and stuff like that . . . I mean you can look at her—you can stand a six-year-old blond girl or boy there, it would be the same effect. It would be like—ok, I fight for that. . . . I do it for the kids and the girls. Men don't do that for themselves, men do that for children and girls. (Interview, Dennis and Saga, April 11, 2012)

Like Burdi, Dennis draws from mythological imagery (here the riding female Valkyrie deities from Norse mythology) to describe Saga as a godlike icon of the nationalist cause, a euhemerized figurehead towering above an army of activists. Both men also exclude her from participating in the activities of male insiders. Dennis develops this thinking by simultaneously elevating women like Saga to the status of icons while likening their agency in the scene to that of children. Though women and children provide inspiration, only adult males are positioned to "fight" for the nationalist cause.

Statements like these reinforce Saga's image as both an embodiment of the national people and as victimized and dependent. Bearing both of these associations, Saga symbolizes a subjugated white population. Indeed, insiders use the discourses surrounding her music as an arena to discuss the oppression of the people they fight for. User "David T. Baldursson," for example, wrote the following on Saga's Facebook fan page on March 1, 2011:

[W]e need Saga in all our countries as her voice is one of pride and survival. We are all facing the same danger: White Genocide. Our people are still too weak and blind to see what really is going on. Saga's voice is waking us up and motivating our folk to stand up. Saga is the embodiment of our pride and purity and should be heard in all our lands.[20]

Baldursson declares Saga a manifestation of the white race, and combines this characterization with a general discussion of white victimization. Other nationalists draw a direct link between Saga's perceived hardship and that of nationalists and the white population at large. Her most notorious fan, Norwegian terrorist Anders Behring Breivik, describes Saga thusly in his manifesto. He writes:

Marxist and multiculturalist character-assassins will claim that Saga is an evil, national-socialist monsterband from hell, due to her success . . . Saga and similar patriotic heroes and heroines of Scandinavia . . . had to face political persecution and demonization for years. Yet they continue their brave struggle to prevent the demographical and cultural genocide of the Scandinavian and European tribes. (2011:847)

Here, Saga's alleged persecution provides Breivik a platform to discuss the unjust treatment of nationalists more generally. And though he concludes his section on Saga by emphasizing her resilience, he, like other nationalists quoted above, presents her as being external to his struggle, writing:

Instead of "physical" revolutionary or democratic resistance, she fights through her music by inspiring the best in us. (ibid.)

Combined, the quotes above from Dennis, Baldursson, Burdi, Breivik, and others depict Saga as encapsulating the physical appearance, the blood, and the population they champion. Additionally, insiders tend to highlight her victimization, and treat it as an opportunity to talk about the marginalization of nationalists, the threats to white pride, and threats to the white race. Saga's music encourages these kinds of interpretations. Pieces like "Symphony of Sorrow" and "Ode to a Dying People" paint her as an entity suffering for the wider white populations' hardships—one with no political agency, no effective means of helping herself. This identity channels gender stereotypes long established in diverse forms of nationalism—stereotypes that imagine women as bearers or embodiments of national essence due in part to their separation from the public sphere, cosmopolitanism, and modernity. But Saga's performance also serves emerging radical-nationalist programs. She supplies vivid expression of a key precondition for the politics of defiant white self-love: she makes a unified, oppressed, and threatened white race audible. And by presenting her suffering as urgent and unresolved, Saga leaves her listeners at a crossroads. The choice of whether and how to respond to her cries is left to them. A response can be made musically—as it was in the song "Symphony of Hatred"—by a chorus of men screaming to save their kind. Or, as activists like Burdi, Baldursson, Dennis, and Breivik imply, responses may come outside of the musical domain.

6

NEW NATIONALISM AND

THE DECLINE OF MUSIC

> The core of Swedishness isn't only barbarism,
> but barbarism is there—you're right about that,
> Prime Minister Reinfeldt. And we will awaken it!
> You shall witness an original Swedish barbarism
> more terrifying than anything in history [cheers,
> shouting]. And barbarians, we will set out in our
> streets and squares, through our cities and our
> countryside. And our enemies will tremble. And
> when the storm has finally settled, we won't need
> to sing about the great days of old; we are going
> to live in them! In a Swedish Sweden—because
> Sweden will remain Swedish! *Sieg Heil!* [*Sieg Heil!*]
> *Sieg Heil!* [*Sieg Heil!*] *Sieg Heil!* [*Sieg Heil!*].[1]

AT THE CONCLUSION of his electrifying speech during the People's March gathering on June 6, 2008, Magnus Söderman foretold a future where fringe nationalists achieve their utmost aspirations. At this event, which would be canceled the following year, Söderman spoke to a community of semimilitant activists that was shrinking, and on behalf of a National Socialist organization—the Nordic Resistance Movement—that he would soon leave. Nonetheless, his speech radiated optimism. His rhetoric and cadences were virtuosic, his tone almost manic. Reveling in then Swedish Prime Minister Fredrik Reinfeldt's offhand statement that "the core of Swedishness is only barbarism,"[2] Söderman prophesized a violent revolution where nationalists would drive their enemies from Sweden's borders. With this victory, he said, they would escape their perpetual stasis, victimhood, and ineffectuality to forge the society of their dreams. Or, as he chose to express it, nationalists would progress from mere "singing" to "living."[3]

The preceding chapters in this book explored the ways nationalists have used new music to pursue their campaigns of reform. Music helped these actors imagine themselves as anti-imperialists, as respectable members of mainstream society, as champions of a folkloric national distinctiveness, as defenders of the oppressed, and above all as non-skinheads. But while New Nationalism has diversified activists' stylistic output, it also spurred an overall decline in musical activity throughout the scene—from identitarians and cultural nationalists to National Socialists like Söderman quoted above. While some use rap, reggae, folk music, and freedom pop to portray themselves as reformed, most are crafting their new identities by declaring disinterest in music as a political tool.

Since the fall of skinheadism, there have never been as many nationalist record labels, bands, or concertgoers. If the Nordic nationalist scene once existed as a musical community—that is, as "a collectivity constructed through and sustained by musical processes" (Shelemay 2011:364)—this is no longer true. Some antecedents to this shift are obvious. Changes in hate speech laws and the rise of online downloading during the late 1990s shackled white nationalist music industries throughout Western Europe and the United States (Dyck 2012). Additionally, nationalist publishing houses, newspapers, and political parties grew to supplant record sales as a source of income.[4] But legal reforms, shifting habits of music consumption, and the emergence of alternative funding sources alone cannot explain the crash of the Nordic countries' nationalist music culture.

In this chapter, I trace the social, ideological, and methodological forces leading insiders to declare investment in music unimportant or dangerous to their cause. My focus is again on discourse, and even in this instance it is a discourse about music with its own characteristics and patterns. Many of the conversations I analyze here address music at large without explicit consideration of the ways styles and traditions may vary. A critical analysis can deconstruct this ostensible universalism, of course. We will see, for example, that insiders' discussions refer more to their own dominant genres of white power and Viking rock, while folk music is often excluded from their generalizations. However, internal inconsistencies and contingencies of this kind do not stop activists from describing music in all-encompassing terms.

The phenomena I investigate in this chapter belong to a broader social and political transformation occurring throughout the west. Nordic radical nationalists' waning investment in music co-occurs with a dwindling of various musical youth subcultures during the late twentieth century. Like punk, metal, rave, and hip-hop scenes, early Nordic radical nationalism was largely a class-based youth collectivity that criticized and resisted sociocultural norms through style and ritual (Hebdige 1979; Brake 1985). While these subcultures transformed youth social behavior, their ability to advance a political cause ultimately seemed insufficient to many participants as well as to their cheerleaders in academia (Weinzierl and Muggleton 2003).

Scholars of oppositional subcultures suggest that these movements' extensive investment in style—be it fashion, music, or art—contributed to their political impotence. Anthropologist Dylan Clark and political theorist Oliver Marchart offer contrasting but complementary expositions of this point. Clark argues that political activism pursued primarily through expressive culture is susceptible to appropriation, decontextualization, and eventually neutralization by its opponents. His analysis focuses on the punk scene, and how its music and fashion were commodified by the same consumer-capitalist forces that punks claimed to fight. Eventually sold back to youths as one of many domesticated cultural options, punk style no longer could shock the mainstream, and therefore could not pursue its political agenda (Clark 2008). Marchart goes a step further than Clark, arguing that "protest through style"—whether appropriated by the mainstream or not—is unable to articulate a comprehensive political platform due to the limitations of the media of expression themselves. He argues that such campaigning

> cannot reasonably be called political "protest" . . . as it lacks any spelled-out political agenda and does not raise any explicit political demands—in other words . . . it remains largely unclear who is protesting against what and why in the first place. (2012:225–26)

Marchart implies that the stylistic medium is problematic, not because it can easily be detached from its social context and intended meaning, but because it fails to detail a compelling political platform.[5]

Both Clark and Marchart suggest that politics conducted via style is not "actual" politics. Statements made through style do not pose a compelling threat to political opponents, nor can expressive culture accommodate the level of specificity needed to establish broad political mobilization in a complex society. Subcultures relying on expressive culture to voice their resistance are doomed to become functionally apolitical. While scholars like Wood (2000) and Anderson (2009) emphasize that subcultures are persistently undermined by in-group schisms and generational turnover, Clark and Marchart assert that these movements will necessarily frustrate and disappoint politically ambitious insiders. Indeed, Clark argues that it was only when later generations of punks shifted the medium of their activities from style to street demonstrations, occupations, and boycotts—to genuine protest—that they regained the ability to antagonize. Relinquishing their investment in music and fashion made them a post-subculture whose actions are not as easily appropriated and neutralized, an "articulated" movement where "the threatening pose has been replaced with the actual threat" (Clark 2008:234). Marchart adds that by evolving beyond a model of protest through style, former subcultures gain greater potential to form alliances with other movements. This prompts them to formulate their agenda in terms that stretch beyond the interests of their narrow demographic—to "mature" by transforming into a more universal, and therefore politically formidable, cause (2012).

At first glance, Clark's and Marchart's theories may appear unsuited to describing early radical nationalism. Relative to metal, punk, or rave communities, nationalist skinheads presented detailed political grievances and desired reforms, albeit most often through music. The broader nationalist scene also included multiple organizations officially committed to parliamentary activism. But the messaging in white power music and Viking rock was vague and unrealistic in its ambitions. Further, political parties—like the Nordic Reich Party, National Socialist Front, or Vigrid—often functioned as, if not youth subcultures per se, then as insular interest groups. Their declared aspirations for mass appeal appeared insincere, with few participants showing interest in escaping social marginalization. This was even true of the early Sweden Democrats. Current parliamentarian Richard Jomshof recalled of the organization during its first years, "it sometimes felt more like a social club than a political party" (cited in Leandersson 2008:181). Former party member Tommy Funebo similarly remarked, "the older generation saw the Sweden Democrats as an end in itself, it almost felt like a kind of religious phenomenon" (cited in Ekman and Poohl 2010:341).

Many reformist nationalists contend that heavy investment in music helped cultivate the scene's problematic social habits and political impotence. Like subculturalism scholars Clark and Marchart, these activists consider music an obstacle in the pursuit of real political action—be it genuine parliamentary advance or revolution[6]—and accordingly regard downplaying the artform as a step in the "articulation" or "maturation" of their cause. But music's negative impact on the nationalist scene diverges from that of other subcultures. Nordic radical nationalists faced little danger of having their primary instruments of protest—white power music and Viking rock—co-opted and neutralized by the mainstream. While music's inability to enact compelling political action subjected punk subculture to outside appropriation, its primary harm to the nationalist scene would instead be felt internally.

The nationalist voices I present here characterize music as a source of social and intellectual aimlessness—as, in the words of Jacques Attali, "a refuge for residual irrationality" in a rationalizing world (1985:6). They deem the expressive form irrational in two senses. First, they claim that music leads insiders to stray from their declared political values and ideals. Second, they characterize it as an emotional phenomenon disconnected from intellectual activity. Both irrationalities—one of disorder and deviance, the other of emotion and passion—prompt reformist nationalists to reject music. Because the expressive form associates activists with a wide variety of values and identities, it jeopardizes efforts to project a clear and consistent image. Further, as an allegedly passion-based endeavor, music cannot support the particular image most New Nationalists seek—that of erudition and professionalism.

In the following pages I examine these two conceptions of irrationality and their relationship to music's decline in the scene. But I will first introduce us to the transition from an old, musical nationalism to a new, nonmusical nationalism by profiling a veteran insider who lived it.

Wither Music

I first met Anna Svensson at a Stockholm bar during the summer of 2013. She walked into the murky establishment late in the evening after her friend Daniel Friberg and I had spent hours drinking and chatting. Like Daniel, Anna is an identitarian, and she is an increasingly prominent writer on the blog portal Motpol. Little about our introduction could have revealed her politics to me, however. For while Daniel and I had been fraternizing, she had been attending a concert in Stockholm's largest arena featuring Barbadian American pop megastar Rihanna.

The apparent mismatch between Anna's choice of leisure activity and her declared political views puzzled me. Well aware that Nordic nationalists patronized a wide range of music styles (see chapter 3), I was nonetheless shocked by her inclination to participate in this mass spectacle—an event seemingly the musical and social epitome of everything nationalists, and identitarians in particular, rage against. The mixed-race performer Rihanna combines risqué lyrics, highly produced R & B and hip-hop instrumental backings, and raunchy stage performances in her shows. She and her music seemed far too commercial, too decadent, too black, or—conversely—too rootless to resonate with any form of Nordic radical nationalism. And indeed Anna would not try to reconcile her musical taste and ideology. For when I expressed my confusion to her a year later, she nonchalantly acknowledged and dismissed the issue, remarking, "Ah, for me, music is just entertainment."

It hasn't always been that way. Anna is one of many contemporary activists whose strategic and ideological investment in music has declined. Her career moved from National Socialist groupuscules into the core of reformed radical nationalism. In the process, music went from being a central to a peripheral concern in her activism.

Anna entered radical nationalism via subcultural and highly musical activist circles in late 1990s Stockholm. She recalls:

> I started hanging out with other nationalists through an older female friend who got into that stuff when she was 14 years old and a punk. I was 15 or 16 when I started to go with her and her friends to concerts and stuff. (Interview, Anna Svensson, November 8, 2014)

Anna's circle of nationalist friends coalesced around the online magazine Info14.[7] The magazine was closely associated with American-inspired neo-Nazi organizations, and was among those forces contesting the rise of the Nordic League, identitarianism, and Daniel Friberg.

She and a female friend would also wade into the nationalist music scene. Singing together as a duo, and with an instrumental backing provided by members of metal group Fyrdung, they called themselves Asynja—after a collectivity of female goddesses in the Old Norse mythological pantheon. They began recording in 2005, and in step with the character of their nationalist faction, Asynja's lyrics were unabashedly race-nationalist, occasionally borrowing from the writings of American militant neo-Nazi David Lane.

While fully entrenched in the dominant culture of turn-of-the-century radical nationalism, Anna nonetheless regarded herself an outsider in her own faction. As Nordic ethnonationalists began to divide between National Socialists and identitarians, she occasionally found herself drawn in both directions—socially to the former, and ideologically to the latter. She had a burgeoning interest in journalism, and this led her to write for the National Socialist site Info14 as well as print and online publications produced by the increasingly identitarian Nordic Press. For example, Anna authored articles for the Press-affiliated magazine *Nordic Freedom* (*Nordisk Frihet*) in 2004, and briefly had a blog on Motpol when it opened in 2006.

After making this initial foray into the identitarian world, however, ideological and social pressures led her to recoil. She explains:

> I quit with that because Motpol seemed obscure at the time. It felt like it was full of bizarre esoterics. Plus, my crowd disliked basically everything about the whole "new intellectualism." (ibid.)

Anna rebounded from her brief involvement with identitarianism by investing more heavily in the activist forms of her original faction. She provided backup vocals on multiple white-power recordings, and her band Asynja released its first full-length album in 2007. During the years surrounding this release, Anna went on concert tours throughout Sweden and Germany—the bulk of which were patronized by race-nationalist skinheads.

Though Asynja was well received in skinhead circles, the band emerged as the Viking rock and white-power music industry in the Nordic countries began to crumble (see chapter 1). White power's downfall in the Nordic countries would eventually reach Anna when her band's label, Nordvind Records, folded in 2009. As broader industry trends inhibited her music making, she also began to lose interest in this activism. She experienced her tours with Asynja as exciting, but also taxing due to the boorish nature of the communities at her shows and the unrefined conditions under which they traveled. Further, she grew to regard these music-centered efforts as unproductive from an activist standpoint, and recalls:

> [I]t felt like nothing was developing, people were ideologically unaware, it was mostly vulgar slurs and strange ideas, it felt counterproductive and very consensus-driven. (ibid.)

Anna abandoned formal activism. She never recanted on her political ideals, but she felt that the nationalist scene as it existed offered no avenues through which she could express herself faithfully.

While no longer connected with any organization or group, Anna maintained her extensive circle of friends in the scene. By 2011, she had come into contact with Daniel Friberg, whose identitarian initiatives were increasingly untethered from the ethnonationalist establishment and ascendant amid the music industry's downturn (see chapter 2). The reformism of his projects carried more appeal to her at this time than they did earlier. Without the social pressure to mobilize against identitarianism, she claims to have been able to assess the school more honestly. And what she found appeared the ideal alternative to the nationalism she had grown up in. Anna explained:

> Identitarianism has a real intellectual and philosophical foundation. It wasn't a bunch of angry skinheads who established the *Nouvelle Droite*, but French academics who relied on philosophical training. It is a much more interesting milieu if you are interested in philosophy, intellectual history, and political discussion. (ibid.)

She began attending identitarian events in 2012, and by 2013 had revived her earlier blog on Motpol. Alongside her migration from establishment to reformist circles, her medium of activism shifted from music to political writing.

While she does not regret her earlier activism, she blames the musical practices of early radical nationalism for perpetuating ignorance, social isolation, and political ineffectuality. Contemporary activists throughout the scene are turning away from music for these same reasons.

Irrationality I: Deviance and Disorder

> Virtually everything about music . . . possesses a distinctly real potential for subversion, however modest, of the status quo, and everyone knows it. To nail down, measure, and hence to control music's potential for subversiveness requires a great deal of effort.
>
> (LEPPERT 2005:102)

When Anna Svensson characterized music as "just entertainment," she was juxtaposing the artform with "politics," implying that any engagement with ideas and identities through music does not qualify as genuine political action. As listeners, she suggested, individuals are free to traffic in a plurality of identities and agendas, trusting that exposure to this material will have little lasting impact on themselves or their cause. A nationalist, in other words, can enjoy music she deems hostile to her values and still be a good nationalist.

Svensson's thinking is hardly eccentric. Instead, it resonates with widely held sentiments in western society condemning the effort to align music and politics as both distasteful and inauspicious (Bohlman 2011). Attempts to politicize musical behavior conflict with ideologies of free expression and notions that musical preference is an involuntary phenomenon. And by asserting the artform's political neutrality, activists imply that they hold no responsibility for messages in the music they produce or consume. They give themselves license to engage with a limitless variety of identities and agendas in music, making it likely that when we peer into their musical lives we will find, not a reflection of a coherent political platform, but rather a chaos of contradictory agendas, claims, and values.

As a purveyor of deviance and disorder, music becomes a potential threat to political campaigning—especially when those who do not find political significance in music share space with those who do. Activists committed to crafting, projecting, and maintaining particular images of their cause risk seeing those efforts thwarted by listeners' and artists' erratic musical engagements. Indeed, while music has helped unify the Nordic nationalist scene and focus its activism throughout the past decades, it has also perpetuated social and ideological rule-breaking.

Like their ideals, nationalists' understanding of deviance shifts considerably across time and among factions. Depending on the context, chief offenses can range from cooperation with Jews, Marxists, or Islamicists to celebration of prereformist nationalism in form of open anti-Semitism, violence, or skinheadism. Nationalist music has agitated many such taboos. Early white-power music seldom confined its messaging to accepted dogmas. For example, some National Socialist activists felt their Holocaust revisionism and claims to chivalry were sabotaged by music that celebrated mass murder of Jews during World War II or petty assaults on contemporary immigrant groups. Accusations of a mismatch between declared ideology and song lyrics frequently surfaced in the white-power music magazine *Nordland* during the late 1990s. The following published letter, from an anonymous reader, is representative of the criticisms directed toward the white-power music establishment:

You often read in your newspaper that National Socialism is the one and only healthy ideology, that you fight for a harmonious society and that it is

Zionist-owned media that portray you as violent soccer hooligans and that you don't support race-based hatred. That isn't exactly the understanding one gets when you listen to recordings that *Nordland* sells.... Pluton Svea [sings] about race-based hatred quite a bit and praises the holocaust. It is funny to celebrate something that never happened. (1997, no. 9)

For this reader, white power music perpetuated counterproductive, violent behavior while also endorsing mainstream understandings of the Holocaust's historicity.

Nordland's editors frequently asserted that the Holocaust had never taken place. But they nonetheless defended selling and promoting music voicing the opposite stance. They wrote in response to the anonymous reader:

You should not treat music as political propaganda that always is 100% correct. We must remember that even the artistic part remains in music. (1997, no. 9)

The editors here ask listeners to permit the expressive form freedom to follow its own creative paths, implying that what is "artistic" cannot be confined to political creeds.

While music occasionally subverted the hardline positions of National Socialists, it also frustrated nationalists' later attempts to project a more refined image of themselves. Cultural nationalists' and identitarians' persistent attraction to race-nationalist or hooliganistic music compromised their claims to moderation and sophistication. This has been especially true for the Sweden Democrats. The party's leadership has maintained an unofficial prohibition of music voicing racial or ethnonationalism, anti-Semitism, or violence at its events since the late 1990s. Such music, while violating the Sweden Democrats' declared ideological platform, also links the party to its skinhead past and thereby sabotages its claims to have reformed itself.

Leaders have never specified which music may and may not be used at their events, but an episode in January 2009 helped illuminate this boundary. Then, two undercover reporters infiltrated a gathering of Sweden Democrats on a ferry from Stockholm to Tallinn. The infiltrators filmed both leaders and rank-and-file members drinking alcohol and singing songs by two ethnonationalist acts: Fyrdung and Svensk Ungdom.[8] One leading politician on the ferry was filmed singing Svensk Ungdom's song "Sweden Has Fallen" (*Sverige har fallit*) from memory—a song whose plain anti-Semitism conflicts with the Sweden Democrats' official ideology. One of the verses describes an apparent Jew thusly:

You'll find him hard at work, profiteering and bargaining
our cosmopolitan[9] can talk shit!
With his snout in the air, he sniffs his way forward,

> through bazaars and entertainment and glam.
> But he goes on the attack, and you're paralyzed,
> he always gets his way.
> He spits on all honor and he snorts at morality,
> he is greedy, deceitful, and slick.

When confronted by journalists after the tapes were exposed, the politicians claimed to have sung the songs with a sense of irony. They further asserted that many party members had a general interest in provocative, political songs, and that they also tend to sing the communist "International" at private gatherings (*Sydsvenskan*, April 7, 2012). But given the party's history, the episode stoked speculation that the Sweden Democrats' overtures to cultural nationalism were nothing but a public façade—that through music they were revealing their true ethnonationalist selves.

Leading Sweden Democrat Mattias Karlsson told me he was deeply disappointed in his colleagues on the ferry, but he does not believe their behavior reflects a hidden ideology. He explained:

> I think that for some in Sweden it can be like—there has never been a cultural nationalist subculture that has been nearly as strong as the race nationalist. Since Ultima Thule, not much has happened. . . . And since the rest of society, to such a small extent—in popular culture—sings about themes that can in any way speak to nationalists—history, tradition, solidarity—then I can absolutely imagine that certain cultural nationalists have listened to individual songs that you don't think are the most radical, but instead sing about pride for the country, or some part of history. You think like, "I don't like the band, but this song is actually pretty good." (Interview, Mattias Karlsson, April 9, 2012)

Karlsson here attempted to defend those instances when cultural nationalists venture beyond their declared ideological home via music. However, his comments suggest that music poses a constant threat to the Sweden Democrats. Lacking a sensational subculture that corresponds to their particular brand of nationalism, these moderates will often find themselves seduced by ethnonationalist song.

Party members' musical tastes thus presents a potential liability for public relations. Fallout from the ferry scandal intensified anxiety about music-making at party functions and social events. Prohibitions of deviant music remain unofficial; announcing and specifying them might signal to outside critics that there is a pervasive problem inside the party. But the heightened concern for music after the scandal, combined with the continued ambiguity of the Sweden Democrats' musical code, contributed to a decrease in all kinds of music-making at gatherings. One active member of the party's youth organization explained his experience of the change to me:

> You never know what the media would react to if they infiltrate us. They could go crazy over something that isn't even that bad, just because they are looking for every opportunity to call us racists. And they don't really know what they are talking about. Even if it were a problematic song, they don't know how I think about it. You know, it isn't like everybody who listens to ghetto rap, for example, really wants to rape women and shoot police officers and so on. But now it feels like nobody [in the party] wants to take that chance. But then it is like, why even sing any songs? If you continue like that, then we could end up in a place where we can't say anything. Then you've given our enemies control over how we act. (Interview, anonymous, March 30, 2011)[10]

As our conversation continued, this individual characterized the leadership's reaction to the ferry scandal as caving to liberalism. He was not only defending his own interests with this critique. Dozens of Sweden Democrats—from different factions of the party—have told me in personal conversations that they listen to the music of certain ethnonationalist bands in private. They often assert, however, that they most enjoy songs that do not conflict with their visions of an ostensibly more inclusive, nonracist nationalism. The piece praised most frequently in these conversations is Svensk Ungdom's track "Questions for Father" (*Frågor till far*), which, in contrast to the band's song "Sweden Has Fallen," lacks direct references to ethnicity, and therefore in isolation does not conflict with the party's declared cultural nationalism. With an acoustic singer songwriter flavor, its lyrics ring:

> Do you remember the times that I never got to see,
> when the people were happy, when the people were one?
> So tell me father, how does it feel today
> as you sit in the wreckage of what once was?
>
> When you grew up, tell me, how was it then?
> Did people attack girls at will?
> Did you stroll down the street listening carefully,
> without hearing a single word you understood?
> Were you ever forced to walk home alone
> after having been robbed and beaten by foreign men?
>
> Tell me, how could you let this happen?
> You've blinded yourself to that which the blind could see.

Does this feel good, dear father?
Are you proud, are you happy?
And where will you stand in our struggle today?

Activists have told me that no other song better captures their understandings of Sweden's destruction at the hands of immigration and multiculturalism. One mentioned that upon first hearing "Questions for Father," he laid down on the floor of his apartment and sobbed. No decree from the Sweden Democrats' leadership, I imagine, could prevent songs like this from appealing to a wide cross-section of its members. The main divide in the party exists, not between those who like and do not like such music, but rather between those who are willing to express their problematic and complicated affinity for it in public and those who are not.

The experiences of early white-power music fans and latter-day Sweden Democrats reveal how music's perceived status as harmless entertainment, involuntary personal taste, or a domain of uncontrollable free expression renders it a precarious accessory to political campaigning. Activists striving to craft a particular identity—whether of an old or new nationalism—must be cautious when dealing with an expressive form such as music, the creation and reception of which they cannot easily steer. Compounding these dangers, the deviance we see in nationalists' listening habits extends to the conversations they have about music. When discussing music, nationalists voice interpretations and worldviews that they otherwise condemn. Specifically, they are willing to deconstruct the notion of purity in music with argumentation they would seldom tolerate in discussions of race, ethnicity, or culture at large.[11] Consider the following exchange I had with singer Saga about whether the music she performed needed to be Swedish:

SAGA (S): Looking back at music, everything originates from something, there are always influences in every music, because rap is a really new music style, it's a lot newer than reggae, and pop and stuff like that. It all originates from something. . . . Unless you play folk music, it is not Swedish, I mean pop is not Swedish. Rock is not Swedish, but I'm Swedish—I'm singing, I make it my version, but I can't claim that for my country.

BT: But is that a problem, to go out and play, and speak and be part of a movement that is aiming to preserve the Swedish?

S: With pop music? Well, then I think they'd have to ban all music styles except for, as I said, folk music. And I mean who listens to that? Seriously? Seriously? [author points at himself] You do? [laughs]. No offense. (Interview, Saga and Dennis, July 28, 2011)

Music, according to Saga, is a domain defined by mutual exchange and influence, and is therefore resistant to agendas of purity and isolation. Swedish folk music seems an exception to this scheme. But because so few people enjoy this genre, it need not be taken into consideration. Saga's description places her close to the conceptual framework many nationalists claim to oppose. In one sense, it is a denial of the existence of the distinctly Swedish. In another sense, it is a statement that the Swedish is undesirable and insufficient.

I found Saga's thoughts on music and identity to be common among contemporary activists, including those in radical nationalism's more moderate wing, such as former political secretary for the Sweden Democrats, Linus Bylund. Bylund is coauthor of the party's two election songs produced for the 2006 and 2010 national parliamentary campaigns. Each of these songs adopted an unremarkable pop format, with light drums, guitars, smooth vocals, and catchy, upbeat melodies. Like Nordic Youth's reggae track and Saga's "freedom pop" style more generally, these election songs were aimed at attracting new participants and breaking with the previous molds for nationalist music-making. But the lack of markedly Swedish musical material seemed especially problematic in Bylund's case, given that the Sweden Democrats claim the preservation and promotion of Swedish culture as their central cause. For that reason, I pressed him to defend his creations. His response followed a progression similar to Saga's.

> BT: I was thinking about the election song, is it important that the music itself is Swedish?
>
> LINUS BYLUND (LB): I guess it isn't. Like, it is hard to say what is and isn't Swedish in terms of music, modern music that is. . . . You can't really say that about any music—modern—because even if we say that "we are now being globalized," in the world of music, globalization has been going on since the 1600s, 1500s. I mean a symphony, a melody written by someone in Austria or someone in Tokyo, it isn't certain that there will be a big difference. (Interview, Linus Bylund, May 24, 2012)

Exchange the words "Swedish culture" or "Swedish people" for "Swedish music" in Bylund's statement, and you will have a classic example of the argumentation nationalists of all stripes rage against: Were a prominent non-nationalist public figure to state, "[I]t is very hard to say what in modern [culture] is Swedish. You can't really say that about any [culture]," it would most certainly appear in nationalist blogs and magazines followed by words of condemnation. It would be treated as yet another example of elites' efforts to deny and erase national difference.

Perhaps sensing this potential conflict, Bylund began to question his own characterizations. I asked him again whether his nationalist ideals had any bearing on the style of music he produced. He replied:

> For me, it is really unimportant, because the type of music—but, it isn't unimportant—but—I can't think of any music genre that would be impossible to use. (ibid.)

While affirming that he is open to using any kind of music for his activism, he retreated from the statement that musical style is "unimportant." As we continued, however, and as I referenced the discussion of Nordic Youth's reggae song "Imagine" (*Tänk*) (see chapter 3), he renewed his defense of his own musical creations. Again, his argumentation parallels Saga's:

> BT: Those who were very upset by Nordic Youth's reggae song, they thought that the songwriters betrayed their own Swedish heritage, because they had said, "no, what is Swedish isn't good enough."
>
> LB: Yes, I can accept that point, but then I would want to know what you would do instead. Because in that case it is nyckelharpa and flute, if you want to be very strict. (ibid.)

Here, Bylund shifts to accept the notion that some music is essentially Swedish. However, he also implied that using Swedish folk music to produce public campaign songs, like the Sweden Democrats' election songs or Nordic Youth's debut song, was unrealistic. After our taped interview had ended, we continued to talk about the attacks on Nordic Youth's reggae song. I described how one critic had compared that organization's actions to former socialist party leader Mona Sahlin and her statements that Swedes have no culture of their own and need importation (see chapter 1). When phrased in this way, Bylund paused, and said, with more earnestness than before, that he agreed with that criticism.

Bylund thus grew hesitant when I placed his statements about music in a broader discussion of "culture"—a discussion that he and his fellow party members are more accustomed to participating in. We may be tempted to attribute both his and Saga's dismissal of Swedish folk music wholly to their agendas of reaching new audiences and recruiting new sympathizers—to agendas of metapolitics. But were this their only motivation, they would not have needed to deconstruct the notion of pure music genres. What the above examples instead suggest is that these nationalists—like the identitarian activist Anna Svensson—tolerate a degree of cosmopolitanism in music that they reject in other domains, even though for Bylund this instinct simultaneously feels problematic.

Irrationality II: Emotion and Passion

Thus far I have explored impressions that the intractability of music's creation and appeal cripples nationalist campaigning. Music's inherent cosmopolitanism and the allegedly involuntary nature of musical taste give it standing potential to foment deviance. But these same properties also lead activists to see a parallel kind of irrationality in music, one born less from the expressive form's chaotic disregard for extramusical social and political order, and more from its perceived status as an emotional, rather than intellectual, endeavor.

Claims that music addresses itself to the heart but not the mind appear in historically, geographically, and culturally diverse contexts and among actors with varied understandings of "emotion" and "intellect," as well as of music.[13] Nordic radical nationalists often distinguish "emotional" and "intellectual" pursuits by their ability to provide insight into political philosophy and contemporary policy issues. Whereas the former kindles love for nation and people, contempt toward opponents, and resolve for activism, the latter offers tools for analyzing and contesting the sociopolitical status quo.

Activists have long celebrated music for its ability to incite passion. But some blame music and the allegedly heightened emotionalism it channels for stoking Nordic nationalism's woes. Semimilitant Norwegian white nationalist Thorgrim Bredesen voiced this position during one of our conversations. Bredesen has been a consistent critic of established activist methods in both Norway and Sweden, and he argued that whatever goods emerge from music provide little benefit to nationalist political campaigns:

THORGRIM BREDESEN (TB): I can go to a concert and it doesn't do anything for me. People say things like, "yeah it gives us energy, it makes us Vikings, ready for the fight." No it doesn't. You stand in a field for a few hours, get drunk, shout into the air, and nothing is different when it's over. You haven't done anything or changed anything. If it did, Sweden and Germany would be white again. . . .

BT: But what does change things, what should people be doing instead?

TB: Getting involved. Handing out leaflets like I was saying. Starting an organization, become a leader. But just being angry, even in a big group, that won't do anything. (Interview, Thorgrim Bredesen, July 6, 2011)

Here Bredesen claims that the emotions produced by music—principally anger—do not advance the nationalist cause. He attempts to defend that statement by mentioning that the expansive nationalist music cultures in Sweden and Germany have not produced appreciable political gains. Instead, he portrays musical events as a distraction leaving activists mired in aimless emotion, an activity that exacerbates the scene's imbalance between feelings on the one hand and productive actions on the other.

A far different kind of nationalist, Sweden Democrat ideologue Mattias Karlsson, characterizes music in ways similar to Bredesen. Karlsson assigns music to a collection of emotionally stimulating pursuits that can bring individuals to nationalism, but that are less effective—even counterproductive—in efforts to affect political change. For him, reforming the Sweden Democrats involves distancing the party from emotional expression, and focusing it instead on parliamentary politics and current policy issues. This agenda may help normalize the nationalist perspective in Swedish politics, and, similarly, help the organization attract a more diverse membership. Emotional appeal, he argues, is personal, mysterious, and ineffable, and thereby a poor avenue through which to unite a larger community. Concrete political agendas, in contrast, can be arrived at for various reasons. He described his thinking to me:

> Nationalism has a personal, emotional side. You have to separate that. If you are working in the political sphere, you have to follow the theoretical aspects, what ever is politically interesting. What I as an individual have for personal, emotional feelings, that is something else. . . . You should be able to embrace our political ideology without feeling like I do. You should be able to—on purely rationalistic, logical grounds—reason your way to thinking, "yes, this is the best political course. Personally I don't care that much about old traditions, and I don't have an especially good relationship with my family, and I don't think that Sweden is any more beautiful than any other country, but for society's best this is nonetheless good." That has to be possible. We can't expect everyone who wants to get involved in the party or vote for us to have our emotional connection. (Interview, Mattias Karlsson, May 20, 2011)

Musical experience fueled the emotional aspect of Karlsson's nationalism. Like many of his fellow party members, he claims that Viking rock band Ultima Thule was a core source of inspiration for his political engagement. But music does not provide political nourishment or guidance in his mind, and for that reason he aspires to reduce the involvement of music—Ultima Thule in particular—in the party's activities. He explained,

> MK: Not everyone in the leadership likes Ultima Thule and Viking rock. Björn [Söder], for example, I don't think he ever was listening to them or part of that scene. And we need more of that. It is important for our party to be open and not connected to any kind of subculture. You shouldn't have to

like Ultima Thule in order to be a Sweden Democrat—I don't really want that music to have any kind of special relationship with the organization.

BT: But you've said that Ultima Thule played a big role in your awakening as a nationalist. Isn't it important to have that same source in the party?

MK: Not really. I mean Ultima Thule isn't going to show us what laws to support, or what political strategies are best. They're on an emotional level, and they've done a lot for me on an emotional level, but they don't appeal to everyone in the party, which is totally fine. It's even a good thing so long as we all arrive at the same political positions. (ibid.)

Karlsson suggests that placing music at the center of the party would create a community of passion, emotion, and taste—one that would necessarily be less open to newcomers, and politically less formidable. I suspect that an additional motivation for Karlsson to downplay references to Ultima Thule in the party's culture is that doing so will cut one of the remaining ties between the Sweden Democrats and the rest of the nationalist scene, as well as to 1990s skinheadism.

Though much of our exchange focused on the impact of Viking rock, his discussion suggested that he opposed the growth of any particular musical behavior in the party. This stance of course conflicts with another of his agendas, namely, that of using folk music to rebrand the Sweden Democrats and stoke patriotic sentiment among Swedes more generally (see chapter 4). How could he promote folk music while claiming that no particular genre should receive special treatment in the party? When I asked Karlsson, he laughed, and said, "I guess it would be okay if we had a Swedish folk music subculture" (ibid.). His irreverent answer exposed how he reconciled pursuing pro- and antimusic agendas simultaneously. Like Saga and fellow Sweden Democrat Linus Bylund, Karlsson implicitly dismissed the possibility that folk music could appeal to a large audience. Therefore, it need not be included in a broader theory of music and political activism.

Conceived as a source of emotion, music not only fails to produce concrete revolutionary or parliamentary action but also obstructs the reformist drive toward intellectualization. Insiders agitating to create a more learned nationalism have frequently targeted music on account of its alleged status as irrational, emotional behavior and experience. Prominent National Socialist writer and activist Björn Björkqvist has advanced this critique throughout his career. For example, he wrote the following in a 1997 letter published in *Nordland* magazine:

The Swedish national movement has, for some years, gotten stuck and stood and stamped in the exact same place with white power music playing as loud as possible. Music is and will remain a strong weapon in the fight for the white race's survival, but it alone is not enough. Music recruits new fighters but it does not provide any ideological schooling. (1997, no. 6)

Björkqvist here describes music as an important but insufficient tool in the nationalist cause because of its inability to deepen activists intellectually. When I spoke to him fifteen years later about his letter, he added that he believes political movements are weakened when any music style achieves a role of preponderance like that of white power in early radical nationalism. He said, "As long as music is the main activity in a movement, you know that people aren't there for the politics and the ideas, and as soon as the music falls out of fashion, those people will leave. And that's exactly what happened [in Sweden's national movement]" (Interview, Björn Björkqvist, July 23, 2013). Individuals engaging with nationalist music, according to him, are thus not engaging with actual nationalist ideas. Journalism and literature were his ideal antidotes to the scene's overinvestment in music, and he would go on to serve as editor for various newspapers, including *The Swedish National Socialist* (*Den Svenske Nationalsocialisten*) and *The Realist* (*Realisten*).

The opposition between music and intellect became most formalized in the Nordic League empire. In chapter 2 we saw how this influential identitarian publishing and retail network assigned music to the category of "inspirational" products, while literature formed their "educational" offerings. According to Nordic League founder Daniel Friberg, that designation justified minimizing investment in music. Insiders in the early nationalist scene, he contends, had an abundance of passion and emotion—of "inspiration"—but no means of interpreting those feelings or translating them into gainful action. This lack of intellectual guidance led early nationalists to embrace an irrelevant Third Reich nostalgia and a decadent music culture (Interview, Daniel Friberg, June 30, 2014). He claimed that nationalists' tendency to invest music with educational or genuinely political content was an outgrowth of their naïveté as strategists. Things, however, are changing. He explains:

This new movement that is growing does not have the same need for open political declarations as the [old] national movement had before. Then, if someone heard a musician performing, the natural question was "oh, is the musician a nationalist?" It was very important for them to confirm that all musicians belonged to their own milieu. But it isn't as important for the new movement. They rather consider the music itself, the emotions it stirs, rather than the artists' opinions. (ibid.)

Friberg considers the emerging attitudes toward music as a sign of progress. As he sees it, demanding political expression in music—or political solidarity with its creators—is antithetical to showing respect for "the music itself" and "the emotions it stirs." He thinks a more harmonious activism emerges when practices that can only provide emotional stimulation are recognized and treated accordingly. When insiders instead look to the emotional domain for political and ideological guidance, they deprive themselves of both authentic emotional experience and intellectual growth.

Indeed, Friberg believes that early nationalism's misguided investment in music caused tangible harm, in part because it positioned musicians—bearers of emotional experience—as political and intellectual leaders. As he put it:

> I think it is hard to build a serious political movement when you are so focused on concerts, partying, and selling CDs. And if you look at the Swedish national movement, some of these musicians had a completely inappropriate level of influence. They became idols for a lot of young nationalists. At the same time, they were pretty poor role models. They behaved like any other rock stars, and it is pretty dangerous for a political movement to have rock stars as trendsetters and idols. (ibid.)

Friberg believes that reformism is correcting this misplaced investment. If musicians were venerated in the old nationalism, his circle has instead lifted philosophers as its foremost celebrities. He added, "If there are idols in the identitarian movement, that would be Ernst Jünger and Julius Evola, and I think that is a positive change" (ibid.).

Sound Reasoning

As Nordic radical nationalism works to rationalize itself—to gain greater control over its image, to form more coherent political platforms, to cultivate and project intellectualism, and to operate effectively as a political force—music resists that agenda. Deemed irrational on account of its alleged uncontrollability and production of passion over knowledge, nationalists blame music for cultivating an activism of disorder and senselessness. For these insiders, freeing themselves of the expressive form advances their efforts to build a new scene based on discipline, erudition, and professionalism.

Music's downgraded role in official nationalist activism does not mean that it will cease to impact the lives of insiders. Nor has it lost the potential to shape the course of the nationalist cause. The perceived irrationality and inconsequence of music, while problematic for collective activism, serves individual needs. Nationalists permit themselves to say, do, and be things in music that they otherwise disallow. The potential for ideological deviance in music that so concerns nationalist leaders may provide individuals a necessary respite from the rigid lifestyle demands they place upon themselves.

Nationalists continue to experience professional setbacks, social exclusion, and even violent attacks as a result of their activism. They may also feel psychologically wearied by their bracing revulsion toward the society they live in or, alternately, feel burdened by their self-imposed orthodoxy and imperative to resist the status quo in all ways and at all times. By allowing a temporary escape from their programs, music makes the pressures of activism more manageable. Though nationalism might become more electorally viable by washing its public profile and social habits of music, insiders' ability to maintain resolve may rely on music's continued presence in their private lives—on their ability to commit occasional heresies under the guise of consuming meaningless entertainment.

But music's alleged irrationality not only gives nationalists' cover to engage with a wide rage of styles, it also allows them to discuss human behavior in ways they otherwise cannot. As we saw with Saga and Sweden Democrat Linus Bylund, nationalists declare the futility of attempts to resist globalization and human hybridity when discussing music. Statements like "looking back at music, everything originates from something, there are always influences in every music" and "it is hard to say what is and isn't Swedish in terms of music" could not be expressed regarding other domains of culture or identity without considerable political risk. Were an activist to question the distinctness of languages, cultures, identities, ethnicities, or races, their engagement in the scene would thereafter appear unintelligible. Put another way, if this discourse ever "matures" or "articulates"—if insiders ever transfer these ideas from the domain of music into that of politics at large—then they will cease to be nationalists.

"Ethnopluralism sounds nice with the whole idea that races come together and agree not to interfere with each other and so on."

"Yes."

"The problem is though, for that to work, I would have to be ok with the fact that they do all these horrible things to themselves in Africa and places like that. And I'm not sure that I *can* be ok with that."

"I see."

"It's that. . .that. . .goddamn white altruism."

"Yes, yes."

. . .

"Back then, you were trying to bring these new ideas, this *Nouvelle Droite* stuff, into the movement."

"Yes."

"And I tried my best to stop you."

"Yes, yes."

"But you did it anyway. Haha."

"Haha. Yes, I suppose I did."

July 23, 2013. On a cool summer evening at a bar called Axela in Stockholm's hip Söder district, Magnus Söderman and Daniel Friberg reminisced about their past. They talked about their lives growing up as nationalists, shared stories of confrontations with leftists, and discussed the ways the scene had changed in recent years. The two have very different personalities, and this is apparent both in their careers as activists and in the way they spoke to each other that evening. Söderman, Nordic ethnonationalism's great orator, drove the conversation, while Friberg, a background figure whose works are far better known than his name, was curt, accommodating, and affirming. Laughs and compliments also dotted their exchange—they clearly enjoyed each other's company.

It was the type of meeting that could never have taken place just five years earlier. Then, these two men belonged to warring factions in the nationalist scene. Söderman was a spokesperson for Sweden's leading militant National Socialist organization. Friberg, on the other hand, spearheaded the Nordic League and other identitarian organizations pursuing reform. The conflict between their respective camps spawned public condemnations—the most memorable of which came in Söderman's speeches—and acts of violence.

What had changed? Söderman had. He hadn't embraced the Sweden Democrats, identitarianism, or ethnopluralism, and he remained a committed white nationalist and admirer of historic National Socialism. But in 2011 he left the Nordic Resistance Movement after having grown deeply critical of established forms of nationalist activism. He shifted his efforts from street campaigns to education, founding a think tank in 2011, initiating an Internet radio program in 2012, and publishing two books by 2013. In other words, though Söderman retained his previous ideology, he had invested in activist strategies and modes of expression that Friberg had long promoted. He had become a New Nationalist. And now he was poised to collaborate with actors he once abhorred. Friberg, for his part, was eager to welcome Söderman: he would later dub the evening at Axela "a great gathering of three intelligent men."

Yes, I was there too. I joined these nationalist veterans while on a return visit to the field during the summer of 2013. I had of course been thinking about the nationalists of the North during my intervening months at home in the United States. Hardly a meal or party had gone by without my mentioning them, and their music was playing everywhere I went. All of this led some of my friends and family to wonder whether I had "gone native" during my years of fieldwork. Undoubtedly, I had gained a new relationship to the people I studied. But the empathy and excitement I felt in anticipation of reconnecting with them instead revealed that, at some point during my research, I had separated my consultants from their ideology. They had become people to me, individuals filled with histories, aspirations, and sorrows, the sums of which were so much larger than any political campaign or subcultural identity.

I first encountered Nordic radical nationalism during a time of transition, a time when an old nationalism died and a new one was born. Those activists traversing the gap needed to understand who they were and what they wanted to be. Though they would not agree on a common vision, they shared a distaste for their past. They had all become anti-skinheads, and they expressed this through music. However, my return trips to the field in 2013 and 2014 showed me that the process of reform is still evolving, and in ways we might not expect.

Production of rap and reggae has all but halted. Nordic Youth—makers of the smash reggae track "Imagine"—have focused on nonmusical spectacles in recent years, save the production of a forgettable rap song in early 2014 by an affiliated duo calling themselves "Karl Skidmarxx and Goy Boy." Similarly, rapper Zyklon Boom has nearly disappeared. Interest in his works rose briefly in July 2012 when he released a much-celebrated single, "The Online-Hate Demon" ("*Näthatsdemonen*"). Expanding on his drive to defy political boundaries, his song argues that mainstream rightist and leftist forces in Sweden share contempt for a free Internet. With rhetorical finesse, the rapper incarnates this shared sentiment in the figure of a two-handed demon, with a free-market right(ist) hand struggling to stop file-sharing and a left hand fearful that the Internet provides a platform for unfettered xenophobia and sexism. Played by the rapper himself, the demon seeks greater control of the Internet to prosecute illegal downloading and maintain profits, as well as to silence criticism of minorities and impose radical gender politics—here manifest in Sweden's new gender-neutral pronoun, *hen*. He raps:

> Am I a filthy pig from the recording industry?
> An aroma-therapist or a journalist sipping red wine?
> Growth is your duty, just like China after Mao,
> Question us and you're taking a step towards Utøyja and Dachau.
> Free are those who lack father, land, and friend,
> but who can buy what they want and have a passport that says "*hen*."
> The left hand stands—the right with a fist—
> for "tolerance," "surveillance," "equality," and slavery.

He's getting better. But as anticipation for his work has been growing, and as Daniel Friberg and Arktos Publishing committed to producing a full-length album of any new material, his production dwindled—likewise his blogging. There is chatter throughout the scene about fatherhood, about threats from antifascists in his hometown, and about a crushing work schedule to make ends meet. Nobody knows for sure.

Saga also seemed to have vanished. Fallout from the Breivik attacks had a devastating impact on her career and private life. The intense, negative media exposure she received in the summer of 2011 led her employer to reassign her to a less public position, one that dropped her annual salary by almost two-thirds. Due to the loss of income, Saga and her German boyfriend Dennis were forced to sell their apartment in Germany and live full-time with her parents in Sweden.

I may have contributed to her troubles. I was the first to tell Saga that the terrorist celebrated her extensively in his manifesto. Just four days after the attack, I began giving interviews about Breivik's interest in her to Swedish and Norwegian radio, synopses of which appeared in most Swedish national and local newspapers. Additionally, I authored an op-ed in Norway's *Dagbladet* newspaper, and was interviewed by Sweden's largest evening paper *Aftonbladet* for an article that was showcased on the paper's front page, shown in Figure 7.1. In these statements, I argued that Breivik's interest in Saga offered insight into his thinking—particularly that the people he fought for was a racial one. But I did not seek to portray her as an accomplice to his crimes. In a letter published in Sweden's *Lira* magazine (no. 5, 2011), for example, I challenged what I understood to be unfounded attacks on her. Still, regardless of my intentions or the content of my claims, I had used my credentials to highlight her music's role in inspiring one of the most gruesome attacks ever in the Nordic countries. It appears today that increased professional and personal hardships for Saga were the only noteworthy outcomes of my actions.

By the time I returned to Sweden in 2013, Saga's various online pages had been dormant for more than a year, though the number of fans on her Facebook page continued to rise. Likewise, her musical output had essentially ceased. Save a 2012 performance at the massive white-nationalist festival Magyar Sziget in Hungary, Saga had not given any public concerts. Nor had she voluntarily released any new music since the Breivik attacks in 2011. The last track she had produced was a ballad titled "Impossible Battles." She uploaded a demo version of the song online on June 10, 2010, promising at the time that a polished recording would someday follow as an official release. Indeed, the vocals, likewise the poetry, lack the craft Saga achieves in some of her other pieces. But her reluctance to continue with this project may lie in the song's messages that seem to take on new meaning in Breivik's wake. In it, she sings:

You know my dreams and you know my truth.
And as long as you are with me,
I will keep this fight alive.
I will keep this fight alive.
I will keep this fight alive.
I will keep this fight alive.

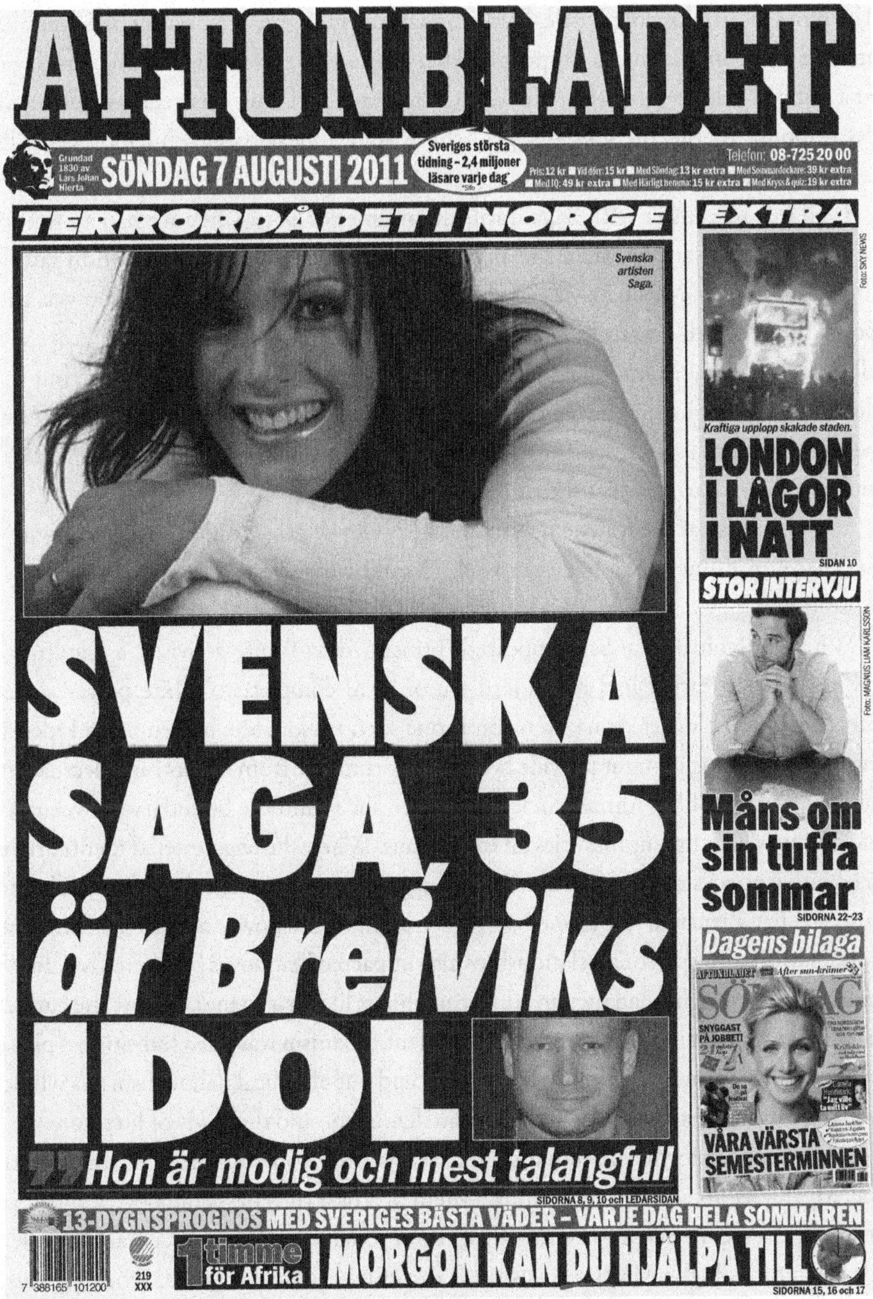
AFTONBLADET

Grundad 1830 av Lars Johan Hierta

SÖNDAG 7 AUGUSTI 2011

Sveriges största tidning – 2,4 miljoner läsare varje dag*
*Sifo

Telefon: 08-725 20 00
Pris: 12 kr ■ Vid dörr: 15 kr ■ Med Söndag: 13 kr extra ■ Med Sommardeckare: 39 kr extra ■ Med IQ: 49 kr extra ■ Med Härligt hemma: 15 kr extra ■ Med Kryss & quiz: 19 kr extra

TERRORDÅDET I NORGE

Svenska artisten Saga.

SVENSKA SAGA, 35 är Breiviks IDOL

”Hon är modig och mest talangfull

SIDORNA 8, 9, 10 och LEDARSIDAN

EXTRA

Foto: SKY NEWS

Kraftiga upplopp skakade staden.

LONDON I LÅGOR I NATT

SIDAN 10

STOR INTERVJU

Foto: MAGNUS LIAM KARLSSON

Måns om sin tuffa sommar

SIDORNA 22–23

Dagens bilaga

AFTONBLADET After sun-krämer SÖNDAG

SNYGGAST PÅ JOBBET!

VÅRA VÄRSTA SEMESTERMINNEN

13-DYGNSPROGNOS MED SVERIGES BÄSTA VÄDER – VARJE DAG HELA SOMMAREN

7 388165 101200

219 XXX

1 timme för Afrika I MORGON KAN DU HJÄLPA TILL

SIDORNA 15, 16 och 17

FIGURE 7.1 Front page of *Aftonbladet*, August 7, 2011. The headline reads, "Swede Saga, 35, Is Breivik's Idol."

The lyrics to "Impossible Battles" are comparatively vague, celebrating perseverance at large and committing to support listeners in an unnamed cause. If this was Saga's first official release after the attacks in Norway—and this was seen as her musical response to the Breivik episode—she would appear to have unapologetically embraced her most notorious fan.

I did not reconnect with Saga until the summer of 2014 when we had a number of phone conversations. Then she and Dennis seemed happily ensconced in family life and new jobs. Music may be a part of her future; she doesn't really know at this point. Breivik had certainly made recording and touring less appealing. Any new albums on the way? One called *Weapons of Choice* came out earlier that year, but she didn't release it. She said her old record label Midgård had assembled it without her permission from scratch studio recordings, including that for "Impossible Battles," and she planned to sue over the ordeal.

Was she upset at me for the newspaper interviews? No. Could I make it down to her place for dinner? No, not that week. Would we make tentative plans for later? Absolutely.

While individuals like Saga appeared disinclined to future activism, a handful of those I studied earlier had renounced nationalism completely. White power singer turned Motpol blogger Anna Svensson is one such person. She had embraced identitarianism thinking it might provide her with a forum free from the anti-intellectualism and chauvinism of her former circles. However, she found the boundary between her old and new activist communities all too porous. When she encountered identitarians celebrating attacks on refugee housing, or suggesting that women shouldn't be able to vote, she felt alienated, just as she had earlier in the white power music establishment. Issues surrounding personal relationships also impacted her moves (women have always been more forthright than men in admitting things like that to me). In 2015 she cut her ties to the scene. In retrospect, it seems that identitarianism was but a transitional phase in her journey from race-revolutionary circles and out of radical nationalism as a whole. Today she is interested in environmentalism, feminism, and the study of literature.

I don't expect former nationalists like Anna Svensson to remain in touch with me. My questions and musings remind them of a past they desperately seek distance from. There are others, however, with whom I remain in close contact, and Sweden Democrat ideologue Mattias Karlsson is the chief example. I am far from the only outside observer who admires his erudition, curiosity, and humility, and our shared passion for the Swedish provides ample fuel for continued exchange. However, keeping in touch with him became more difficult following the Sweden Democrats' considerable advance during the 2014 elections. From October of that year and until March 2015, Karlsson served as party chairman while leader Jimmie Åkesson took a medical leave of absence. His short tenure included two major political battles:

the first was against all other parties in parliament, who united to blunt the Sweden Democrats' influence; the second was against a wing of his own party. He drove a campaign that ejected a dozen of his fellow party members, including the leadership of the Sweden Democrats' youth organization, whom he accused of harboring sympathies and connections with identitarianism. The battle over the expulsions played out in public social media and led to heated confrontations with party outsider Daniel Friberg, whom Karlsson called a "Nazi and an enemy of democracy" (*Nyheter Idag*, March 13, 2015). In response, Friberg accused Karlsson of stifling free debate within the party and of cultivating mistrust and secrecy.

Increased administrative duties and the burdens of strife hindered Karlsson's ability to advance his cultural campaign. When we first met in late 2010, he was engulfed in an intense public battle over his party's interest in Swedish folk music. The predominately left-leaning folk music establishment lashed out at the Sweden Democrats, and after months of demonstrations, television debates, and op-ed articles, there were indications, such as the cartoon shown in Figure 7.2, that these folk musicians' rejection of the party had registered in the popular consciousness.

As actors outside the party challenged Karlsson's campaign, his internal resources began to crumble. His cultural organization Gimle went dormant in 2012. One reason for this was the political turmoil experienced by the organization's co-founder, Erik Almqvist, who in 2013 was forced to resign from the party after video footage surfaced of him shouting racial slurs in downtown Stockholm and threatening a man with an iron bar. Almqvist relocated to Hungary, and Gimle Festival—with its folk dancing, mead, and motocross bike racing—has never been held since. Shortly after the iron bar scandal stripped Karlsson of one of his partners, master fiddler Marie

FIGURE 7.2 Illustration by Magnus Bard in the Swedish newspaper *Dagens Nyheter*. The figure in the center is Sweden Democrats' party leader Jimmie Åkesson, and he leads a procession of dancers in Nazi-like clothing opposite a disapproving group of folk musicians. Here, Åkesson says, "ONE—TWO—THREE—AAAND—HOP-STEP." Published June 5, 2011.

Stensby—the Sweden Democrats' sole insider to the folk music community—was also prompted to leave the party due to scandal. In December 2013, a media expose alleged she had posted unsightly comments about refugee children in an online chat forum.[1] Today she finds herself alienated from both her former folk music circle as well as the political movement she sacrificed so much to join.

When we meet, Mattias Karlsson and I often discuss music and his frustrated aspirations to start a nationalist cultural renaissance. One of the more memorable occasions came during an evening at his home in summer 2013. His then wife Gabriella was celebrating her birthday with a costume party, and the two had invited me to join them along with a large group of friends—mostly fellow party members. Mattias was Julius Caesar and Gabriella was Arwen from the *Lord of the Rings*. As is my wont, I lied and said I had forgotten to bring a costume.

That night Karlsson voiced his disappointment over the scandals that had rocked his party and stunted his extraparliamentary projects—snarling with sarcasm at one of the belligerents in the iron bar episode, Kent Ekeroth, who was in attendance that evening dressed appropriately as a pirate. But Karlsson also said he was committed to reviving his earlier cause of prying folk music from "cultural Marxists" and using it to inspire Swedish pride. It struck me that he felt more passion for this metapolitical initiative, as he continues to describe it, than for parliamentary work.

The evening would not be devoted to discussing politics, however. Karlsson had printed booklets filled with lyrics to classic Swedish drinking songs, as well as pieces by popular mid-century singer songwriters—music he calls "new folk music." With toasts and smiles we worked our way through the booklets, singing until the late summer sunset. As night fell, as glasses were emptied and refilled, and as the assembly began to thin, our repertoire shifted—first to nineteenth-century romantic nationalist hymns, and finally to Viking rock favorites by Ultima Thule. Printed lyrics were not necessary; we all knew these songs by heart.

The music of the old nationalism lives on, indeed. When activists gather in informal settings and their inhibitions ease, there you can expect to hear skinheadism—Ultima Thule for the moderates and white power standards for those on the fringes. This is not because they secretly yearn to be what they once were. Rather, they cling to this music because it commemorates their involvement in that decadent movement sprung in the streets and schoolyards of 1990s Scandinavia, one that was the epitome of aimlessness and destruction, but that now finds itself on the brink of real political power. These nationalists are proud of their history, and even prouder to have overcome it.

The whisper of skinhead song resounds amid New Nationalism's silence. While 1990s nationalist favorites retain their popularity today, the same cannot be said of the alternative music projects emerging in the post-skinhead era that I have studied in this book. Campaigns to create a new sound for the scene—efforts to rebrand nationalism through rap, reggae, folk music, and "freedom pop"—have stalled. Circumstances prevent nationalism's musical innovators from carrying on their work, but I see little demand in the scene for replacement Zyklon Booms or Sagas. Nationalism's moment of reform via music may be passing.

I suspect that just as the arrival of alternative styles proclaimed a new era for Nordic nationalism, so too does their speedy disappearance. A growing attitude in the scene may be starving reformist music of necessary fuel. I encountered this attitude in virtually everyone I spoke to on my return visits. They were eager to talk about the booming readership of their newspapers and online magazines, as well as increased sales for their publishing houses. They noted that many nationalist online personalities were deanonymizing themselves by writing under their real names. They relished election results in the region that placed anti-immigrant parties in Denmark, Norway, and Finland in positions of power, and they knew that the Sweden Democrats—despite nonstop scandals and relentless public condemnation—would increase their standing during the 2014 election and begin vying to become the largest party in the country. They celebrated political developments in Hungary and France, where robust, dynamic, radical nationalisms succeeded in penetrating the mainstream. They even spoke about the rise of figures like Vladimir Putin and Donald Trump, and the prospects for a new anti-liberal order in the west.

The nationalist scene, in other words, bruned thick with an optimism I'd never seen before. Its once intense backward glance is shifting forward as its members stand before a future for the Nordic region and for Europe they believe is theirs for the taking. Whether their confidence is justified I cannot say, but musical projects devoted to grappling with the scene's past seem passé. Their focus today lies on an anticipated liberation from the underground, a freedom to ignore rather than deny their stereotypes, and an escape from the need to apologize. Will new songs emerge to articulate this attitude? Perhaps. My thoughts go to the Sweden Democrats' official election anthem. Void of sorrow and indignation, full of pomp and swagger, the nationalists sing:

> Nothing is stronger than an idea when its time has come.
> Nobody is stronger than we are at the daybreak.
> Nobody can push down our love—we have it in our sights.
> Our heart, beating proud,
> Come hear our merry song!

Notes

1. The tax populism party New Democracy held a handful of seats in Sweden's parliament from 1991 to 1994 with an anti-immigrant platform. I follow Ekman and Poohl (2010), however, in separating that party from the wider nationalist scene in Sweden. Social connections between New Democracy and nationalists were weak, and the party's anti-immigrant stance emerged gradually throughout their brief period of representation.

2. See the 2014 report from the United Nations High Commissioner for Refugees, available online, http://www.unhcr.org/5329b15a9.html, accessed June 19, 2015.

3. I base this claim on the Anti-Defamation League's 2005 database of white power bands throughout the globe (http://archive.adl.org/learn/ext_us/music_country.asp), and 2005 population estimates from the United Nations (http://www.un.org/en/development/desa/population/) and the Office for National Statistics (http://www.ons.gov.uk). Sweden, with 44 white power bands and a population of 9,041,000, had a per-capita rate of 205,000. Note that the Anti-Defamation League's 2005 database has a number of flaws, such as making multiple entries for a single band that changed its name, the omission of prominent acts, and the inclusion of groups whose status as "white power" I find questionable. I explore the genre of white power in further detail later in this chapter.

4. All translations from Swedish, Norwegian, and German in this book are my own unless otherwise noted.

5. Scholars like historian Roger Griffin (1996, 2000, 2003, 2006) and political scientists Anton Shekhovstov (2009:437) and Tamir Bar-On (2013) observe such a three-part division—by various names—among similar populations throughout Europe. However, their analyses focus on methodological rather than ideological distinctions, and separate the population into the categories

of militant revolutionaries, party politicians, and propagandists or intellectual activists. These scholars build their models to argue that a core ideology—fascism—unites a broader population, and that this ideology is expressed and pursued in different ways. With the analysis I am building here, I instead suggest that the apparent differences in ideology are significant and can therefore combine with methodological differences to serve as a basis for understanding fragmentation in the broader population.

6. This group originally called itself the Swedish Resistance Movement. For the sake of clarity I refer to them in this book at all times by their current name, the Nordic Resistance Movement.

7. See Carr (1997), Bonilla-Silva and Forman (2000), Gallagher (2003a), Forman and Lewis (2004), and Bonilla-Silva (2006).

8. Arnstad relies on the work of historian Roger Griffin to label the Sweden Democrats "fascists." Griffin defines fascism as a mythic brand of populist ultranationalism centered on fomenting a people's rebirth—or palingenisis (1993:41). But the Sweden Democrats cannot be regarded as fascists in this sense. Whereas Arnstad sees in the party's programs a drive toward palingenetic nationalism, Rydgren (2010) and Hübinette and Lundström (2011) were closer to the truth when they described the Sweden Democrats' yearnings as ultimately nostalgic in nature. Assessed in isolation of other nationalists, the party's ideology today resembles generic forms of what Rydgren (2006) and Mudde (2007) call "radical right-wing populism." However, this label has its own drawbacks in the Nordic context that I outline below.

9. Michael Freeden's article (1998) remains one of the more cogent statements on the limitations of treating nationalism as an ideology in itself. See also Smith (2010:26–27).

10. Note however, that the term "radical" maintains an association with the political left in popular discourse (Ignazi 2003).

11. I use this term in place of an insider expression "the national movement" (*den nationella rörelsen*) which I discuss later in this chapter. The term "the national movement" typically refers to initiatives and organizations connected with the explosion of youth-based nationalist activism in 1980s Sweden. Nordic nationalists like the Sweden Democrats and adherents of the French-inspired intellectual school identitarianism now deny association with the national movement and its contemporary celebrants. Scholars have tended to place the Sweden Democrats within the national movement nonetheless (e.g., Larsson 2001; Hamrud 2011:3). But to do so today is to disregard the thinking of insiders—of both Sweden Democrats and other nationalists. Scholars recognizing the limitation of the term "movement" often replace it with "milieu" (e.g., Lööw 2015). I prefer "scene" rather than "milieu" primarily because of the former's common association with expressive culture and ritualistic behavior.

12. The seemingly endless search for these movements' ideological "core concepts" (Freeden 1997; Ball 1999) has become a taken-for-granted pursuit for most scholars throughout the past decades.

13. Most of this research took place between 2010 and 2012 in Sweden, where I moved between cities with especially active nationalist communities: Stockholm, Gothenburg, Malmö, Lund, Västerås, Eskilstuna, Kalmar, Helsingborg, Nyköping, Linköping, and Umeå. My fieldwork also included visits to Oslo and Agder in Norway and Copenhagen and Århus in Denmark. As they do throughout Europe and the United States, radical nationalists in the Nordic countries maintain an extensive Internet presence (Eatwell 1996; Schafer 2002; Copsey 2003; and Deland, Hertzberg, and Hvitfeld 2010). Accordingly, online discussion forums, blogs, and news media were my main sources for information about nationalist gatherings and forging connections with

insiders. Seeking insight into all prominent factions of Nordic radical nationalism, I assembled a broad contact base of informants that covered major political parties like the Sweden Democrats, the Danish People's Party, and the Norwegian Progress Party, as well as smaller parties and organizations like the National Democrats, the Party of the Danes, the Skåne Party, Nordic Youth, the Organization of National Youth, the Party of the Swedes, Midgård Records, Arktos Publishing, Motpol.nu, Vigrid, and the Nordic Resistance Movement. Though I investigated broader transformations and trends, influential insiders also shape nationalist music-making and imbue it with meaning peculiar to their own experiences, values, and ambitions. Accordingly, I paid added attention to a handful of individuals in my research, particularly singer Saga, blogger and rapper Solguru, producer Daniel Friberg, and the Sweden Democrats' ideologue Mattias Karlsson.

14. See early works by Heléne Lööw (e.g. 1998) and Katrine Fangen (1999) in Scandinavia; and Raphael Ezekiel (1995), Kathleen Blee (2002), Mattias Gardell (2003), and Pete Simi and Robert Futrell (2010) in the United States. Note also Goodwin's call (2006) for increased attention to the insider perspective in studies of European anti-immigrant parties.

15. These trends are especially pronounced in scholarship on more moderate nationalist forces. For examples relating to the Sweden Democrats, see Thulin (2007), Grönqvist (2008), Sannerstedt (2008), Hällström and Nilsson (2010), Urvell and Carlsen (2010), Hågård (2011), Rydgren and Ruth (2011), Thorell (2012), Arneback (2013), Norocel (2013), and Widfeldt (2014).

16. Available online, http://www.nordfront.se/nazistexpert-kontaktar-motstandsrorelsen-om-statlig-utredning.smr, accessed February 7, 2013.

17. Like Katrine Fangen (1998b:262), I assumed that attempting to portray myself as a sympathizer would have made me more suspicious to insiders.

18. I almost always refer to nationalists by their real names in this book. I use pseudonyms or list sources as "anonymous" only in those instances where informants asked for it, or when I feel they will be appreciably compromised in their personal or professional lives should they be linked to their quotes.

19. As a scholar of American white nationalism, Raphael Ezekiel, wrote, "it takes no effort to speak glibly about a stereotype" (1995:xxxv).

20. Lassiter declares the do-no-harm policy the "ethical and moral commitment [that] transcends all else" (2005:91; see also Graves and Shields 1991; Fluehr-Lobban 2003).

21. See Cook (2003) and Hale (2006).

22. Reports like these are far too often dismissed by liberal voices as part of nationalists' ploy to cultivate a martyr complex. Former Swedish Prime Minister Fredrik Reinfeldt even made a back-handed endorsement of such attacks when he said in 2010 that the Sweden Democrats should expect violent reactions to their politics (*Expressen*, September 15, 2010).

23. Malmberg, Anderson, and Östh (2011) offer a compelling study suggesting that racial segregation in Sweden may be far more severe than state agencies—who refuse to take statistics on race—may realize.

24. For an English-language introduction to the Second World War in the Nordic countries, see Nordstrom (2000) and Vehviläinen (2002).

25. For a treatment of historical National Socialism and fascism in Sweden, see Lööw (1998, 2004) and Berggren (2002).

26. Office of the Administration, "Statens offentliga utredningar 1974:69–70." See also Opper (1983) and Hill (1996).

27. Various immigrant groups and activists allege that official commitments to multiculturalism most often fail to translate into concrete action. For instance, Rasoul Nejadmehr, one of a

handful of publicly financed "multicultural consultants" throughout the country, argued that, throughout the 1980s, 1990s, and into the twenty-first century, Swedish society has advanced a policy of assimilationism under the guise of the euphemism "integration" (Interview, Rasoul Nejadmehr, January 21, 2011). A sufficient treatment of these criticisms is beyond the scope of this book.

28. Sweden's commitment to generous refugee policies has wavered in the past, however. Following a period of growth and steadily increasing living standards, Sweden's economy fell into a crisis during the early 1990s. The burst of a 1980s real estate bubble, combined with an international recession and rising interest rates, sent unemployment skyrocketing. Growing unemployment and the subsequent increase of state expenditures and decrease in revenues placed major strain on the country's famed "Swedish model" welfare system. Likewise, the government's efforts to buy almost 25% of bank assets increased the national debt dramatically (Bergmark and Palme 2003:109–111). Wages dropped during the decade, and are yet to fully recover. Leading politicians, such as Social Democrat and future prime minister Göran Persson, responded to the crisis with vaguely nativist language, suggesting that the solution to Sweden's problem was a return to its core Lutheran values of careful spending and responsibility (Andersson 2009:237). Others focused, not only on the virtues of Swedishness, but also on the allegedly destructive impact of immigration. A notable example of this was Social Democrat Sverker Åström who, in a famous op-ed published in *Dagens Nyheter* on August 21, 1990, argued that Sweden should be free to make decisions about accepting refugees based on whether those migrants will serve Sweden (and not whether Sweden can serve them). Contemporaneous developments provided fodder for such claims: the stream of non-Nordic immigrants continued to expand during the 1990s. The country received nearly 70,000 non-Nordic immigrants—many of them refugees—in 1994 alone (Bergmark and Palme 2003). Expressions like Åström's op-ed may have legitimized the notion that immigration caused the economic crisis (Ålund and Schierup 1991:9, 1993; Pred 2000).

29. For an introduction to the so-called groupuscular right elsewhere in Europe, see Bale (2002).

30. Trends in media production during the 1990s reveal music's central role at the time. Whereas the scene produced numerous publications treating militarism, political opponents, and historical Nazism, the most widely read periodical was the white power music magazine *Nordland*. Founded in 1995, the magazine published album reviews, concert information, and musician interviews, paying only marginal attention to nonmusical topics. *Nordland's* overall project was multifaceted, and included a record label that produced prominent Swedish white power acts like Division S, Svastika, Triskelon, and Pluton Svea. Additionally, *Nordland* organized concerts that drew upward of a thousand people, making these events some of the largest radical nationalist gatherings in the Nordic countries at the time (Wåg 2010).

31. Viking rock differs fundamentally from Viking metal in its sound, lyrical themes, and political associations. Whereas Viking rock is tied to organized nationalist and conservative politics, links between organized politics and the Viking metal scene—as well as the associated subgenre National Socialist Black Metal—are inconsistent (Purcell 2003; Spracklen 2010).

32. This title is taken from the motto of Hitler's SS force, "Meine Ehre heißt Treue."

33. The expression "Svensson" is here used to refer to a generic, ethnic Swedish male.

34. Sound clips with translated texts of many of the songs treated in this book can be found on the Youtube channel "SCAN 3301".

35. Note, however, that I am not using the term "New Nationalism" as Bohlman does. Whereas he uses it to describe European society at a larger scale, I refer only to the organized anti-immigrant forces treated in this book.

36. See Carby (1992), hooks (1992), Hill (1994), Frankenberg (1993, 2001), Dyer (1997), Nayak (2002), Gallagher (2003b), and Baum (2006).

37. Gallagher (2000), Sacks and Lindholm (2002), Kauffman (2006), and Cornell and Hartmann (2007).

38. Available online, http://www.frihet.nu/forum/1421414548/1325828286.html, accessed May 27, 2011.

39. Available online, http://www.nationell.nu/2011/11/02/tv-reklamliknande-film-infor-demonstrationen-den-10-december/, accessed September 24, 2012.

CHAPTER 2

1. My analysis here diverges from scholars like Rydgren (2005), who treat the emergence of right-wing populist, cultural nationalist parties like the Sweden Democrats as the main engine of cultural and intellectual change in radical nationalist circles. Despite the innovation and novelty of those parties, their output does not always function as a unifying force among nationalists more broadly. Identitarianism's output, in contrast, serves as an antidote to skinheadism throughout the scene.

2. See Hainsworth and Mitchell (2000), Rydgren (2004), McCulloch (2006), Hervik (2011), and Bar-On (2014) for case studies examining the school's influence on political parties.

3. The war-era fascist organization The New Swedish Movement, for example, called on ethnostates to pursue a common, nonhierarchical separatism, or a "mutual nationalism" (*samnationalism*)—an agenda that anticipates the notion of ethnopluralism I discuss later in this chapter. See also Christopher Rangne of White Aryan Resistance (*Vitt ariskt motstånd*) in Teitelbaum (2013:83).

4. Kicker gangs held a reputation in 1990s Sweden for perpetuating violence on a par with soccer hooligan groups (Nilsson and Åstrand 2007:13; Van Offer 2000:56).

5. For examples of these early complaints, see Teitelbaum (2013:87–89).

6. A watershed moment in this shift came on January 3, 1998, when Swedish police stormed a concert north of Stockholm in Brottby, arresting scores of attendees as well as members of the Swedish white-power bands Vit Aggression, Svastika, Pluton Svea, and the American group Max Resist. Christian Dalsgaard, a police officer leading the raids, reported that they were acting under orders from the state to intervene more forcefully in racist activities (*Expressen*, January 4, 1998). The band Max Resist would later immortalize the event through the song "The Battle of Brottby."

7. Production companies that survived this crash never regained their former strength, and some of their subsequent marketing campaigns bear a distinctively defensive posture, attempting to entice customers with what at times seem like calls for charity. Sweden's Midgård Records, for example, began posting a web banner on their home page in the late 2000s that stated, "Don't let the Swedish scene die out—buy your music!" Available online, accessed December 2, 2011, www.midgaardshop.com.

8. Mats Nilsson—neo-Nazi leader from Mattias Karlsson's hometown—was sentenced to a year in prison in 2000 as an accessory to a bank robbery and double murder of two police officers (*Aftonbladet*, January 18, 2000).

9. These four activists met while serving as the editorial staff for the newspaper of the newly founded Swedish Resistance Movement (later the Nordic Resistance Movement) in 1999, which was in turn derived from the white-power music magazine *Nordland*. Their departure from the Swedish Resistance Movement in 2001, and subsequent founding of the Nordic Press, followed a series of personal and ideological disputes with the Movement's increasingly radicalized leadership. Mattias Wåg has called the four men "the Nordland group." The label is somewhat a misnomer given that Friberg and Berg never worked at *Nordland*, despite Wåg's claim to the contrary (see Wåg 2010:106).

10. Available online, accessed July 10, 2012, http://web.archive.org/web/20040810070901/http://www.nordiskaforlaget.se/info/.

11. Note also that the Press's annual festival, the Nordic Festival (*Nordiska festivalen*), showcased leading international music acts who, though not standard white-power punk, nonetheless voiced sympathy with historic National Socialism.

12. This work is largely responsible for the discourse criticizing "cultural Marxism" in contemporary Swedish ethnonationalism. Further, via its attention to the way the Frankfurt School impacted political common-sense in the west, *Culture of Critique* seems to anticipate the arrival and celebration of *Nouvelle Droite* metapolitics in the Nordic countries.

13. Available online, accessed October 24, 2011, http://www.racialcompact.com/racialgoldenrule.html.

14. Available online, accessed July 12, 2012, www.preservationist-books.com.

15. Such as the American journal *Telos*.

16. For a thorough examination of the *Nouvelle Droite* and its history, see Taguieff (1993) and Bar-On (2007; 2013).

17. Despite their admiration for the premodern, activists of the *Nouvelle Droite* typically renounce any agenda to replicate past society in any comprehensive sense. Rather, many advocate reconciling trajectories of technological progress with traditional, pluralistic social models. This leads commentators like Tamir Bar-On to describe the *Nouvelle Droite*'s agenda as one of creating an "alternative modernity" (2013)—thereby making the school an example of fascism according to Roger Griffin's definition.

18. For this reason, few ardent insiders to this school call themselves nationalists.

19. However, the universality of this thinking spurred an internal schism within the *Nouvelle Droite* initiated by Guillaume Faye. Faye criticized De Benoist and others for relativizing the achievements, and even the superiority, of European society.

20. Tomislav Sunic claims that the school understands culture as including "popular myths and popular modern sensibilities," as well as educational and media institutions (Sunic 2011 [2009]:70–71). Michael O'Mera devotes a chapter to the topic (2011), though this aims to define culture more generally rather than explaining how the *Nouvelle Droite* uses the concept.

21. The spread of the school's ideas, along with those corresponding concepts in the United States, has been described as a movement of "heterophelia" (Taguieff 2001 [1987]), "the New Racism" (Gordon and Klug 1986; Berbrier 1998, 2000), or "differential racism" (Balibar 2002).

22. Exceptions to this trend include the Hungarian political parties Fidesz and Jobbik.

23. German sociologist Henning Eichberg coined the term in 1973 to describe his vision for a new approach to foreign aid that would cultivate difference among nonwestern peoples.

Ethnopluralism, as Eichberg first used it, undermined ethnocentrism and western imperialism (1973, 2011:151–55), and today he recalls intending the term to refer to cultural and social, rather than ethnic or racial, pluralism (personal communication, Henning Eichberg, July 1, 2012). Attracted to the *Nouvelle Droite*'s anti-imperialist stance, Eichberg published a series of articles introducing ethnopluralism in the German *Nouvelle Droite* (see Krebs 1982) and its journal *Junges Forum*, and may have discussed the term in a brief letter correspondence with Alain de Benoist in the mid-1970s (ibid.). Throughout the 1970s, Eichberg slowly disassociated from the right, and eventually abandoned the scene entirely. His term, however, lived on, starting in *Nouvelle Droite* Germany and France, and later throughout European radical nationalism. Activists in these circles would add inherited biological traits to the "ethno" of Eichberg's term. De Benoist began applying the term to the French *Nouvelle Droite*'s preexisting ideology of the right to ethnic difference. Ethnopluralism for him was a demand for ethnic separatism born, not out of assumed superiority of one ethnic group, but out of a belief in the inherent value of preserving ethnic diversity. He nonetheless used the term infrequently, and does not use it today (personal communication, Alain de Benoist, July 15, 2012).

24. Indeed, Spektorowski claims that the school's emphasis on a right to difference is itself borrowed conceptual material from the left (2003:115).

25. Note that usage of the term "identitarian" is far from uniform. I have derived this broad explanation from conversations with insiders.

26. Likely the first published material in the Nordic countries showing influence of the *Nouvelle Droite* was the manifesto of the conservative organization Engelbrek. The organization was founded in 2001, and its leaders included future CEO of *National Today* (*Nationell idag*) Björn Herstad. Herstad himself had come in contact with *Nouvelle Droite* literature first during the late 1990s (personal communication, Björn Herstad, June 22, 2014).

27. Available online, accessed June 2, 2014, http://web.archive.org/web/20050308025324/http://www.nordiskaforbundet.se/forbundet.asp.

28. The League also participated less formally—often through its subsidiaries—in other events like the Salem March.

29. Members of the Nordic League produced only the Scandinavian-language pages, whereas activists abroad operating with relative autonomy wrote other pages. Adam Klein calls the site "white nationalist" or "white power" (2010:93, 147). But such overriding classifications fail to register the rhetorical strategies and ideological positions that vary from article to article, and especially between languages. For example, the English and Hungarian versions of Metapedia are far more open in their criticism of Jews than the original Swedish version. The English page even features a small Star-of-David icon next to the name of every Jewish individual, which in turn links to a page on Judaism.

30. Available online, accessed July 4, 2014, http://www.metapedia.org.

31. Available online, accessed July 15, 2012, http://sv.metapedia.org/wiki/Nordisk.nu.

32. Note that many nationalists also communicate through the extensive non-nationalist discussion forum, Flashback. Flashback began showing signs of supplanting Nordisk.nu as the premier online discussion venue in mid-2013.

33. Subsequent turnover strengthened this trajectory. That same year, the League's lead computer programmer Lars Lindén left the organization citing interpersonal disputes. When leaving, he took the Nordic League's customer register—which he planned to share with a rival National Socialist website—as well as vital tax documents. League members would later break

into Lindén's apartment in Munkedal, Sweden and retake their customer register at gunpoint. However, they struggled to extract their tax documents, and this left the organization in danger of defaulting and being stripped of its projects, including all web pages. Sensing the challenge involved in resolving the situation, Lennart Berg and Anders Lagerström sold their share of the Nordic League to Daniel Friberg. Friberg thereafter hired outside consultants who managed to reproduce the company's tax documents in time for declaration.

34. Available online, accessed July 13, 2012, http://web.archive.org/web/20081222150832/ http://www.nordiskaforbundet.se/artikel.asp?aID=110. Note also that despite its celebration of the past, the manifesto explicitly embraces leading identitarian thinker Guillaume Faye and his concept of archeofuturism. Indeed, it continues to describe culture as something that "develops in parallel with the tribe's ability to respond to current and future challenges in dialogue with those [challenges] from the past, without losing its traditional foundation." But in a divergence from Faye, the manifesto makes no statement of European superiority. Rather, most of its language addresses the topic of identity in universal terms. This hesitation to espouse Eurocentrism may derive from the early influence of Richard McCulloch's writings in the Nordic Press.

35. Video of speech available online, accessed August 27, 2016, http://www.info14.com/media. php?id=94.

36. Available online, accessed July 30, 2012, http://solguru.motpol.nu/?p=72.

37. Jens Rydgren, in his otherwise solid study, overlooks this ideological distinction and its social importance within the nationalist scene when he labels the Sweden Democrats "ethnopluralists" (2006:109).

38. Available online, accessed July 25, 2012, http://web.archive.org/web/20060809162147/ http://www.nd.se/mal/default.asp.

39. McCulloch suggests that the differences between his approach and those of parties like the National Democrats derive from the contrasting sociopolitical situations in Europe and the United States. He says of the culture-race compound concept of ethnicity, "Obviously, this concept doesn't apply very well in the American context, but in the European context it is very important. The different native populations of Europe have ethnic differences that have little to do with race but much to do with cultural, national and linguistic identity and heritage, to which they are very attached and which are very much worth preserving, i.e., they should be regarded as valuable and important. They are an essential component of the human richness of Europe. But these differences, such an important part of the human richness of Europe, barely exist in the Euro-American population. So while I support the 'ethnopluralist' preservation of the nationally and culturally distinct, if not always so racially distinct, native populations of Europe, I don't regard its national and cultural component as relevant to the Euro-American situation, where such national and cultural distinctions barely exist" (electronic message, Richard McCulloch, July 2, 2012).

40. Available online, accessed July 19, 2014, http://web.archive.org/web/20091208051113/; http://www.vigridtvedt.net/.

41. Available online, accessed July 17, 2014, http://web.archive.org/web/20120407062328/; http://www.vigridtvedt.net/metapoli.htm.

42. Available online, accessed June 14, 2014, http://sv.metapedia.org/wiki/Nationalsocialism.

43. These similarities indicated that the Swedish politicians were inspired by identitarians, thereby providing ammunition to antiracist activists who accuse the Sweden Democrats of harboring secret ethnonationalist sympathies. See, e.g., *Resume* (May 30, 2014).

CHAPTER 3

1. The quote in the first opening epigraph was posted on April 29, 2007. Available online, http://www.nordisk.nu/showthread.php?t=269, accessed February 19, 2012. The second quote was posted February 7, 2010. Available online, http://nordiskungdom.se/nio-dagar-med-nu-och-atta-dagar-med-laten-tank/, accessed October 30, 2011.

2. Note that while insiders' understandings of whiteness and Nordicness are not entirely overlapping, the discourses I analyze in this chapter have treated these categories as synonymous. I believe that this derives from the fact that, in discussing global popular musics, these nationalists traffic in the North American black/white divide. Further, the attempts to establish musical whiteness—examined toward the end of this chapter—never referenced European populations with whom Nordic ethnonationalists are hesitant to identify, such as Southern Europeans or Ashkenazi Jews.

3. This point was made by Paul Gilroy (1994) and Tony Mitchell (2001a), the latter arguing against Tricia Rose (1994).

4. Available online, http://solguru.motpol.nu/?page_id=2, accessed February 2, 2011.

5. Note that by calling Zyklon Boom apolitical, I do not mean to suggest that this music qualifies as what Anton Shekhovstov calls "apoliteic music"—a form of European nationalist neo-folk that rejects political activism (2009).

6. This title references ultratraditionalist and identitarian idol Julius Evola's book *Ride the Tiger* (2003 [1961]).

7. Kajikawa anticipates such identification when he astutely points out the ways Eminem's project resonated with the conservative backlash against the perceived excesses of progressive identity politics in the United States (2015:138–40).

8. Available online, http://www.stormfront.org/forum/t827233-2/, accessed February 17, 2012.

9. These two German rap scenes coalesced around the albums *Krauts with Attitude* (1991) and *Cartel* (1995), respectively.

10. I am unaware of any significant white nationalist rap scene in the United States. The only acts to gain major recognition were the New York–based group Neo-Hate, active only during 2001, and a rapper named Paleface from San Francisco, whose song "O'Shea Jackson (Diss Therapy)" is mentioned in *Vibe*, September 1993, 29.

11. Originally attributed to an interview on the now-defunct Italian online magazine, Perimento.com. Available in French translation online, accessed December 4, 2011, http://infosuds.free.fr/082001/enquete_bc.htm.

12. Originally attributed to an interview on the now-defunct Polish nationalist site, InfoPatria. Available in French translation online, accessed December 12, 2011, http://infosuds.free.fr/082001/enquete_bc.htm. My thanks to Aleysia Whitmore for her help with this translation. All mistakes are my own.

13. Nationalist organizations seldom target reggae specifically, though they may include the genre under the umbrella of "Afro-American music" or even "American ghetto culture." When reggae is mentioned, it is often associated with drug use. For example, Magnus Söderman, former activist in the militant Nordic Resistance Movement, wrote "A reggae festival has been taking place in Uppsala since last Thursday. And just like last year's festival, drugs are flowing freely. That isn't so strange, given that reggae is synonymous with drugs" (*Nationellt Motstånd*, August 12, 2007).

14. The associations described by this nationalist were reinforced in mainstream Swedish popular culture. A pair of films directed by Daniel Frisell during the 1990s—*The Seekers* (*Sökarna*) in 1993 and *November 30th* (*30:e November*) in 1995—portrayed a politicized opposition between white power/Viking rock and rap in the public consciousness. Both *The Seekers* and *November 30th* examine the rise of skinhead culture and its antagonisms with immigrant groups during the 1990s. These films paired skinhead youth gangs with Ultima Thule's music, while hip-hop—often the Latin Kings—accompanies immigrants.

15. Available online, accessed August 21, 2014, http://www.nordisk.nu/showthread.php?t=21 216&page=2&highlight=zyklon.

16. Written February 1, 2010. Available online, accessed May 27, 2011, http://www.nationell. nu/2010/01/31/nordisk-ungdom-lanserades-i-goteborg/.

17. Written April 30, 2007. Available online, http://www.nordisk.nu/showthread.php?t=269, accessed February 19, 2011.

18. Available online, accessed October 30, 2011, http://www.dn.se/blogg/pa-stan/2010/02/ 26/fredriks-kronika-det-finns-en-framtid-for-nazistisk-reggae-2570/.

19. Written April 21, 2007. Available online, accessed February 19, 2012, http://www.nordisk. nu/showthread.php?t=269.

20. Written January 15, 2007. Available online, accessed February 19, 2012, http://oskorei. motpol.nu/?p=349.

21. Available online, accessed February 19, 2012, http://www.anus.com/tribes/snus/nihilism/ artiklar/alexis/svartvit/.

22. Note that the claims of "Alexis" hold some merit. Bronx hip-hop pioneer Afrika Bambaataa, for example, admired Kraftwerk and borrowed material from the German group in his own productions. See Chang (2005) for an account of early hip-hop history.

23. Transcript available online, accessed March 2, 2012, http://natvan.com/free-speech/ fs954b.html.

24. See second quote opening this chapter.

25. Written February 1, 2010. Available online, accessed May 27, 2011, http://www.frihet.nu/ forum/1421414548/1325828286.html.

26. Written February 1, 2010. Available online, accessed May 27, 2011, http://www.frihet.nu/ forum/1421414548/1325828286.html.

27. Viktor Sjölund would later tell me that he was not opposed to all use of reggae in nationalist music. Rather, he objected to the fact that a nationalist organization used the genre to announce and define itself. In his mind, reggae may be included in the scene, but it should not represent it (Interview, Viktor Sjölund, April 12, 2012).

28. Written February 1, 2010. Available online, accessed May 27, 2011, http://www.frihet.nu/ forum/1421414548/1325828286.html.

29. Written February 2, 2010. Available online, accessed May 27, 2011, http://www.frihet.nu/ forum/1421414548/1325828286.html.

30. Written Febrary 3, 2010. Available online, accessed May 27, 2011, http://www.frihet.nu/ forum/1421414548/1325828286.html.

31. Available online, accessed May 27, 2011, http://www.frihet.nu/forum/1421414548/ 1325828286.html.

32. Written May 1, 2007. Available online, accessed February 19, 2012, http://www.nordisk.nu/ showthread.php?t=269&page=11&highlight=zyklon+boom.

CHAPTER 4

1. Prolific folk music scholar and performer Sven Ahlbäck groups 1700s and 1800s dance traditions and herding styles together under the heading "older folk music" (1995). Kaminsky (2012a) explores definitions of folk music among practitioners in Sweden. See also Bohlman (1988).

2. Note that Swedish nationalists tend not to use the term when referring to genres of neofolk music popular among other European nationalists (see Shekhovstov 2009).

3. For more information on early ultraconservative interest in Swedish folk music, see Ling (1980), Roempke (1980), Kaminsky (2012b), and Teitelbaum (2013).

4. Note that Andersson's phraseology here is borrowed from an interview with Owens in the American music magazine *Resistance* (1996, no. 6).

5. Other, somewhat less engaged nationalists include Angelika Bengtsson and Runar Filper in the Sweden Democrats, Andreas Johansson in Nordic Youth, and free nationalist Johan Björnsson.

6. One exception is white power band Storm's cover of the Swedish war-era National Socialist anthem "Friheten leve." Their 1998 cover on the album *European Guard* features an introduction with nyckelharpa.

7. Such as the solo melody in Röde Orm's track "Vårt Land."

8. When visiting nationalist events, I often asked music vendors why they did not carry any Swedish folk music recordings. Most thought the genre should be included in their offerings, and had no explanation as to why it was not.

9. Balder's writings began to subside at the start of the 1990s, and instead the topics he wrote about were often discussed in a new feature called "Fun Culture" (*Kul Kultur*).

10. Available online, accessed May 27, 2012, http://web.archive.org/web/20021124154536/; http://sverigedemokraterna.se/

11. Available online, accessed May 27, 2012, http://web.archive.org/web/19991013170835/; http://www.sverigedemokraterna.se/sd/

12. See article, "SD vill ha en mer centralstyrd kulturpolitik" (Kulturnytt, October 21, 2010), and program *Morgon* on P1 radio, October 27, 2010.

13. Motion to Riksdagen, 2010/11:SD300

14. Available online, accessed June 14, 2012, http://sverigesradio.se/sida/artikel.aspx?program id=2487&artikel=4102334.

15. Skansen is an outdoor folk park in central Stockholm showcasing rural culture from around the country.

16. I interviewed Hans Rydberg on March 29, 2011, more than twenty years after Sundberg wrote this article. Rydberg did not recall having told Sundberg, nor having ever thought, that large numbers of nationalists were attending his dances.

17. When the Sweden Democrats achieved their symbolic and strategic victory by entering the national parliament during the 2010 elections, they did so receiving only 334,053 votes (or 5.7% of the total vote). The National Democrats received 1,141 votes (0.02% of the total vote), and the Party of the Swedes received 681 votes (0.01% of the total vote). Available online, accessed June 5, 2012, http://www.val.se/val/val2010/slutresultat/R/rike/index.html.

18. Like rightist commentators of earlier generations, many revivalists were thus invested in the perceived purity of folk music. The new celebration of a "pure" folk music prompted musicologist Jan Ling to warn leftists that such rhetoric might make the genre appealing to their political opposites once again (1979). The most direct articulation of the far left agenda in the folk music

revival was an academic publication, *Folket har aldrig segrat till fiendens musik: Musikpolitiska artiklar* (The People Have Never Triumphed by Marching to the Enemy's Music: Articles on Music Politics) (Fiskvik et al. 1977).

19. See "Kulturkrig med knätofs," *Aftonbladet* (January 17, 2011).

20. Available online, accessed June 21, 2012, http://www.limmud.org/home/mission/.

21. Available online, accessed May 23, 2012, https://www.flashback.org/p35839566#p35839566.

22. For example, in an interview with Minister of Culture Lena Adelsohn Liljeroth published in *Folk music & dans* (2011, no. 1:11), he criticized the minister for her statements that no specifically Swedish culture exists. Those criticisms prompted the minister to express regret over her previous statements.

23. Available online, accessed March 19, 2011, http://www.nationellidag.se/visa/default.asp?dokID=1304.

CHAPTER 5

1. This website, with the address http://www.adp.fptoday.com/musicfem.htm, is no longer online. I am grateful to Les Back for providing me with a printed image of the page as it appeared on June 15, 1998. See also Back (2002:116).

2. Of these tracks, only two were written by Saga. The other ten songs were written by figures including Ian Stuart Donaldson of Skrewdriver, Canadian white power band RaHoWa (short for Racial Holy War), or based on the poetry of late American white nationalist David Lane. Breivik may have been aware of this. See Teitelbaum (2014).

3. She has performed for festivals arranged by the Nordic League (see chapter 2), though this was before that organization made its sharpest turn toward identitarianism.

4. Emily Turner-Graham, in an otherwise compelling essay on Saga, appears to miss this start of Saga's recording career (2012:107).

5. Donaldson alternated between singing "Once a nation, and now we're run by Jews," and "Once a nation, and now we're run by whom?" in this track. Saga chose the latter text when she recorded "Free My Land" on her second tribute album in 2000.

6. See Kandiyoti (1991:8), Collier (1997), and Yuval-Davis (1996, 1997).

7. See Dobratz and Shanks Meile (1997), Ferber (1998, 2004), Rogers and Litt (2004), and Anahita (2006).

8. Scholars like Von Hofer (2000), Lundgren et al. (2002), and Lovett and Kelly (2009) attempt to qualify Sweden's ranking by tracing it to international differences in defining and reporting rape rather than the prevalence of sexual assault in any absolute sense.

9. Available online, accessed March 23, 2016, https://www.youtube.com/watch?v=tiODoQR5040.

10. See Fangen (1998a).

11. Available online, accessed May 5, 2012, http://midgaardshop.com/om-oss.

12. Written August 17, 2009. Available online, accessed May 10, 2012, http://www.nordisk.nu/showthread.php?t=37464&page=3&highlight=Frigg.

13. This term positions the genre as ideologically, but not musically, similar to white power punk and metal, which insiders increasingly refer to as "freedom rock."

14. See, e.g., user "brandr" on nationell.nu, August 7, 2011. Available online, accessed March 14, 2012, http://www.nationell.nu/2011/08/06/saga-i-expressen-da-var-jag-mer-extrem/.

15. Available online, accessed May 8, 2012, http://www.facebook.com/pages/Saga/249159933080.

16. This is true even of the Swedish band Vinterdis, whose singer Johanna has been hostile toward Saga and her music in public interviews (Interview available online, accessed May 10, 2012, http://revoltns.blogspot.com/2009_07_01_archive.html).

17. A video of this concert is available online, http://www.youtube.com/watch?v=4b2KAMZsjto.

18. Serbian act Sadko & Third Way's cover of "Ode to a Dying People" offers one example of this.

19. Blee appears to observe this common composite identity when she names one persona of women in American white nationalist circles as "goddess/victim" (2002:115–16).

20. Available online, accessed May 8, 2012, http://www.facebook.com/pages/Saga/249159933080.

CHAPTER 6

1. Available online, accessed March 23, 2016, https://www.youtube.com/watch?v=qZOl7MhQNkY

2. See this quote in *Dagens Nyheter*, November 15, 2006.

3. Söderman's reference to "great days of old [*fornstora dar*]" in this final statement references a line in the second verse of Sweden's national anthem "Du Gamla, Du Fria."

4. Book production has become more profitable thanks to the rise of print-on-demand technology, and Daniel Friberg's pan-Scandinavian Arktos Publishing has exploited this opportunity most effectively. Newspaper producers in Sweden have successfully tapped into public media funding. Amid intense public outcry, the newspaper *National Today* (*Nationell Idag*) received 2,400,000SEK (approx. $370,000) of tax money to support their operations in 2009 and had that support renewed in 2011 and 2012. But the greatest nonmusical fundraising success in the scene has been the electoral triumphs of the Sweden Democrats. Following their entry into parliament in 2010, for example, the party received 110,000,000SEK (approx. $16,500,000) in public support.

5. See also Woo (2009).

6. Note that nationalists advocating metapolitics would agree with the statement that politics via style is not real politics. Metapolitics is intended to prepare for future political action. However, there are some key distinctions between subcultural protest and metapolitics, such that some activists see the transition from the former to the latter as progress. Whereas subcultures cling to a single style and use it to disassociate from society at large, those pursuing metapolitics seek to employ all media available in order to reach a wide audience. For more on metapolitics, see chapter 2.

7. The number 14 in the title is a reference to American white nationalist David Lane and his famed fourteen-word statement, "we must secure the existence of our people and a future for white children" (see Michael 2009).

8. Available online, accessed July 27 2012, http://sverigesradio.se/sida/artikel.aspx?programid=83&artikel=2747308.

9. The word "cosmopolitan," along with "the gold," "the money," "moneychangers," or "the liars," is frequently used in ethnonationalist circles to refer to Jews.

10. This individual suggests that his celebration of a given set of song lyrics ought not be taken at face value—that lyrics may speak to him in ways beyond their literal meaning. As such, his thoughts call to mind Potter's writing about the "unserious seriousness" in hip-hop poetics and the potential for lyrics to be at once insincere in their surface-level content and deeply earnest in their underlying social critique (1995:84; see also Knudsen 2011:85). The potential for listeners to derive unarticulated messages from music provides an additional means by which the control of musical experience by political actors seems inauspicious.

11. We encountered similar discourses in chapter 3, where insiders described a broad cross-section of genres as politically and ethnically neutral.

12. See Sahlin's interview in *Euroturk* magazine, 2002, no. 2.

13. One of the more lucid examples of this thinking in the history of European music comes from the writings of sixteenth-century Italian humanist Girolamo Mei (see Tanay 2006).

EPILOGUE

1. Available online, accessed Septemer 4, 2016, http://www.dn.se/nyheter/sverige/sds-marie-stensby-hoppar-av/.

Bibliography

Ahkell, Jah. 1981. *Rasta: Emperor Haile Selassie and the Rastafarians*. Port of Spain: Black Starliner.

Ahlbäck, Sven. 1995. *Tonspråket i den äldre svensk folkmusik* [Tonal Language in Older Swedish Folk Music]. Stockholm: Royal College of Music.

Åkesson, Jimmie. 2010. 99 Förslag för ett bättre Sverige: Sverigedemokraternas kontrakt med väljarna, 2010–2014 [99 Proposals for a Better Sweden: The Swede Democrats' Contract with the Voters, 2010–2014]. Press Document.

Ålund, Aleksandra, and Carl-Ulrik Schierup. 1991. *Paradoxes of Multiculturalism*. Aldershot: Avebury.

Ålund, Aleksandra, and Carl-Ulrik Schierup. 1993. "The Thorny Road to Europe: Swedish Immigrant Policy In Transition." In John Wrench and John Solomos (eds), *Racism and Migration in Western Europe*. Providence: Berg, 99–114.

Anahita, Sine. 2006. Blogging the Borders: Virtual Skinheads, Hypermasculinity, and Heteronormativity. *Journal of Political and Military Sociology* 34(1):143–64.

Anderson, Tammy L. 2009. Understanding the Alteration and Decline of a Music Scene: Observations from Rave Culture. *Sociological Forum* 24(2):307–36.

Andersson, Jenny. 2009. Nordic Nostalgia and Nordic Light: The Swedish Model as Utopia 1930–2007. *Scandinavian Journal of History* 34(3):229–45.

Andersson, Jenny, and Mary Hilson. 2009. Images of Sweden and the Nordic Countries. *Scandinavian Journal of History* 34(3):219-28.

Andersson, Reinhold. 2001 [1964]. *Beskrivning av Svenska Folkdanser* [Description of Swedish Folk Dances]. Part 1. Hudiksvall: Kommuntrykeriet.

Arneback, Emma. 2013. "Bemötanden av främlingsfientlighet i gymnasieskolan [Confronting Xenophobia in Secondary School]." In M. Deland, P. Fuehrer, and F. Hertzberg (eds), Det vita fältet II. Samtida forskning om högerextremism [The White Field II: Contemporary Research on Right-Wing Extremism]. Special issue of *Arkiv. Tidskrift för samhällsanalys* 2:139–65.

Arnstad, Henrik. 2013. *Älskade fascism: De svartbruna rörelsernas ideologi och historia* [Beloved Fascism: The Black-Brown Movements' Ideology and History]. Stockholm: Norstedts.

Asad, Talal (ed). 1973. *Anthropology and the Colonial Encounter*. Atlantic Highlands: Humanities Press.

Attali, Jacques. 1985 [1977]. *Noise: The Political Economy of Music*. Translated by Brian Massumi. Manchester: Manchester University Press.

Baacke, Dieter, Michaela Thier, Christian Gruninger, and Frank Lindemann. 1994. *Rock von Rechts* [Rock from the Right]. Bielefeld: AJZ-Druck& Verlag.

Back, Les. 2000. Voices of Hate: Black Music and the Complexities of Racism. *Black Music Research Journal* 20(2):127–49.

Back, Les. 2002. "Wagner and Power Chords: Skinheadism, White Power Music and the Internet." In Vron Ware and Les Back (eds), *Out of Whiteness: Color, Politics, and Culture*. Chicago: University of Chicago Press, 94–132.

Backes, Uwe. 2010. *Political Extremes: A Conceptual History from Antiquity to the Present*. New York: Routledge.

Bale, Jeffrey M. 2002. "National Revolutionary" Groupuscules and the Resurgence of "Left-Wing" Fascism: The Case of France's Nouvelle Résistance. *Patterns of Prejudice* 36(3):26–49.

Balibar, Étienne. 2002. "Finns det en 'nyrasism?'" [Is There a "New Racism?"]. In Étienne Balibar och Immanuel Wallerstein (eds), *Ras, nation, klass* [Race, Nation, Class]. Stockholm: Daidalos, 33–47.

Ball, Terence. 1999. From "Core" to "Sore" Concepts: Ideological Innovation and Conceptual Change. *Journal of Political Ideologies* 4(3):391–96.

Bar-On, Tamir. 2007. *Where Have All the Fascists Gone?* Aldershot: Ashgate Publishing.

Bar-On, Tamir. 2013. *Rethinking the French New Right: Alternatives to Modernity*. London: Routledge.

Batson, Charles R. 2009. Panique Celtique: Manau's Celtic Rap, Breton Cultural Expression, and Contestatory Performance in Contemporary France. *French Politics, Culture & Society* 27(2):63–83.

Baum, Bruce. 2006. *The Rise and Fall of the Caucasian Race: A Political History of Racial Identity*. New York: New York University Press.

Bauman, Zygmunt. 1994. Från pilgrim till turist [From Pilgrim to Tourist]. *Moderna Tider* 47(3):34–37.

Beaudry, Nicole. 2008. "The Challenges of Human Relations in Ethnographic Inquiry: Examples from Arctic and Subarctic Fieldwork." In Gregory Barz and Timothy Cooley (eds), *Shadows in the Field: New Perspectives for Fieldwork in Ethnomusicology*. Oxford: Oxford University Press, 224–45.

Beckwith, Karl. 2002. "'Black Metal Is for White People': Constructs of Colour and Identity with the Extreme Metal Scene." *M/C: A Journal of Media and Culture* 5(3). Available online, accessed December 4, 2012, http://journal.media-culture.org.au/0207/blackmetal.php.

Berbrier, Mitch. 1998. "Half the Battle": Cultural Resonance, Framing Processes, and Ethnic Affectations in Contemporary White Separatist Rhetoric. *Social Problems* 45(4):431–50.

Berbrier, Mitch. 2000. The Victim Ideology of White Supremacists and White Separatists in the United States. *Sociological Focus* 33(2):175–91.

Berggren, Henrik, and Lars Trägårdh. 2009. *Är svensken människa? Gemenskap och oberoende i det moderna Sverige* [Is the Swede a Human?: Community and Independence in Modern Sweden]. Stockholm: Norstedts.

Berggren, Lena. 2002. Swedish Fascism—Why Bother? *Journal of Contemporary Politics* 37(3):395–417.

Bergmark, Åke, and Joakim Palme. 2003. Welfare and the Unemployment Crisis: Sweden in the 1990s. *International Journal of Social Welfare* 12:108–22.

Betz, Hans-Georg. 1999. Contemporary Right-Wing Radicalism in Europe. *Contemporary European History* 8(2):299–316.

Bjørgo, Tore. 2000. "Främlingsfientliga ungdomsgäng: Våldsutövare, processer och lokalsamhällets reaktioner [Xenophobic Youth Gangs: Perpetrators of Violence, Processes, and Local Reactions]." In Ingrid Sahlin and Malin Åkerström (eds), *Det lokala våldet: Om rädsla, rasism och socialkontroll* [Local Violence: On Fear, Racism, and Social Control]. Malmö: Liber, 71–106.

Bjurström, E. 1997. The Struggle for Ethnicity: Swedish Youth Styles and the Construction of Ethnic Identities. *Young: Nordic Journal of Youth Research* 5(3):44–58.

Blee, Kathleen. 2002. *Inside Organized Racism: Women and the Hate Movement.* Berkeley: University of California Press.

Blee, Kathleen. 2004. "Women and Organized Racism." In Abby L. Ferber (ed), *Home Grown Hate: Gender and Organized Racism.* New York: Routledge, 46–70.

Bohlman, Philip V. 1988. *The Study of Folk Music in the Modern World.* Bloomington: Indiana University Press.

Bohlman, Philip V. 2002. Landscape—Region—Nation—Reich: German Folk Song in the Nexus of National Identity. In Celia Applegate and Pamela Potter (eds), *Music and German National Identity.* Chicago: University of Chicago Press, 105–27.

Bohlman, Philip V. 2011. *Music, Nationalism, and the Making of the New Europe.* 2nd ed. New York and London: Routledge.

Bonilla-Silva, Eduardo. 2006. *Racism without Racists.* 2nd ed. Lanham, MD: Rowman & Littlefield.

Bonilla-Silva, Eduardo, and Tyrone Forman. 2000. "I'm not a racist, but. . .: Mapping White College Students' Racial Ideology in the USA." *Discourse & Society* 11(1):50–85.

Bonnett, Alastair. 2002. A White World? Whiteness and the Meaning of Modernity in Latin America and Japan. In Cynthia Levine-Rasky (ed), *Working through Whiteness: International Perspectives.* Albany: State University of New York Press, 69–106.

Born, Georgina, and David Hesmondhalgh. 2000. "On Difference, Representation, and Appropriation in Music." In Georgina Born and David Hesmondhalgh (eds), *Western Music and Its Others.* Berkeley: University of California Press, 1–58.

Brake, Mike. 1985. *Comparative Youth Culture: The Sociology of Youth Cultures and Youth Subcultures in America, Britain, and Canada.* London: Routledge.

Breivik, Anders (psyd. Andrew Berwick). 2010. *2083: A Declaration of European Independence.* N.p.:N.p.

Briggs, Charles. 1992. "Since I am a Woman, I will Chastise My Relatives": Gender, Reported Speech, and the (Re)production of Social Relations in Warao Ritual Wailing. *American Ethnologist* 19(2):337–61.

Brottsförebyggande rådet (BRÅ) [The Swedish National Council for Crime Prevention]. 2005. Brottslighet bland personer födda i Sverige och i utlandet [Crime among Persons Born in Sweden and Abroad]. Published Report.

Brown, Timothy S. 2004. Subcultures, Pop Music and Politics: Skinheads and "Nazi Rock" in England and Germany. *Journal of Social History* 38(1):157–78.

Brown, Timothy S. 2006. "'Keeping It Real' in a Different 'Hood: (African-) Americanization and Hip-hop in Germany." In Dipannita Basu and Sidney J. Lemelle (eds), *The Vinyl Ain't Final: Hip Hop and the Globalization of Black Popular Culture*. London: Pluto Press, 137–50.

Caraveli, Ana. 1986. "The Bitter Wounding: The Lament as Social Protest in Rural Greece." In Jill Dubisch (ed), *Gender and Power in Rural Greece*. Princeton: Princeton University Press, 169–94.

Carby, Hazel V. 1992. "The Multicultural Wars." In Gina Dent (ed), *Black Popular Culture*. Seattle: Bay Press, 187–99.

Carr, Leslie. 1997. *Colorblind Racism*. Thousand Oaks: Sage.

Ceasar, Julia (pseud). 2010. *Världsmästerna. När Sverige blev mångkulturellt* [World Champions: When Sweden Became Multicultural]. Visby: Books on Demand.

Chang, Jeff. 2005. *Can't Stop, Won't Stop: A History of the Hip-Hop Generation*. New York: St. Martin's Press.

Chatterjee, Partha. 1986. Colonialism, Nationalism, and Colonialized Women: The Contest in India. *American Ethnologist* 16(4):622–33.

Chatterjee, Partha. 1993. *The Nation and Its Fragments: Colonial and Postcolonial Histories*. Princeton: Princeton University Press.

Christians, Clifford G. 2000. "Ethics and Politics in Qualitative Research." In Norman K. Denzin and Yvonna S. Lincoln (eds), *The Sage Handbook of Qualitative Research*. 3rd ed. London: Sage Books, 109–38.

Collier, Jane Fishburn. 1997. *From Duty to Desire: Remaking Families in a Spanish Village*. Princeton: Princeton University Press.

Condry, Ian. 2006. *Hip-Hop Japan: Rap and the Paths of Cultural Globalization*. Durham, NC: Duke University Press.

Cook, Samuel. 2006. *Monacans and Miners: Native American and Coal Mining Communities in Appalachia*. Lincoln: University of Nebraska Press.

Cooley, Timothy. 2003. Theorizing Fieldwork Impact: Malinowski, Peasant-Love, and Friendship. *British Journal of Ethnomusicology* 12(1):1–17.

Copsey, N. 2003. "Extremism on the Net: The Extreme Right and the Value of the Internet." In R. Gibson, P. Nixon, and S. Ward (eds), *Political Parties and the Internet: Net Gain?* London: Routledge, 218–33.

Cornell, Stephen Ellicott, and Douglas Hartmann. 2007. *Ethnicity and Race: Making Identities in a Changing World*. London: Sage.

Corte, Ugo, and Bob Edwards. 2008. White Power Music and the Mobilization of Racist Social Movements. *Music and Arts in Action* 1(1):4–20.

Crook, Larry N. 1993. Black Consciousness, *Samba Reggae*, and the Re-Africanization of Bahian Carnival Music in Brazil. *The World of Music* 35.

Davis, Michael J. 2009. Was That Racist or Not? I Can't Tell: The Music of Prussian Blue. PhD diss., University of Tennessee.

De Benoist, Alain. 2004. *On Being a Pagan*. Atlanta: Ultra.

De Benoist, Alain. 2011 [2009]. "The New Right: Forty Years After." Guest foreword. In Tomislav Sunic, *Against Democracy and Equality: The European New Right*. London: Arktos Media, 15–29.

De Benoist, Alain, and Charles Champetier. 1999. The French New Right in the Year 2000. Translated by Martin Bendelow and Francis Green. *Telos* 115:117–44.

DeClair, Edward G. 1999. *Politics on the Fringe: The People, Policies, and Organization of the French Front National.* Durham: Duke University Press.

Deland, Mats, Fredrik Hertzberg, and Thomas Hvitfeldt. 2010. "Introduction." In Deland, Mats, Fredrik Hertzberg, and Thomas Hvitfeldt (eds), *Det vita fältet: Samtida forskning om högerextremism* [The White Field: Contemporary Research on Right-Wing Extremism]. Uppsala: University of Uppsala Department of History, 5–13.

Denzin, Norman. 1997. *Interpretive Ethnography: Ethnographic Practices for the 21st Century.* London: Sage Books.

Diamanti, I. 1996. "The Northern League: From Regional Party to Party of the Government." In S. Parker and S. Gundle (eds), *The New Italian Republic: From the Fall of the Berlin Wall to Berlusconi.* London: Routledge, 113–29.

Doane, Ashley W., Jr. 1997. Dominant Group Ethnic Identity in the United States: The Role of "Hidden" Ethnicity in Intergroup Relations. *Sociological Quarterly* 38(3):375–97.

Dobrats, Betty A., and Stephanie L. Shanks-Meile. 1997. *White Power! White Pride! The White Separatist Movement in the United States.* New York: Twayne.

Dominguez, Virginia R. 1986. *White by Definition: Social Classification in Creole Louisiana.* New Brunswick, NJ: Rutgers University Press.

Dornbusch, Christian, and Jan Raabe. 2008. "Protestnoten für Deutschland." In Andreas Speit and Andrea Röpke (eds), *Neonazis in Nadelstreifen: Die NPD auf dem Weg in die Mitte der Gesellschaft* [Neo-Nazis in Pinstripes: The NPD on the Way toward Society's Mainstream]. Berlin: Christoph Links Verlag, 169–92.

Dyck, Kristen. 2012. "Race and Nation in White Power Music." Ph.D. diss., Washington State University.

Dyer, Richard. 1997. *White.* London: Routledge.

Eatwell, Rodger. 1996. Surfing the Great Wave: The Internet, Extremism, and Problems of Control. *Patterns of Prejudice* 30(1):61–71.

Eatwell, Rodger. 2000. The Rebirth of the Extreme Right in Western Europe? *Parliamentary Affairs* 53(3):407–25.

Eichberg, Henning. 1973. *Ethnopluralismus: eine Kritik d. naiven Ethnozentrismus u. d. Entwicklungshilfe* [Ethnopluralism: A Critique of Naïve Ethnocentrism and Foreign Aid]. Hamburg: Verlag Deutsch-Europäischer Studien.

Eichberg, Henning. 2011. *Minderheit und Mehrheit* [Minority ad Majority]. Berlin: LIT Verlag.

Ekman, Mikael, and Daniel Poohl. 2010. *Ut ur garderoben: En kritisk granskning av Sverigedemokraterna* [Out of the Closet: A Critical Examination of the Sweden Democrats]. Stockholm: Natur & Kultur.

Elflein, Dietmar. 1998. From Krauts with Attitudes to Turks with Attitudes: Some Aspects of Hip-Hop History in Germany. *Popular Music* 17(3):255–65.

Elliston, Deborah. 2000. Geographies of Gender and Politics: The Place of Difference in Polynesian Nationalism. *Cultural Anthropology* 15(2):171–216.

Elliston, Deborah. 2004. A Passion for the Nation: Masculinity, Modernity, and Nationalist Struggle. *American Ethnologist* 31(4):606–30.

Evola, Julius. 2003 [1961]. *Ride the Tiger: A Survival Manual for the Aristocrats of the Soul.* Translated by Joscelyn Godwin and Constance Fontana. Rochester, VT: Inner Traditions.

Eysenck, Hans Jürgen. 1954. *The Psychology of Politics*. London: Routledge.

Ezekiel, Raphael S. 1995. *The Racist Mind: Portraits of American Neo-Nazis and Klansmen*. New York: Viking Press.

Fangen, Katrine. 1998a. Living Out Our Ethnic Instincts: Ideological Beliefs among Right-Wing Activists in Norway. In Jeffrey Kaplan and Tore Bjørgo (eds), *Nation and Race*. Boston: Northeastern University Press, 202–30.

Fangen, Katrine. 1998b. Fangens dilemma. *Nytt Norsk Tidsskrift* 15(3): 257–69.

Fangen, Katrine. 1999. On the Margins of Life: Life Stories of Radical Nationalists. *Acta Sociologica* 42(4):357–75.

Fangen, Katrine. 2001. *En bok om nynazister* [A Book about Neo-Nazis]. Oslo: Universitetsforlaget.

Faye, Guillaume. 2010. *Archeofuturism: European Visions of the Post-Catastrophic Age*. London: Arktos Media.

Faye, Guillaume. 2011. *Why We Fight: Manifesto of the European Resistance*. London: Arktos Media.

Feld, Steven, and Aaron Fox. 1994. Music and Language. *Annual Review of Anthropology* 23:25–53.

Ferber, Abby L. 1998. *White Man Falling: Race, Gender, and White Supremacy*. Lanham, MD: Rowman & Littlefield.

Ferber, Abby L. 2004. "Introduction." In Abby Ferber (ed), *Home-Grown Hate: Gender and Organized Racism*. New York: Routledge, 1–17.

Fish, Stanley. 1997. Boutique Multiculturalism, or Why Liberals Are Incapable of Thinking about Hate Speech. *Critical Inquiry* 23(2):378–95.

Fiskvik, Sæmund, et al. 1977. *Folket har aldrig segrat till fiendens musik: Musikpolitiska artiklar* [The People Have Never Achieved Victory by Marching to the Enemy's Music: Articles on Music Politics]. Stockholm: Oktoberförlaget.

Fleischer, Rasmus. 2003. "Etnopluralism: Om Nationaldemokraterna och framväxten av en ny rasism" [Ethnopluralism: On the National Democrats and the Growth of a New Racism]. C-level paper, Södertörn University College, Institute for Contemporary History.

Fluehr-Lobban, Carolyn (ed). 2003. *Ethics and the Profession of Anthropology: Dialogue for Ethically Conscious Practice*. Walnut Creek, CA: AltaMira.

Forman, T. A., and A. E. Lewis. 2004. "White Racial Apathy: The Anatomy of Racism and Prejudice in the Post-Civil Rights Era." Paper presented at the annual meeting of the American Sociological Association, San Francisco, CA.

Frankenberg, Ruth. 1993. *White Women, Race Matters: The Social Construction of Whiteness*. Minneapolis: University of Minnesota Press.

Frankenberg, Ruth. 2001. "The Mirage of an Unmarked Whiteness." In Birgit Brander Rasmussen, Eric Klinenberg, Irene J. Nexica, and Matt Wray (eds), *The Making and Unmaking of Whiteness*. Durham: Duke University Press, 72–96.

Fraser, Andrew. 2011. *The WASP Question*. London: Arktos Media.

Freeden, Michael. 1997. Ideologies and Conceptual History. *Journal of Political Ideologies* 2(1):3–12.

Freeden, Michael. 1998. Is Nationalism a Distinct Ideology? *Political Studies*. 46(4):748–65.

Frith, Simon. 1996. "Music and Identity." In Stuart Hall and Paul Gilroy (eds), *Questions of Cultural Identity*. London: Sage, 108–50.

Futrell, Robert, Peter Simi, and Simon Gottschalk. 2006. Understanding Music in Movements: The White Power Music Scene. *Sociological Quarterly* 47:275–304.

Gallagher, Charles A. 2000. "White Like Me?" In France Winddance Twine and Jonathan W. Warren (eds), *Racing Research, Researching Race: Methodological Dilemmas in Critical Race Studies*. New York: New York University Press, 67–92.

Gallagher, Charles A. 2003a. Colorblind Privilege: The Social and Political Functions of Erasing the Color Line in Post Race America. *Race, Gender & Class* 10(4):22–37.

Gallagher, Charles A. 2003b. "Playing the White Ethnic Card: Using Ethnic Identity to Deny Contemporary Racism." In Ashley Woody Doane and Eduardo Bonilla-Silva (eds), *White Out: The Continuing Significance of Racism*. New York: Routledge, 145–58.

Gardell, Mattias. 2003. *Gods of the Blood: The Pagan Revival and White Separatism*. Durham, NC: Duke University Press.

Garpelin, Anders, Sverker Lindblad, and Fritjof Sahlström. 1995. Vikings and Hip-Hoppers in the Classroom: An Explorative Case Study of Cultural Conflict in an Educational Setting. *Young* 3(3). Available online, accessed January 19, 2013, http://logic.itsc.cuhk.edu.hk/~b114299/young/1995/95_3_artikkel_Garpelin.htm.

Geertz, Clifford. 1998. Deep Hanging Out. *New York Review of Books*, October 22, 69–72.

Gellner, Ernst. 1983. *Nations and Nationalism*. Ithaca, NY: Cornell University Press.

Gellner, Ernst. 1985. *Relativism and the Social Sciences*. Cambridge: Cambridge University Press.

Gibson, Rachel. 2002. *The Growth of Anti-Immigrant Parties in Western Europe*. Lewiston: Edwin Mellon Press.

Gilroy, Paul. 1994. "After the Love Has Gone": Bio-politics and Ethno-poetics in the Black Public Sphere. *Public Culture* 7(1):49–77.

Givens, Terri G. 2004. The Radical Right Gender Gap. *Comparative Political Studies* 37(1):30–54.

Gladney, Dru C. 2004. *Dislocating China: Muslims, Minorities, and Other Subaltern Subjects*. Chicago: University of Chicago Press.

Goluboff, Sascha. 2008. Patriarchy through Lamentation in Azerbaijan. *American Ethnologist* 35(1):81–94.

Goodwin, Matthew. 2006. The Rise and Faults of Internalist Perspective in Extreme Right Studies. *Representation* 42(4):347–64.

Goodriche-Clarke, Nicholas. 2002. *Black Sun: Aryan Cults, Esoteric Nazism and the Politics of Identity*. New York: New York University Press.

Gordon, Paul, and Francesca Klug. 1986. *New Right, New Racism*. London: Searchlight Publications.

Graves, William III, and Mark A. Shields. 1991. "Rethinking Moral Responsibility in Fieldwork: The Situated Negotiation of Research Ethics in Anthropology and Sociology." In Carolyn Fluehr-Lobban (ed), *Ethics and the Profession of Anthropology: Dialogue for a New Era*. Philadelphia: University of Pennsylvania Press, 132–51.

Green-Pedersen, Christoffer, and Pontus Odmalm. 2008. Going Different Ways? Right-Wing Parties and the Immigrant Issue in Denmark and Sweden. *Journal of European Public Policy* 15(3):367–81.

Griffin, Roger. 1993. *The Nature of Fascism*. London: Routledge.

Griffin, Roger. 2000. Between Metapolitics and *Apoliteia*: The Nouvelle Droite's Strategy for Conserving the Fascist Vision in the "Interregnum." *Modern and Contemporary France* 8(1):35–53.

Griffin, Roger. 2003. From Slime Mould to Rhizome: An Introduction to the Groupuscular Right. *Patterns of Prejudice* 31(1):27–50.

Griffin, Roger. 2006. "Fascism's New Faces (and Facelessness) in the Post-Fascist Epoch." In Roger Griffin, Werner Loh, and Andreas Umland (eds), *Fascism Past and Present, West and East: An International Debate on Concepts and Cases in the Comparative Study of the Extreme Right*. Stuttgart: ibidem-Verlag, 29–67.

Griffiths, Marc. 1995. *Boss Sounds: Classic Skinhead Reggae*. Dunoon: S.T. Publishing.

Grönqvist, Björn. 2008. Sverigedemokraterna och skolan: En studie av hur Sverigedemokraterna behandlas i samhällskunskapsundervisningen på gymnasiet [The Sweden Democrats and the School: A Study of How the Sweden Democrats Are Discussed in Social Science Classes in Secondary School]. M.A. thesis, Karlstad University.

Güngör, Murat, and Hannes Loh. 2002. *Fear of a Kanak Planet: HipHop zwischen Weltkultur und Nazi-Rap* [Fear of a Kanak Planet: Hip Hop between World Culture and Nazi Rap]. Höfen: Hannibal.

Hågård, Henrik. 2011. Diskutera tills de lärt sig, om lärares syn på värdegrundsarbete och främlingsfientlighet [Discuss It until They Have Learned: On Teachers' Views of Values and Xenophobia]. M.A. thesis, Gothenburg University.

Hainsworth, Paul, and Paul Mitchell. 2000. France: The National Front from Crossroads to Crossroads? *Parliamentary Affairs* 53(3):443–56.

Hale, Charles R. 2006. Activist Research vs. Cultural Critique: Indigenous Land Rights and the Contradictions of Politically Engaged Anthropology. *Cultural Anthropology* 21(1):96–120.

Hamrud, Annika. 2011. Sverigedemokraternas användning av begreppet "svenskfientlighet"—en diskursanalys [The Sweden Democrats' Use of the Term "Anti-Swedishness"—A Discourse Analysis]. C-level paper, Södertörn University.

Harding, Susan. 2001. *The Book of Jerry Falwell: Fundamentalist Language and Politics*. Princeton: Princeton University Press.

Healy, Murray. 1996. *Gay Skins: Class, Masculinity, and Queer Appropriation*. London: Cassell.

Hebdige, Dick. 1988. *Subculture: The Meaning of Style*. London: Routledge.

Hellier-Tinoco, Ruth. 2003. Experiencing People: Relationships, Responsibility and Reciprocity. *British Journal of Ethnomusicology* 12(1):19–34.

Hellström, Anders, and Thomas Nilsson. 2010. "We Are the Good Guys": Ideological Positioning of the Nationalist Party Sverigedemokraterna in Contemporary Swedish Politics. *Ethnicities* 10(1):55–76.

Hervik, Peter. 2011. *The Annoying Difference: The Emergence of Danish Neonationalism, Neoracism, and Populism in the Post-1989 World*. New York: Berghahn Books.

Hess, Mickey. 2007. *Is Hip Hop Dead? The Past, Present, and Future of America's Most Wanted Music*. Westport, CT: Praeger.

Hewitt, Roger. 2005. *White Backlash and the Politics of Multiculturalism*. Cambridge: Cambridge University Press.

Hill, Jane H. 1994. "The Incorporative Power of Whiteness." Paper delivered at the American Ethnological Society meetings, Santa Barbara, California.

Hill, Margareth. 1996. *Invandrarbarns möjligheter: om hemspråksundervisning och språkutveckling* [Possibilities for Immigrants' Children: About Home Language Education and Linguistic Development]. Mölndal: Institutionen för pedagogik, Göteborgs universitet.

hooks, bell. 1992. *Black Looks: Race and Representation*. Boston: South End Press.

van Hofer, Hanns. 2000. Criminal Violence and Youth in Sweden: A Long-Term Perspective. *Journal of Scandinavian Studies in Criminology and Crime Prevention* 1(1):56–72.

Holmes, Douglas, and George Marcus. 2008. Collaboration Today and the Re-Imagination of the Classic Scene of Fieldwork Encounter. *Collaborative Anthropologies* 1(1):81–101.

Hübinette, Tobias. 2012. "'Words That Wound': Swedish Whiteness and Its Inability to Accommodate Minority Experiences." In Kristín Loftsdóttir and Lars Jensen (eds), *Whiteness and Postcolonialism in the Nordic Region: Exceptionalism, Migrant Others and National Identities.* Burlington: Ashgate, 43–56.

Hübinette, Tobias, and Catrin Lundström. 2011. Sweden after the Recent Election: The Double-Binding Power of Swedish Whiteness through the Mourning and the Loss of "Old Sweden" and the Passing of "Good Sweden." *NORA—Nordic Journal of Feminist and Gender Research* 19(1):42–52.

Hudson, Robert. 2003. Songs of Seduction: Popular Music and Serbian Nationalism. *Patterns of Prejudice* 37(2):157–76.

Husbands, Christopher. 1992. "Belgium: Flemish Legions on the March." In P. Hainsworth (ed), *The Extreme Right in Europe and the USA.* London: Pinter, 126–50.

Ignazi, Piero. *Extreme Right-Wing Parties in Western Europe.* Oxford: Oxford University Press.

Ingazi, Piero, and Colette Ysmal. 1992. New and Old Extreme Right Parties: The French Front National and the Italian Movemento Sociale. *European Journal of Political Research* 22(1):101–21.

Inglehart, Ronald, and Pippa Norris. 2003. *Rising Tide: Gender Equality and Cultural Change around the World.* Cambridge: Cambridge University Press.

Irwin, John. 1977. *Scene.* Beverly Hills: Sage Publications.

Jalving, Mikael. 2011. *Absolut Sverige: En rejse i tavshedens rige* [Absolute Sweden: A Journey in the Kingdom of Silence]. Århus: Jyllands-Posten Forlag.

Johansson, Alf. 2001. "Inledning [Introduction]." In Alf W. Johansson (ed), *Vad är Sverige? Reflektionen kring svensk nationell identitet* [What Is Sweden? Reflections on Swedish National Identity]. Stockholm: Prisma, 7–17.

Johnson, Carol, Steve Patten, and Hans-Georg Betz. 2005. "Identitarian Politics and Populism in Canada and the Antipodes." In Jens Rydgren (ed), *Movements of Exclusion: Radical Right-Wing Populism in the Western World.* New York: Nova Sciences Publishers, 85–100.

Jones, Simon. 1988. *Black Culture, White Youth: The Reggae Tradition from Jamaica to the United Kingdom.* Houndmills: Macmillan Education.

Kajikawa, Loren. 2009. Eminem's "My Name Is": Signifying Whiteness, RearticulatingRace. *Journal of the Society for American Music* 3(3):341–65.

Kajikawa, Loren. 2015. *Sounding Race in Rap Songs.* Oakland: University of California Press.

Kaminsky, David. 2012a. *Swedish Folk Music in the Twenty-First Century: On the Nature of a Tradition in a Folkless Nation.* Lanham, MD: Lexington Books.

Kaminsky, David. 2012b. Keeping Sweden Swedish: Folk Music, Right-Wing Nationalism, and the Immigration Debate. *Journal of Folklore Research* 49(1):73–96.

Kandiyoti, Deniz. 1991. "Introduction." In Deniz Kandiyoti (ed), *Women, Islam, and The State.* Philadelphia: Temple University Press, 1–21.

Kauffman, Eric. 2006. The Dominant Ethnic Moment: Towards the Abolition of "Whiteness?" *Ethnicities* 6(2):231–53.

Keeler, Ward. 2009. What's Burmese about Burmese Rap?: Why Some Expressive Forms Go Global. *American Ethnologist* 36(1):2–19.

Kemper, Robert V., and Anya Royce. 2002. "Preface." In Robert Van Kemper and Anya Royce (eds), *Chronicling Cultures: Long-Term Field Research in Anthropology*. Walnut Creek, CA.: AltaMira, vii–x.

Kimmel, Michael S. 2004. "Foreword." In Abby L. Ferber (ed), *Home Grown Hate: Gender and Organized Racism*. New York: Routledge, 46–70.

King, Stephen A. 2002. *Reggae, Rastafari, and the Rhetoric of Social Control*. Jackson: University Press of Mississippi.

Kirsch, Stuart. 2002. Anthropology and Advocacy: A Case Study of the Campaign against the Ok Tedi Mine. *Critique of Anthropology* 22:175–200.

Kitschelt, Herbert. 1995. *The Radical Right in Western Europe: A Comparative Analysis*. Ann Arbor: University of Michigan Press.

Kitwana, Bakari. 2005. *Why White Kids Love Hip Hop*. New York: Basic Civitas.

Klein, Adam. 2010. *A Space for Hate: The White Power Movement's Adaptation into Cyberspace*. Duluth: Litwin Books.

Klein, Barbro. 2000. The Moral Content of Tradition: Homecraft, Ethnology, and Swedish Life in the Twentieth Century. *Western Folklore* 59(2):171–95.

Knudsen, Jan Sverre. 2010. "'Playing with Words as if It Was a Rap Game': Hip-hop Street Language in Oslo." In Bente Ailin Svendsen and Pia Quist (eds), *Multilingual Urban Scandinavia*. Bristol: Multilingual Matters, 156–69.

Knudsen, Jan Sverre. 2011. Music of the Multiethnic Minority: A Postnational Perspective. *MAIA—Music and Arts in Action* 3(3):77–91.

Krebs, Pierre. 1982. *Die Europäische Wiedergeburt* [The European Rebirth]. Tübingen: Grabert-Verlag.

Kronja, Ivana. 2004. Turbo Folk and Dance Music in 1990s Serbia: Media, Ideology and the Production of Spectacle. *Anthropology of Eastern Europe Review* 22(1):103–14.

Kulick, Don. 2006. Theory in Furs: Masochist Anthropology. *Current Anthropology* 47(6):933–52.

LaChapelle, Peter. 2011. "'Dances Partake of the Racial Characteristics of the People Who Dance Them': Nordicism, Antisemitism, and Henry Ford's Old-TimeMusic and Dance Revival." In Bruce Zuckerman, John Kun, and Lisa Ansell (eds), *The Song Is Not the Same: Jews and American Popular Music*. West Lafayette: Purdue University Press, 29–70.

Lagerlöf, David. 2012. "The Rise and Fall of Swedish White Power Music." In Anton Shekhovtsov and Paul Jackson (eds), *White Power Music: Scenes of the Extreme-Right Cultural Resistance*. Northampton: University of Northampton, 35–46.

Lange, Anders, Heléne Lööw, and Stéphane Bruchfeld, and Ebba Hedlund. 1997. Utsathet för etniskt och politiskt relaterat hot m.m., spridning av rasistisk och antirasistisk propaganda samt attityder till demokrati m.m., bland skolelever [Vulnerability for Ethnic and Politically Related Threats etc.: The Spread of Racist and Antiracist Propaganda, as Well as Attitudes toward Democracy]. Report for CEIFO/BRÅ.

LaRouche, Lyndon H. 1982. *Olof Palme and the Neo-Nazi International*. New York: Executive Intelligence Firm.

Larsson, Stieg, and Mikael Ekman. 2001. *Sverigedemokraterna: Den nationella rörelsen* [The Sweden Democrats: The National Movement]. Stockholm: Ordfront Förlag.

Lassiter, Luke Eric. 2005. *The Chicago Guide to Collaborative Ethnography*. Chicago: University of Chicago Press.

Leandersson, Jens (ed). 2008. *20 röster om 20 år—Sverigedemokraterna 1988–2008*. N.p.: Blåsippa förlag.

Lee, Martin. 1997. *The Beast Reawakens*. Toronto: Little, Brown.

Leppert, Richard D. 2005. Music "Pushed to the Edge of Existence": Adorno, Listening, and the Question of Hope. *Cultural Critique* 60:92–133.

Ling, Jan. 1979. "Folkmusik—en brygd [Folk Music—a Brew]." *Fataburen* 34:9–34.

Ling, Jan. 1980. "'Upp, bröder, kring bildningens fana:' Om folkmusikens historia och ideologi" ["Up, Brothers, around the Banner of Education:" On Folk Music's History and Ideology]. In Jan Ling, Gunnar Ternhag, and Märta Ramsten (eds), *Folkmusikboken* [The Folk Music Book]. Stockholm: Prisma, 44–65.

Löfgren, Orvar. 1979. "Känslans Förvandling: Tiden, naturen och hemmet i den borgerliga kulturen [The Change of Emotion: Time, Nature, and the Home in Bourgeois Culture]." In Jonas Frykman and Orvar Löfgren (eds), *Den Kultiverade Männsikan* [The Cultivated Human]. Malmö: Gleerups, 21–127.

Löfgren, Orvar. 1993. Nationella arenor [National Arenas]. In *Försvenskningen av Sverige* [The Swedifying of Sweden], by Billy Ehn, Jonas Frykman, and Orvar Löfgren. Stockholm: Natur och Kultur, 22–117.

Löfgren, Orvar. 2000. The Disappearance and Return of the National: The Swedish Experience 1950–2000. In Perrti J. Anntonen (ed), *Folklore, Heritage Politics and Ethnic Diversity: A Festschrift for Barbro Klein*. Botkyrka: Multicultural Center, 230–52.

Lööw, Heléne. 1998a. *Nazismen i Sverige 1980–1997: Den rasistiska undergroundrörelsen: Musiken, myterna, riterna* [Nazism in Sweden 1980–1997: The Racist Underground Movement: Music, Myths, Rites.] Stockholm: Ordfront Förlag.

Lööw, Heléne. 1998b. "White Power Rock 'n' Roll: A Growing Industry." In Jeffrey Kaplan and Tore Bjørgo (eds), *Nation and Race: The Developing Euro-American Racist Subculture*. Boston: Northeastern University Press, 126–47.

Lööw, Heléne. 2004. *Nazismen i Sverige 1924–1979* [Nazism in Sweden 1924–1979]. Stockholm: Ordfront Förlag.

Lööw, Heléne. 2015. *Nazismen I Sverige 2000—2014* [Nazism in Sweden 2000—2014]. Stockholm: Ordfront Förlag.

Lööw, Heléne, and Lotta Nilsson. 2001. Hets mot folkgrupp [Hate Speech]. BRÅ Report.

Lott, Eric. 1993. *Love and Theft: Blackface Minstrelsy and the American Working Class*. New York: Oxford University Press.

Love, Nancy. 2009. "Privileged Intersections: The Race, Class, and Gender Politics of Prussian Blue." Paper presented at the Western Political Science Association Annual Meeting, Vancouver, BC, Canada, March 19.

Lovett, Jo, and Liz Kelly. 2009. Different Systems, Similar Outcomes?: Tracking Attrition in Reported Rape Cases across Europe. Report for Child and Women Abuse Studies Unit, London Metropolitan University.

Lundberg, Dan, Krister Malm, and Owe Ronström. 2000. *Musik—Medier—Mångkultur: Förändringar i svenska musiklandskap* [Music—Media—Multiculture: Changes in Swedish Musical Landscapes]. Hedemora: Gidlunds.

Lundgren, E., G. Heimer, J. Westerstrand, and A. Kalliokoski. 2002. *Captured Queen: Men's Violence against Women in "Equal" Sweden—A Prevalence Study*. Stockholm: Fritzes Offentliga Publikationer.

Lundquist, Dag. 2010. "Mellan myt och verklighet [Between Myth and Reality]." In Mats Deland, Fredrik Hertzberg, and Thomas Hvitfeldt (eds), *Det vita fältet: Samtida forskning om högerextremism* [The White Field: Contemporary Research on Right-Wing Extremism]. Uppsala: University of Uppsala Department of History, 127–54.

Lundström, Anna. 1995. "'Vi äger gatorna i kväll!' Om hyllandet av Karl XII i Stockholm den 30 November 1991" ["We Own the Streets Tonight!" On the Celebration of Karl XII in Sotkcholm on November 30, 1991]. In Barbro Klein (ed), *Gatan är vår! Ritualer på offentliga platser* [The Street Is Ours! Rituals in Public Places]. Stockholm: Carlssons, 134–61.

MacDonald, Kevin. 1994. *A People That Shall Dwell Alone: Judaism as a Group Evolutionary Strategy*. Westport, CT: Praeger.

MacDonald, Kevin. 1998a. *Separation and Its Discontents: Toward an Evolutionary Theory of Anti-Semitism*. Westport, CT: Praeger.

MacDonald, Kevin. 1998b. *The Culture of Critique: An Evolutionary Analysis of Jewish Involvement in Twentieth-Century Intellectual and Political Movements*. Westport, CT: Praeger.

MacDonald, Kevin. 2006–2007. Psychology and White Ethnocentrism. *Occidental Quarterly* 6(4):7–46.

Malmberg, Bo, Eva Anderson, and John Östh. 2011. "How Does Segregation Vary between Different Urban Areas? Using a K-Nearest Neighbor Approach to Segregation Measurement." Unpublished conference paper. Enhr Conference, Toulouse.

Marchart, Oliver. 2003. "Bridging the Macro-Micro Gap: Is There Such a Thing as Subcultural Politics?" In David Muggleton and Rupert Weinzierl (eds), *The Post-Subcultures Reader*. Oxford: Berg, 83-97.

Marchart, Oliver. 2012. Elements of Protest: Politics and Culture in Laclau's Theory of Populist Reason. *Cultural Studies* 26(2–3):223–41.

Marcus, George. 1998. *Ethnography through Thick and Thin*. Princeton: Princeton University Press.

Marcus, J. 1995. *The National Front and French Politics*. London: Macmillan.

Mareš, Miroslav, and Josef Smolík. 2012. "White Power Music and Interconnected Issues in the Czech Republic, 1999–2011." In Anton Shekhovtsov and Paul Jackson (eds), *White Power Music: Scenes of the Extreme-Right Cultural Resistance*. Northhampton: University of Northampton, 71–83.

Marshall, George. 1991. *Spirit of 69: A Skinhead Bible*. Dunoon: S. T. Publishing.

Matsson, Pontus. 2009. *Sverigedemokraterna: In på bara skinnet* [The Sweden Democrats: In the Bare Skin]. Stockholm: Natur och Kultur.

McClintock, Anne. 1997. "No Longer in a Future Heaven: Gender, Race, and Nationalism." In Anne McClintock, Aamir Mufti, and Ella Shohat (eds), *Dangerous Liaisons, Gender, Nation, and Postcolonial Perspectives*. Minneapolis: University of Minnesota Press, 89–112.

McCulloch, Richard. 1994. *The Racial Compact: A Call for Racial Rights, Preservation, and Independence*. N.p.: Towncourt.

McCulloch, Tom. 2006. The Nouvelle Droite in the 1980s and 1990s: Ideology and Entryism, the Relationship with the Front National. *French Politics* 4(2):158–78.

Mercer, Kobena. 1990. "Black Hair/Style Politics." In Russell Ferguson et al. (eds), *Out There: Marginalization and Contemporary Culture*. Cambridge, MA: MIT Press, 247–64.

Mercer, Kobena. 1994. *Welcome to the Jungle: New Positions in Black Cultural Studies*. New York: Routledge.

Merkl, Peter, and Leonard Weinberg (eds). 1997. *The Revival of Right-Wing Extremism in the 90s*. London: Frank Cass.

Meyer, Michael. 1993. *The Politics of Music in the Third Reich*. New York: P. Lang.

Michael, George 2009. David Lane and the Fourteen Words. *Totalitarian Movements and Political Religions* 10(1):43–61.

Middleton, Jason, and Roger Beebe. 2002. The Racial Politics of Hybridity and Neo-Eclecticism in Contemporary Popular Music. *Popular Music* 21(2):159–72.

Mikenberg, Michael. 1997. "The New Right in France and Germany: Nouvelle Droite, Neue Rechte, and the New Right Radical Parties." In Peter Merkl and Leonard Weinberg (eds), *The Revival of Right-Wing Extremism in the 90s*. London: Frank Cass, 65–90.

Miller, David L. 1974. *The New Polytheism*. New York: Harper & Row.

Milles, Karen. 2008. *Jämställt språk* [Gender-Equal Language]. Stockholm: Nordstedts Akademiska Förlag.

Mitchell, Tony. 2001a. "Introduction: Another Root—Hip Hop Outside the USA." In Tony Mitchell (ed), *Global Noise: Rap and Hip Hop Outside the USA*. Middletown: Wesleyan University Press, 1–38.

Mitchell, Tony. 2001b. "Kia Kaha! (Be Strong!): Maori and Pacific Islander Hip-Hop in Aoteraroa-New Zealand." In Tony Mitchell (ed), *Global Noise: Rap and Hip Hop Outside the USA*. Middletown: Wesleyan University Press, 280–305.

Mitra, S. 1988. The National Front in France—A Single Issue Movement? *West European Politics* 11(2):47–64.

Mudde, Cas. 2007. *Populist Radical Right Parties in Europe*. Cambridge: Cambridge University Press.

Nairn, Tom. 1977. *The Break-up of Britain: Crisis and Neonationalism*. London: NLB.

Nairn, Tom. 1998. *Faces of Nationalism: Janus Revisited*. London: Verso.

Nayak, Anoop. 2002. "In Whitest England: New Subject Positions for White Youth in the Post-Imperial Moment." In Cynthia Levine-Rasky (ed), *Working through Whiteness: International Perspectives*. Albany: State University of New York Press, 241–68.

Negus, Keith, and Patria Roman Velazquez. 2002. Belonging and Detachment: Musical Experience and the Limits of Identity. *Poetics* 30(1):133–45.

Nilsson, Fredrik, and Peter Åstrand. 2007. Vi är igen jävla kickersgäng: En studie om hur huliganer organiserar sig, vidmakthåller gemenskap via symboler, samt vilka premisser som måste uppfyllas för att komma med i en "firma" [We Are Not a Fucking Kickers Gang: A Study on How Hooligans Organize Themselves, Maintain Community via Symbols, and What Conditions Must be Fulfilled to Join a "Firm"]. C-level thesis paper, Örebro Universitet.

Nordstrom, Byron J. 2000. *Scandinavia since 1500*. Minneapolis: University of Minnesota Press.

Norocel, Ov Cristian. 2013. "Give Us Back Sweden!" A Feminist Reading of the (Re)Interpretations of the Folkhem Conceptual Metaphor in Swedish Radical Right Populist Discourse. *NORA—Nordic Journal of Feminist and Gender Research* 21(1):4–20.

Norris, Pippa. 2005. *Radical Right: Voters and Parties in the Electoral Market*. Cambridge: Cambridge University Press.

O'Mera, Michael. 2011. "Prophet of the Fourth Age." Guest foreword. In Guillaume Faye, *Why We Fight: Manifesto of the European Resistance*. London: Arktos Media, 9–18.

Opper, Susan. 1983. Multiculturalism in Sweden: A Case of Assimilation and Integration. *Comparative Education* 19(2):193–212.

Orrenius, Niklas. 2010. *Jag är inte rabiat. Jag äter pizza: En bok om Sverigedemorakterna* [I am Not Rabid. I Eat Pizza: A Book about the Sweden Democrats]. Stockholm: Månpocket.

Pelto, Pertti J., and Gretel H. Pelto. 1973. "Ethnography: The Fieldwork Enterprise." In John Honigmann (ed), *Handbook of Social and Cultural Anthropology*. Chicago: RandMcNally, 241–88.

Perry, Barbara. 2004. "'White Genocide': White Supremacists and the Politics of Reproduction." In Abby Ferber (ed), *Home-Grown Hate: Gender and Organized Racism*. New York: Routledge, 75–95.

Peterson, Abby. 1995. "Walls and Bridges": Youth and the Drama of Immigration in Contemporary Sweden. *Young* 4(4):54–70.

Pieslak, Jonathan. 2015. *Radicalism and Music: An Introduction to the Music Cultures of al-Qa'ida, Racist Skinheads, Christian-Affiliated Radicals, and Eco-Animal Rights Militants*. Middletown: Wesleyan University Press.

Pred, Allan. 2000. *Even in Sweden: Racisms, Racialized Spaces and the Popular Geographical Imagination*. Berkeley: University of California Press.

Prévos, André J. M. 2001. "Postcolonial Popular Music in France: Rap Music and Hip Hop Culture in the 1980s and 1990s." In Tony Mitchell (ed), *Global Noise: Rap and Hip Hop Outside the USA*. Middletown: Wesleyan University Press, 39–56.

Potter, Russell A. 1995. *Spectacular Vernaculars: Hip-Hop and the Politics of Postmodernism*. Albany: State University of New York Press.

Purcell, Natalie J. 2003. *Death Metal Music: The Passion and Politics of a Subculture*. London: McFarland.

Racist Sweden? 1993. Directed by Leon Flamholc. London: Caravan. [Film]

Ramsten, Märta. 1992. *Återklang: Svensk folkmusik i förändring 1950–1980* [Reverberations: Shifts in Swedish Folk Music 1950–1980]. Stockholm: Svenskt Visarkiv.

Ray, Hill. 1988. *The Other Face of Terror: Inside Europe's Neo-Nazi Network*. London: Grafton.

Ridgeway, James. 1990. *Blood in the Face: The Ku Klux Klan, Aryan Nations, Nazi Skin-heads, and the Rise of a New White Culture*. New York: Thunder Mouth's Press.

Roempke, Ville. 1980. " 'Ett nyår för svensk folkmusik': Om spelmansrörelsen" ["A New Year for Swedish Folk Music": On the spelman movement]. In Jan Ling, Gunnar Ternhag, and Märta Ramsten (eds), *Folkmusikboken* [The Folk Music Book]. Stockholm: Prisma, 263–96.

Rogers, JoAnn, and Jacquelyn S. Litt. 2004. "Normalizing Racism: A Case Study of Motherhood in White Supremacy." In Abby Ferber (ed), *Home-Grown Hate: Gender and Organized Racism*. New York: Routledge, 92–107.

Rose, Tricia. 1994. *Black Noise: Rap Music and Black Culture in Contemporary America*. Middletown: Wesleyan University Press.

Rose, Tricia. 2008. *The Hip Hop Wars: What We Talk about When We Talk about Hip Hop—and Why It Matters*. New York: Basic Civitas Books.

Roy, William G. 2010. *Reds, Whites, and Blues: Social Movements, Folk Music, and Race in the United States*. Princeton: Princeton University Press.

Runblom, Harald. 1995. "Immigration to Scandinavia after WWII." In Sven Tägil (ed), *Ethnicity and Nation Building in the Nordic World*. Edwardsville: Southern Illinois University Press, 282–324.

Ryan, Katherine E. 1995. "Evaluation Ethics and Issues of Social Justice: Contributions from Feminist Moral Thinking." In Norman K. Denzin (ed), *Studies in Symbolic Interaction*. Greenwich, CT: JAI, 143–51.

Rydgren, Jens. 2002. Radical Right Populism in Sweden: Still a Failure, but for How Long? *Scandinavian Political Studies* 26(1):27–56.

Rydgren, Jens. 2004. *The Populist Challenge: Political Protest and Ethno-Nationalist Mobilization in France*. New York: Bergham Books.

Rydgren, Jens. 2005. Is Extreme Right-Wing Populism Contagious?: Explaining the Emergence of a New Party Family. *European Journal of Political Research* 44(3):413–37.

Rydgren, Jens. 2006. *From Tax Populism to Ethnic Nationalism: Radical Right-Wing Populism in Sweden*. New York: Berghahn Books.

Rydgren, Jens. 2010. "Den radikala högerns sociologi" [The Sociology of the Radical Right]. In Mats Deland, Fredrik Hertzberg, and Thomas Hvitfeldt (eds), *Det vita fältet: Samtida Forskning om Högerextremism* [The White Field: Contemporary Research on Right-Wing Extremism]. Uppsala: University of Uppsala Department of History, 15–44.

Rydgren, Jens, and Patrick Ruth. 2011. Voting for the Radical Right in Swedish Municipalities: Social Marginality and Ethnic Competition? *Scandinavian Political Studies* 34(3):202–25.

Sacks, Michael Alan, and Marika Lindholm. 2002. "A Room without a View: Social Distance and the Structuring of Privileged Identity." In Cynthia Levine-Rasky (ed), *Working through Whiteness: International Perspectives*. Albany: State University of New York Press, 129–51.

Sannerstedt, Anders. 2008. De okända väljarna—en analys av de skånska väljare som röstade på icke riksdagspartier 2006 [The Unknown Voters: An Analysis of Voters from Skåne Who Voted for Unrepresented Parties, 2006]. In L. Nilsson and R. Antoni, (eds), *Medborgarna, regionen och flernivådemokratin. Skåne 2006* [Citizens, Regions, and Multilevel Democracy. Skåne, 2006]. Göteborg: SOM-institutet: Göteborgs universitet, 49–70.

Schafer, Joseph A. 2002. Spinning a Web of Hate: Web-based Hate Propaganda by Extremist Organizations. *Journal of Criminal Justice and Popular Culture* 9(2):69–88.

Sernhede, Ove. 2002. *AlieNation Is My Nation: Hiphop och unga mäns utanförskap* [AlieNation Is My Nation: Hip Hop and Young Men's Alienation]. Stockholm: Ordfront Förlag.

Sernhede, Ove. 2005. "'Reality Is My nationality': The Global Tribe of Hip Hop and Immigrant Youth in 'the New Sweden." In Ove Sernhede, Mette Andersson, and Yngve Georg Lithman (eds), *Youth, Otherness and the Plural City: Modes of Belonging and Social Life*. Göteborg: Daidalos, 271–90.

Sexton, Jared. 2008. *Amalgamation Schemes: Antiblackness and the Critique of Multiculturalism*. Minneapolis: University of Minnesota Press.

Shekhovtsov, Anton. 2009. Apoliteic Music: Neo-Folk, Martial Industrial and "Metapolitical Fascism." *Patterns of Prejudice* 43(5):431–57.

Shelemay, Kay Kaufman. 2008. "The Ethnomusicologist, Ethnographic Method, and the Transmission of Tradition." In Gregory Barz and Timothy Cooley (eds), *Shadows in the Field: New Perspectives for Fieldwork in Ethnomusicology*. Oxford: Oxford University Press. 141–56.

Shelemay, Kay Kaufman. 2011. Musical Communities: Rethinking the Collective in Music. *Journal of the American Musicological Society* 64(2):349–90.

Sichel, Betty A. 1991. Different Strains and Strands: Feminist Contributions to Ethical Theory. *Newsletter on Feminism* 90:86–92.

Simi, Pete, and Robert Futrell. 2010. *American Swastika: Inside the White Power Movement's Hidden Spaces of Hate*. New York: Rowman & Littlefield.

Skyum-Nielsen, Rune. 2006. *Dansk hiphop kultur siden 1983* [Danish Hip-Hop Culture since 1983]. Copenhagen: Informations Forlag.

Smith, Anthony. 2010. *Nationalism*. 2nd ed. Cambridge: Polity Press.

Söderman, Magnus. 2011. *Till värn för Norden* [In Defense of the North]. N.p.: Logik Förlag.

Spektorowski, Alberto. 2002. The Intellectual New Right, the European Radical Right and the Ideological Challenge to Liberal Democracy. *International Studies* 39(2):165–82.

Spektorowski, Alberto. 2003. The New Right: Ethno-Regionalism, Ethno-Pluralism and the Emergence of a Neo-Fascist "Third Way." *Journal of Political Ideologies* 8(1):111–30.

Spracklen, Karl. 2010. "True Aryan Black Metal: The Meaning of Leisure, Belonging and the Construction of Whiteness in Black Metal Music." In Niall Scott and Imke Von Helden (eds), *The Metal Void*. Oxford: Inter-Disciplinary Press, 81–94.

Spracklen, Karl. "'Nazi Punks Folk Off': Leisure, Nationalism, Cultural Identity, and the Consumption of Metal and Folk Music." In Nigel Copsey and John E. Richardson (eds), *Cultures of Post-War British Fascism*. London: Routledge, 161–76.

Staud, Toralf, and Johannes Radke. 2012. *Neue Nazis. Jenseits der NPD: Populisten, Autonome Nationalisten und der Terror von rechts* [Neo-Nazis. Beyond the NPD: Populists, Autonomous Nationalists and Terror from the Right]. Cologne: Kiepenheuer & Witsch.

Sternhell, Zeev. 1986. *Neither Right nor Left: Fascist Ideology in France*. Princeton: Princeton University Press.

Stokes, Martin. 1994. "Introduction." In Martin Stokes (ed), *Ethnicity, Identity, and Music: The Musical Construction of Place*. Providence: Berg, 1–28.

Sundin, Bosse. 1999. Att väcka och vidmakthålla kärleken till hem och härd. Hemsljödsrörelsen och det tidiga 1900-talets Sverige [To Awaken and Preserve Love for Home and Heart: The Homecraft Movement and Early 1900s Sweden]. In Gunilla Lundahl (ed), *Den vackra nyttan. Om hemslöjd i Sverige* [The Beautiful Utility: On Homecraft in Sweden]. Stockholm: Gidlunds, 89–111.

Sunic, Tomislav. 2011 [1990]. *Against Democracy and Equality: The European New Right*. 3rd ed. London: Arktos Media.

Sweers, Britta. 2004. "The Power to Influence: Minds: German Folk Music during the Nazi Era and After." In Annie Janeiro Randall (ed), *Music, Power, and Politics*. London: Routledge, 65–86.

Sverigedemokraterna [Sweden Democrats]. 2010a. Vår Skuggbudget [Our Budget Proposal]. Report.

Sverigedemokraterna [Sweden Democrats]. 2010b. "Dags att tala klarspråk om våldtäkterna" [Time to Speak Directly about the Rapes]. Report.

Taguieff, Pierre-André. 1993. The New Right's View of European Identity. *Telos* 98–99: 34–54.

Taguieff, Pierre-André. 2001 [1987]. *Forces of Prejudice: On Racism and its Doubles*. Translated by Hassan Melehy. Minneapolis: University of Minnesota Press.

Tanay, Dorit. 2006. The Birth of Opera and the New Science. *The European Legacy: Toward New Paradigms* 11(7):753–64.

Taylor, Charles. 1992. *Multiculturalism and the Politics of Recognition*. Princeton: Princeton University Press.

Teitelbaum, Benjamin R. 2013. "'Come Hear our Merry Song:' Shifts in the Sound of Contemporary Swedish Radical Nationalism." Ph.D. diss., Brown University.

Teitelbaum, Benjamin R. 2014. "The Path of Dreams: Breivik, Music, and Neo-Nazism." In Gro Trondalen, Marie Skanland, and Jan Sverre Knudsen (eds), *Musikken og 22 juli*. Oslo: Norges musikhøgskole, 119–38.

Teitelbaum, Benjamin R. 2016. "Did Breivik Care about Race? The Study of Scandinavian Radical Nationalism." In Ursula Lindquist and Jenny Björklund (eds), *Dimensions of Diversity in Nordic Culture and Society*. Newcastle: Cambridge Scholars Publishing, 131–50.

Templeton, Inez. 2007. "Was ist so Deutsch Daran? Kulturelle Identität in der Berliner HipHop Szene" [What's So German about That? Cultural Identity in the Berlin Hip Hop Seen]. In Karin Bock, Stefan Meier, and Gunter Süss (eds), *Hip Hop Meets Academia*. Beilefeld: Transcript Verlag, 185–95.

Ter Wal, Jessika. 2000. The Discourses of the Extreme Right and Its Ideological Implications: The Case of the Alleanza Nazionale. *Patterns of Prejudice* 34(4):37–51.

Thomas, Robert. 1999. *The Politics of Serbia in the 1990s*. New York: Columbia University Press.

Thorell, Richard. 2012. Sverigedemokraterna i riksdagen: Vilka konsekvenser får det för undervisningen [The Sweden Democrats in Parliament: What are the Consequences for Education]? M.A. thesis, Karlstad University.

Thulin, Marie. 2007. Skolvalet och Sverigedemokraterna [School Elections and the Sweden Democrats]. M.A. thesis, Malmö College.

Titon, Jeff Todd. 2008. "Knowing Fieldwork." In Gregory Barz and Timothy Cooley (eds), *Shadows in the Field: New Perspectives for Fieldwork in Ethnomusicology*. Oxford: Oxford University Press, 25–41.

Torigian, Michael. 1999. The Philosophical Foundations of the French New Right. *Telos* 117:6–44.

Turner-Graham, Emily. 2012. "'Resistance Never Looked This Good': Women in White Power Music." In Anton Shekhovtsov and Paul Jackson (eds), *White Power Music: Scenes of the Extreme-Right Cultural Resistance*. Northampton: University of Northampton, 71–83.

Ullestad, Neal. 1999. American Indian Rap and Reggae: Dancing to the Beat of a Different Drummer. *Popular Music and Society* 23(2):63–90.

Urban, Greg. 1988. Ritual Wailing in Amerindian Brazil. *American Anthropologist* 90(2):385–400.

Urla, Jacqueline. 2001. "'We are All Malcome X!' Negu Gorriak, Hip-Hop, and the Basque Political Imaginary." In Tony Mitchell (ed), *Global Noise: Rap and Hip Hop Outside the USA*. Middletown: Wesleyan University Press, 171–93.

Uvell, Markus, and Erik Meier Carlsen. 2010. *Folkhems populismen: Berättelsen om sverigedemokraternas väljare* [Folkhem Populism: The Story of the Sweden Democrats' Voters]. Stockholm: Timbro.

Vehviläinen, Olli. 2002. *Finland in the Second World War: Between Germany and Russia*. London: Palgrave Macmillan.

Von Beyme, Klaus. 1988. Right-wing Extremism in Post-war Europe. In Klaus von Beyme (ed), *Right-Wing Extremism in Western Europe*. Special issue of *West European Politics* 11(2):2–18.

Von Hofer, Hanns. 2000. Crime Statistics as Constructs: The Case of Swedish Rape Statistics. *European Journal on Criminal Policy and Research* 8(1):77–89.

Wåg, Mathias. 2010. "Nationell kulturkamp—Från vit maktmusik till metapolitik" [National Culture War—From White Power Music to Meta-Politics]. In Mats Deland, Fredrik Hertzberg, and Thomas Hvitfeldt (eds), *Det vita fältet: Samtida forskning om högerextremism* [The White Field: Contemporary Research on Right-Wing Extremism]. Uppsala: University of Uppsala Department of History, 97–125.

Watkins, S. Craig. 2006. *Hip Hop Matters: Politics, Popular Culture, and the Struggle for a Movement*. Boston: Beacon Press.

Ware, Vron. 1996. Island Racism: Gender, Place, and White Power. *Feminist Review* 54(1):65–86.

Ware, Vron, and Les Back. 2002. *Out of Whiteness: Color, Politics, and Culture*. Chicago: University of Chicago Press.

Weismantel, Mary. 2001. *Cholas and Pishtacos: Stories of Race and Sex in the Andes*. Chicago: University of Chicago Press.

Widfeldt, Anders. 2014. *Extreme Right Parties in Scandinavia*. London: Routledge.

Wiegman, Robyn. 1999. Whiteness Studies and the Paradox of Particularity. *Boundary 2* 26(3):115–50.

Wilce, James M. 1998. The Pragmatics of "Madness": Performance Analysis of a Bangladeshi Woman's "Aberrant" Lament. *Culture, Medicine, and Psychiatry* 22(1):1–54.

White, Miles. 2011. *From Jim Crow to Jay Z: Rap, and the Performance of Masculinity*. Urbana: University of Illinois Press.

Wodak, Ruth, and Anton Pelinka. 2002. *The Heider Phenomenon in Austria*. London: Transaction Publishers.

Wolf, Eric, and Joseph Jorgensen. 1970. Anthropology on the Warpath in Thailand. *New York Review* 15(9):26–36.

Woo, Benjamin. 2009. Subculture Theory and the Fetishism of Style. *Stream* 2(1):23–32.

Wood, Robert T. 2000. Threat Transcendence, Ideological Articulation, and Frame of Reference Reconstruction: Preliminary Concepts for a Theory of Subcultural Schism. *Deviant Behavior* 21(1):23–45.

Yousman, Bill. 2003. Blackophilia and Blackophobia: White Youth, the Consumption of Rap Music, and White Supremacy. *Communication Theory* 13(4):366–91.

Yuval-Davis, Nira. 1996. Women and the Biological Reproduction of the "Nation." *Women's Studies International Forum* 19(1–2):17–24.

Yuval-Davis, Nira. 1997. *Gender and Nation*. London: Sage Publications.

Index

"n" = endnote number.

CPSIA information can be obtained
at www.ICGtesting.com
Printed in the USA
BVOW03s0358230617

487554BV00003B/11/P